T0300584

Global Energy Fundamentals

This book provides a rigorous, concise guide to the current status and future prospects of the global energy system. As we move away from fossil fuels and toward clean energy solutions, the complexity of the global energy system has increased. Tagliapietra cuts through this complexity with a multidisciplinary perspective of the system, which encompasses economics, geopolitics, and basic technology. He goes on to explore the main components of the global energy system – oil, natural gas, coal, nuclear energy, bioenergy, hydropower, geothermal energy, wind energy, solar energy, marine energy – as well as energy consumption and energy efficiency. It then provides an in-depth analysis of the pivotal issues of climate change and of energy access in Africa.

SIMONE TAGLIAPIETRA is Research Fellow at Bruegel and at the Università Cattolica del Sacro Cuore. He is also Adjunct Professor at The Johns Hopkins University SAIS Europe and Senior Fellow at the Fondazione Eni Enrico Mattei. He is the author of *Energy Relations in the Euro-Mediterranean* (Palgrave, 2017) and *The Geoeconomics of Sovereign Wealth Funds and Renewable Energy* (Claeys & Casteels, 2012).

Praise for Global Energy Fundamentals

Global Energy Fundamentals aims to provide a well-founded and wide-ranging discourse on energy issues, through a comprehensive, rigorous and fact-based portrayal of its fundamentals.
A multidisciplinary and fact-based approach makes the book a highly valuable reference for both experts as well as for a broader audience seeking to establish the profound knowledge necessary to understand the future debate on energy security, climate change and development policy.

– Ottmar Edenhofer – Director, Potsdam Institute for Climate Impact Research

Energy is a global issue, affecting world affairs, human welfare, pollution and climate. This informative, well written, and easy-to-grasp book provides a guide to the fundamentals of this important subject: resources, technologies, economy and policy, from oil and gas to renewables and universal access. Remarkable, refreshing, and so useful.

– Jean-Michel Glachant – Director, Florence School of Regulation, European University Institute

This book is a real instrument for the daily work. It encompasses a global energy analysis; including its technological, economic, climate and geopolitical aspects. A window and an introduction to understand the greatest challenges of our time, from climate change to access to energy in developing countries.

– Francesco La Camera – Director General, International Renewable Energy Agency

Global Energy Fundamentals offers a concise, up-to-date, authoritative and clearly written account of key features of the global energy system. The author, Simone Tagliapietra, is a highly respected energy expert and an academic researcher. The book covers fossil fuels, nuclear energy, and renewable energy, and puts these energy alternatives in the context of changing technologies, global markets, geopolitics, and the challenges of climate change, decarbonization, and energy access for the world's poor. General readers will obtain an overview of the world energy system and energy specialists will gain new insights on the pathways to sustainable energy for all.

– Jeffrey D. Sachs – University Professor, Columbia University and Director, UN Sustainable Development Solutions Network

This new volume provides a comprehensive, readable, and timely description of the diverse sources of energy supply that exist around the world, with supplementary material on energy demand, climate change, and pressing energy-access issues in Africa.

– Robert N. Stavins – Professor of Energy and Economic Development, John F. Kennedy School of Government, Harvard University

Global Energy Fundamentals

Economics, Politics, and Technology

SIMONE TAGLIAPIETRA

Bruegel, Brussels and Università Cattolica del Sacro Cuore, Milan

CAMBRIDGE
UNIVERSITY PRESS

University Printing House, Cambridge CB2 8BS, United Kingdom

One Liberty Plaza, 20th Floor, New York, NY 10006, USA

477 Williamstown Road, Port Melbourne, VIC 3207, Australia

314–321, 3rd Floor, Plot 3, Splendor Forum, Jasola District Centre, New Delhi – 110025, India

79 Anson Road, #06–04/06, Singapore 079906

Cambridge University Press is part of the University of Cambridge.

It furthers the University's mission by disseminating knowledge in the pursuit of education, learning, and research at the highest international levels of excellence.

www.cambridge.org
Information on this title: www.cambridge.org/9781108495219
DOI: 10.1017/9781108861595

First published 2020

A catalogue record for this publication is available from the British Library.

Library of Congress Cataloging-in-Publication Data
Names: Tagliapietra, Simone, author.
Title: Global energy fundamentals / Simone Tagliapietra, Università Cattolica del Sacro Cuore, Milan.
Description: New York : Cambridge University Press, 2020. | Includes bibliographical references and index.
Identifiers: LCCN 2020025097 (print) | LCCN 2020025098 (ebook) | ISBN 9781108495219 (hardback) | ISBN 9781108861595 (ebook)
Subjects: LCSH: Power resources – Environmental aspects. | Energy industries – Environmental aspects. | Renewable energy sources. | Climatic changes.
Classification: LCC HD9502.A2 T324 2020 (print) | LCC HD9502.A2 (ebook) | DDC 333.79–dc23
LC record available at https://lccn.loc.gov/2020025097
LC ebook record available at https://lccn.loc.gov/2020025098

ISBN 978-1-108-49521-9 Hardback
ISBN 978-1-108-81770-7 Paperback

To the memory of my grandfather,
Vittore Giovanni Tagliapietra

Contents

Figures

Tables

Tables

Preface

Energy is a key prerequisite for modern life and it represents the lifeblood of modern societies. Every international order in modern history has been based on an energy resource: coal was the backdrop for the British Empire in the nineteenth century, oil has been at the core of the subsequent 'American Century', and today many expect China to become the twenty-first century's world renewable energy superpower. That is, the strategic importance of energy is so pervasive as to shape global economic and geopolitical dynamics.

Over the last two decades, the global significance of energy has become even more pronounced as two major issues increasingly gathered international recognition and awareness: climate change and energy access in the developing world.

Global energy supply has always been, and it continues to be, largely based on fossil fuels. Notwithstanding the most recent renewable energy developments, 80 per cent of global energy supply indeed remains based on coal, oil and natural gas. The combustion of these fossil fuels is responsible for around 75 per cent of global greenhouse gas emissions, making energy the largest cause of climate change. A structural response to this major threat to humanity can therefore only come from the energy sector, notably through a global clean energy revolution.

Being that energy is a key prerequisite for modern life, the lack of access to it represents a decisive socio-economic challenge. Today, 840 million people across the world – and notably in sub-Saharan Africa – continue to lack access to electricity, while 2.9 billion people continue to lack access to clean cooking facilities. Providing access to affordable modern energy services to these people represents one of the greatest socio-economic challenges of our time, an essential step to eradicating poverty and to reducing inequalities.

Given the order of magnitude of these challenges, it is important to have a clear understanding of global energy fundamentals. Throughout a decade of work in the field, I have appreciated the importance of a well-informed debate in paving the way for appropriate responses to these challenges. This is the spark that ignited the idea of this book: feeding a wide and honest debate on energy issues, through a rigorous and accessible portrayal of its fundamentals.

On this basis, I developed the book following a multidisciplinary and fact-based approach. Multidisciplinary because the book reviews each component of the global energy system, tackling the major historical, technological, economic, and geopolitical issues characterising it. Fact-based because the book is data-driven in order to be as neutral as possible. The aim of the book is indeed not the one of presenting my personal views on the issue, nor the one of speculating about future, more or less plausible, energy scenarios. Its aim is really the one of providing to the reader all the necessary elements to make up his own views on the current status of the global energy system, and therefore on its potential future developments.

In order to make the book accessible to a wide readership, I tried to adopt simple language, avoiding the jargon that often characterises the debate in the field. In order not to compromise on rigour, I not only utilised the most authoritative data sources in the field, but also made plenty of references to primary literature for those who might wish to delve more deeply into the topics discussed.

The book opens with an introductory chapter presenting the fundamental global energy trends. The succeeding chapters review the main components of the global energy system – oil, natural gas, coal, nuclear energy, bioenergy, hydropower, geothermal energy, wind energy, solar energy, marine energy – as well as energy consumption and energy efficiency. After this examination, the book closes with two chapters offering an in-depth analysis of the pivotal issues of climate change and energy access in Africa.

I very much hope that this book will help the present and next generation of teachers, students, policymakers, and citizens with an interest in energy issues to develop a clearer understanding of the global energy system, so that they may be better able to contribute to the resolution of the urgent, complex, and interacting energy system problems which now face humanity.

Simone Tagliapietra

1   Introduction to Global Energy

1.1   INTRODUCTION TO ENERGY

Energy plays a fundamental role in our societies, as it does in our daily life. Electricity allows the functioning of lighting systems, office machines, as well as of household appliances and electronics. Oil products enable transport, and therefore trade and commerce. Industry depends on energy supply, as does agriculture. In practical terms, without energy we would not be able to carry out basic daily activities such as taking a hot shower in the morning, cooking our breakfast, driving kids to school and then working on our computer, possibly in an adequately air-conditioned office. That is, energy is a key prerequisite for modern life.

But to allow all this, a complex energy infrastructure has to be put in place, frequently linking faraway countries, if not even different continents. Primary energy resources like oil and gas are indeed unevenly distributed round the globe, raising the necessity of transporting them over long distances from the production well to the refuelling station down the road or to the gas stove in our kitchen. Likewise, electricity systems are also based on a complex infrastructure linking generation plants – either fossil fuel or renewable based – and final consumers.

Governments have traditionally played an important role in the energy sector, also driven by energy security and environmental protection concerns. Since energy is vital in our societies, governments have to ensure the availability of energy without interruptions and at an affordable price. This concerns national security. At the same time, governments have increasingly become active in the sector with policies aimed at limiting energy's negative externalities, both in terms of air pollution and in terms of greenhouse-gas emissions – which causes

1

climate change. The Paris Agreement on climate change is a clear example of this activity.

In some developing countries, governments do have an additional task: expanding the access to modern energy. Today, around 840 million people across the world lack access to electricity, while 2.9 billion people (i.e., more than a third of the global population) do not have access to clean cooking facilities – a situation that causes every year 3.8 million deaths around the world due to the indoor air pollution generated by dirty cooking stoves. Sub-Saharan Africa is the global hotspot of this problem, as around 60 per cent of its population lacks access to electricity, and 80 per cent lacks access to clean cooking facilities (IEA et al., 2019). Bridging this modern energy gap represents a fundamental prerequisite to unleash socio-economic development of vast areas of the world, and for this reason energy access has become a top priority of the international development agenda.

The purpose of this introductory chapter is to set the scene for a fuller exposition of these issues in the chapters that follow. The chapter is structured as follows. Section 1.2 provides an overview of world's energy markets focusing on main global and regional demand and supply trends, and it introduces the notion of energy policy. Section 1.3 looks at the climate change challenge in relation to energy. Section 1.4 illustrates the challenge of energy access across the globe. Section 1.5 opens up the energy geopolitics issue by looking at historical events and current problematics.

I.2 GLOBAL ENERGY TRENDS

Global energy demand[1] has more than doubled over the last fifty years, raising from 5,523 million tonnes of oil equivalent[2] (mtoe) in 1971 to

[1]   Based on the International Energy Agency (IEA, 2019e) definition, global energy demand indicates 'the total amount of energy that is available to meet demand in a country or region in a given period of time'. In IEA statistics, this corresponds to total primary energy supply (TPES). TPES is calculated by the IEA by adding together primary energy production and imports, and subtracting exports, bunker fuels, and changes in fuel stocks.

[2]   A tonne of oil equivalent is a normalised unit of energy. As defined by Eurostat (2019), 'by convention it is equivalent to the approximate amount of energy that can be extracted from one tonne of crude oil. It is a standardized unit, assigned a net calorific

13,761 mtoe in 2016.[3] This trend has mainly been the result of an expanding global population (i.e., grown from 3.8 billion to 7.4 billion between 1971 and 2016[4]), alongside an expanding global economy (i.e., expanded from USD 20 trillion to 78 trillion between 1971 and 2016[5]).

Energy demand has evolved differently across world regions, in particular shifting from developed to developing countries. Between 1971 and 2016, the share of developed countries[6] in global energy demand fell from 61 per cent to 38 per cent, while the share of non-OECD Asia (i.e., China, India, and smaller Asian countries like Indonesia, Malaysia, and the Philippines) almost tripled, from 13 per cent to 35 per cent (Figure 1.1).

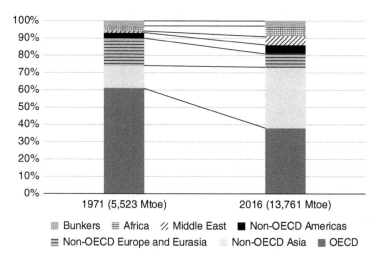

FIGURE I.I Share of global energy demand by region, 1971 and 2016
Source: author's elaboration on International Energy Agency, World Energy Balances database, accessed in June 2019.

value of 41,868 kilojoules/kilogram and may be used to compare the energy from different sources'.

3   IEA, World Energy Balances database, accessed in June 2019.
4   World Bank, World Development Indicators database, accessed in June 2019.
5   World Bank, World Development Indicators database, accessed in June 2019.
6   'Developed countries' are here defined as countries belonging to the Organisation for Economic Co-operation and Development (OECD).

This trend reflects the falling share of developed countries in global gross domestic product (GDP) (i.e., from 81 to 63 per cent of global GDP between 1971 and 2016) and, at the same time, the rising share of China (i.e., from 3 to 15 per cent of global GDP between 1971 and 2016).[7]

It should also be outlined that developed countries have managed over time to make better use of energy by enhancing their levels of energy efficiency. While energy intensity (i.e., the indicator measuring the amount of energy consumed to produce the same amount of wealth, such as a unit of GDP) has decreased in nearly all world regions, the strongest reductions have indeed occurred in developed countries. This has been the result of an economic transition from energy-intensive manufacturing to services, as well as of energy efficiency enhancements. In 2016, developed countries used on average 12 per cent less energy per dollar of GDP than developing countries.[8]

Accounting for 22 per cent of global demand in 2016, China has become the main energy-consuming country in the world, while the United States rank second (with 16 per cent of global demand). India, Russia, and Japan rank third, fourth, and fifth respectively. Together, these five countries account for more than half of global energy demand (Table 1.1).

Fossil fuels have historically been the cornerstone of the global energy system, and they continue to be so today. Representing 81 per cent of global energy supply in 2016, fossil fuels have indeed maintained almost unchanged their share in the global energy supply mix throughout the last fifty years.

While remaining the dominant fuel, the share of oil in the global energy supply mix fell from 44 per cent in 1971 to 32 per cent in 2016. The share of coal has fluctuated at 27 per cent, while the share of natural gas has grown from 16 per cent in 1971 to 22 per cent in 2016. The share of nuclear energy rose from 1 per cent in 1971 to 5 per cent in 2016. Hydro and biofuels have maintained their positions in the mix –

7   World Bank, World Development Indicators database, accessed in June 2019.
8   IEA, World Energy Balances database, accessed in June 2019.

Table 1.1 *Global energy demand by country, 2016*

Country	Energy demand (Mtoe)	Share in world energy demand	
	2016	*2016*	*1971*
China	2,958	22%	7%
United States	2,167	16%	29%
India	862	6%	3%
Russia	732	5%	N/A
Japan	426	3%	5%
Germany	310	2%	6%
Brazil	285	2%	1%
Korea	282	2%	0.3%
Canada	280	2%	3%
Iran	248	2%	3%
Rest of the world	5,211	38%	44%
World	13,761	100%	100%

Source: author's elaboration on International Energy Agency, World Energy Balances database, accessed in June 2019.

respectively at 2 per cent and 10 per cent, while other renewables such as wind and solar have emerged, growing from 0 to 2 per cent of the global supply mix between 1971 and 2016 (Figure 1.2).

Energy supply mixes greatly differ among world regions and individual countries, also as a result of different energy resource endowments. Differences are particularly pronounced in fuels mainly utilised for electricity generation, such as coal, natural gas, hydro, nuclear, and other renewables like wind and solar. In fact, given its predominant role in transportation and its limited substitutability with other fuels, oil is widely utilised across the world. To understand this variety, let's take into consideration the world's top-10 energy-consuming countries (Figure 1.3).

Coal covers 65 per cent of China's energy demand and more than 40 per cent of India's demand. Both countries are endowed with large coal reserves, and respectively contribute to 46 per cent and 9 per cent

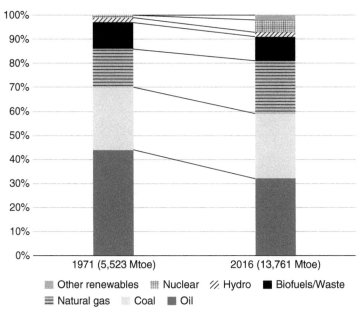

FIGURE 1.2 Share of global energy supply by fuel, 1971 and 2016
Source: author's elaboration on International Energy Agency, World
Energy Balances database, accessed in June 2019.

of global coal production (BP, 2018a). Natural gas covers around
70 per cent of Iran's energy demand and around 50 per cent of
Russia's energy demand. Not by coincidence, the two countries own
the world's largest reserves of natural gas, with a share of respectively
17 per cent and 18 per cent of total global reserves. Hydro is particularly important in the energy mixes of Brazil and Canada, two countries richly endowed with water resources. Brazil also stands out in the
field of biofuels; based on the country's rich forest and energy crop
resources they contribute to more than 30 per cent of the country's
energy mix. The utilisation of nuclear and other renewables such as
wind and solar energy widely differ among countries, but on the basis
of different energy policy choices rather than on the basis of different
natural endowments.

But what are the most energy-consuming sectors of the economy? To answer this question, it is necessary to look at another

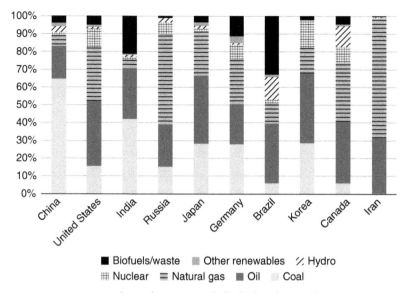

FIGURE I.3 Share of energy supply by fuel in the world's top-10 energy-consuming countries, 2016
Source: author's elaboration on International Energy Agency, World Energy Balances database, accessed in June 2019.

indicator: total final energy consumption. In fact, while the previously utilised global energy demand indicator illustrates the overall energy supply available for use in a country, the total final energy consumption indicator shows the energy that is actually used by final consumers – the energy used in homes, transportation, and businesses. This introduces the concept of energy balance, which clarifies how energy products are transformed into one another and ultimately used. The various relationships among energy products are also outlined in an energy balance. For this reason, the best way to appreciate an energy balance is perhaps the one of representing it in a graphic manner through a Sankey diagram which would offer a clear summary of the main flows of energy in a certain territory, and how they ultimately define its energy balance.

Such a diagram also highlights that substantial losses character-ise the global energy system. That is, when energy is transformed (e.g., when natural gas is burned to produce electricity) or transported (e.g., when electricity is transmitted over long distances), energy losses inevitably occur. A simple example of energy loss is provided in our daily life by an incandescent light bulb, in which most of the input energy is lost in the form of unwanted heat energy.

In terms of final energy consumption, industry has traditionally been – and continues to be – the largest consuming sector in the world (37 per cent of total final energy consumption in 2016), followed by the transport sector (29 per cent) and the residential sector (22 per cent). Other relevant consuming sectors are the commerce and public services sector (8 per cent) and the agriculture and forestry sector (2 per cent).[9]

This introductory overview of the global energy system reveals an important element: natural resource endowment plays a key role in defining a country's energy profile. Should a country be richly endowed with a certain energy resource, it would certainly try to exploit it as much as possible in order to ensure a cheap and secure energy supply to its citizens. Ideally, such as in the case of oil or natural gas, it would also try to export it to global markets in order to get a rent out of it. A recent example of this is represented by the shale gas revolution in the United States. Led by new extraction techniques (i.e., hydraulic fracking and horizontal drilling), since the early 2000s, the development of new sources of shale gas in the United States has offset declines in production from conventional gas reservoirs, completely reshaping the country's energy mix. In 2006, coal provided 50 per cent of total electricity generation in the United States, while gas accounted for less than 20 per cent. In 2016, the share of coal was just over 30 per cent, with natural gas overtaking coal and rising to nearly 35 per cent (BP, 2018a). This is a clear illustration of how energy resource endowment defines a country's energy profile.

But other elements could also play a role in defining a country's energy profile. For instance, environmental considerations can lead a country richly endowed with coal resources to stop using them in order to reduce pollution. As another example, safety concerns can lead a country to close downs its nuclear power plants.

---

[9]   IEA, World Energy Balances database, accessed in June 2019.

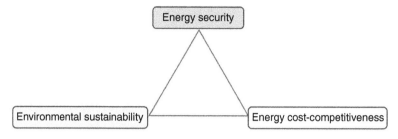

FIGURE I.4 The 'energy policy triangle'
Source: author's elaboration.

All this suggests that a country's energy profile is shaped by the interaction of its natural resource endowment with another key element: its energy policy. Energy policy can be defined as the way adopted by a government to tackle energy development issues, including production, distribution, and consumption. Energy policy can be seen as a triangle, the three vertices of which are represented by three major policy goals: security, cost-competitiveness, and environmental sustainability (Figure 1.4).

Energy security is defined by the IEA (2019d) as

> The uninterrupted availability of energy sources at an affordable price. Energy security has many dimensions: long-term energy security mainly deals with timely investments to supply energy in line with economic developments and sustainable environmental needs. Short-term energy security focuses on the ability of the energy system to react promptly to sudden changes within the supply–demand balance. Lack of energy security is thus linked to the negative economic and social impacts of either physical unavailability of energy, or prices that are not competitive or are overly volatile.

Energy cost-competitiveness relates to the cost of energy, and therefore to the affordability of energy among the population. This entails guaranteeing a level of energy prices that is both internationally competitive and affordable for final consumers. Lack of energy cost-competitiveness can undermine a country's overall economic competitiveness, and it can also push part of the population into energy poverty.

Environmental sustainability relates to the reduction – or, ideally, to the complete mitigation – of the damaging effects of energy exploration, production, and consumption on the environment and on the climate. Energy is indeed the major contributor to climate change and to local air pollution, and it also contributes to other environmental problems spanning from acid rains to water and soil pollution.

In an ideal world, these three components would be perfectly balanced and countries would be able to offer their citizens a secure, cost-competitive, and environmentally sustainable energy system. But, in reality, difficult trade-offs exist between these three components and governments have to make policy choices that will inevitably favour one or two elements over the other(s). Just to give an example, a government deciding to keep burning cheap and domestic coal to ensure energy security and cost-competitiveness would implicitly compromise environmental sustainability. Delivering energy policies which simultaneously address energy security, cost-competitiveness, and environmental sustainability could well be considered as one of the most formidable challenges facing governments in the twenty-first century, particularly in view of facing the existential threat of climate change.

I.3   ENERGY AND CLIMATE CHANGE

As stated by the G20 (2015, p.6) leaders, 'climate change is one of the greatest challenges of our time'. Energy production and use is by far the main contributor to climate change, and for this reason energy and climate change must be considered altogether, as two sides of the same coin.

The most authoritative international scientific body on climate change, the United Nations Intergovernmental Panel on Climate Change (IPCC, 2011b, p.1), defines climate change as 'a change in the state of the climate that can be identified (e.g., using statistical tests) by changes in the mean and/or the variability of its properties, and that persists for an extended period, typically decades or longer. It refers to any change in climate over time, whether due to natural variability or as a result of human activity.' Albeit the earth's climate has changed throughout history,[10] since the Industrial Revolution the average climate has changed at an unprecedented rate. According to the IPCC (2018, p.6), 'human activities are estimated to have caused approximately 1 degree Celsius of global warming above pre-industrial levels'. This has been the result of increased human-made carbon dioxide (CO_2), methane (CH_4), and nitrous oxide emissions (N_2O) – commonly referred altogether as greenhouse gases (GHG) – into the atmosphere.

The physics of climate change is rather simple. As explained by NASA (2019), 'sunlight passes through the atmosphere and warms the earth's surface. This heat is radiated back towards space. Most of the outgoing heat is absorbed by GHG molecules and re-emitted in all directions, warming the surface of the earth and the lower atmosphere, allowing life in the planet'. That is, the earth does require a certain level of this GHG effect. Without enough GHG effect, the earth surface would indeed be largely frozen, with no possibility of life. On the contrary, with too much GHG effect the earth would be too hot to allow life. In short, also as pointed by NASA (2019), 'in order to maintain a stable climate and allow life, the earth must be in a specific energetic equilibrium between the radiation it receives from the sun and the radiation it emits out to space'.

The climate change problem emerged as, after the Industrial Revolution, human activities such as fossil fuels combustion have strengthened this GHG effect, ultimately causing global warming. The large part of this warming occurred since the 1970s, with the six warmest years on record taking place since 2010 (NASA, 2019). Not by coincidence, between 1970 and 2014 global GHG emissions increased by 92 per cent, driven by fossil fuel combustion (Figure 1.5).

[10]   According to NASA (2019), in the last 650,000 years there have been seven cycles of glacial advance and retreat, with the abrupt end of the last ice age about 7,000 years ago marking the beginning of the modern climate era.

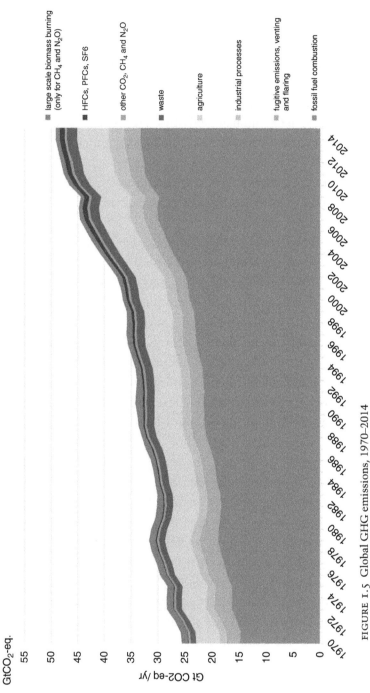

GtCO$_2$-eq.

- large scale biomass burning (only for CH$_4$ and N$_2$O)
- HFCs, PFCs, SF6
- other CO$_2$, CH$_4$ and N$_2$O
- waste
- agriculture
- industrial processes
- fugitive emissions, venting and flaring
- fossil fuel combustion

FIGURE 1.5 Global GHG emissions, 1970–2014
Source: International Energy Agency, CO$_2$ Emissions from Fuel Combustion 2018.

CO_2 is the largest component of GHG emissions, accounting for 73 per cent of the total in 2014, followed by CH_4 (19 per cent), N_2O (6 per cent), and other gases (2 per cent) (IEA, 2018a).

In 2014, the largest sources of GHG emissions were fossil fuel combustion (68 per cent, mainly CO_2), and agriculture (12 per cent, mainly CH_4 and N_2O). Other sources of GHG were CO_2 from industrial processes (6 per cent, mostly cement production) and CO_2 and CH_4 emissions from fuel production (6 per cent). Energy is therefore at the core of the climate change problem, being responsible for 74 per cent of global GHG emissions (IEA, 2018a).[11]

Global GHG emissions have been driven by different regional dynamics over time. Until 2000, the growth in emissions was largely driven by developed countries, particularly led by the United States. Since 2000, developed countries have generally decreased their emissions,[12] while emerging economies have largely increased their emissions. Since 2000, Asia has led global GHG emissions growth, reaching a level of emissions twice that of the Americas and three times that of Europe. China has been the key driver of this trend, contributing to half of Asia's emissions.

It should be outlined that at global level three-quarters of GHG emissions are currently produced in only ten blocks, with the top-three emitting ones – China, the United States, and Europe – contributing to more than half of the world's total emissions. Elsewhere, a hundred countries emit altogether only 3.5 per cent of global GHG emissions.

In December 2015, the 195 parties of the United Nations Framework Convention of Climate Change (UNFCCC) adopted the Paris Agreement, a global agreement aimed at 'holding the increase in

[11] This sums GHG emissions from fossil fuel combustion and GHG emissions from fuel production.

[12] Since 2000, Europe's emissions have decreased by more than 10 per cent, with pronounced decreases in the United Kingdom (–30 per cent), France (–20 per cent), Italy (–20 per cent), Spain (–10 per cent), and Germany (–10 per cent). Meanwhile, the United States' emissions have decreased by 16 per cent (IEA, 2018a). These trends have also been driven by the economic crisis, which in turn has led to a significant delocalisation of industrial processes in developing countries.

the global average temperature to well below 2 degrees Celsius above pre-industrial levels and pursuing efforts to limit the temperature increase to 1.5 degrees Celsius above pre-industrial levels, recognising that this would significantly reduce the risks and impacts of climate change' (UNFCCC, 2015, p.3). The Paris Agreement is the first-ever universal, legally binding, agreement on climate change. Its predecessor, the Kyoto Protocol, was indeed based on a principle of common but differentiated historical responsibilities, which put the obligation to reduce GHG emissions only on developed countries. The Paris Agreement thus represents a coherent response to the new regional GHG emissions dynamics which have emerged since 2000.

However, notwithstanding this unprecedented global commitment, the world is not yet on track to combat climate change. Between 2015 and 2016, global GHG emissions were flat, but they rose again in 2017 and 2018, each year marking a new all-time high (WMO, 2019). Given these trends, scientists estimate the world to be currently on track for a temperature rise of 3 degrees Celsius by the end of the century (IPCC, 2018), a level which would imply higher frequency of extreme weather events, more crop losses, more water shortages, more inundated coastal cities (e.g., from The Hague to Rio de

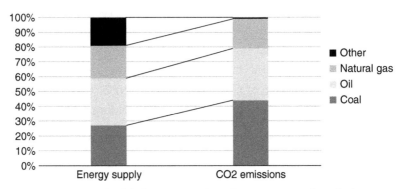

FIGURE I.6 Global energy supply and CO_2 emissions from fuel combustion, 2016
Source: author's elaboration on International Energy Agency (2018a).

Janeiro, from Hong Kong to Venice), more diseases and, in sum, more suffering for millions of people.

Given energy-related CO_2 emissions are significantly responsible for the problem, responding to climate change requires a revolution of the current global energy system. For instance, it is clear that the world's reliance on the most-polluting fossil fuel, coal, should urgently be addressed. Coal indeed contributes to 27 per cent of global energy supply, but to 44 per cent of global CO_2 emissions from fuel combustion (IEA, 2018a) (Figure 1.6).

The profound global energy system transformation required to tackle climate change is generally named global energy transition, to indicate the progressive shift from fossil fuels to the clean energy sources necessary to substantially reduce GHG emissions and avoid a dangerous rise in global temperatures.

I.4   ENERGY ACCESS

Energy is a key enabler of human activities and providing access to affordable modern energy services represents a key prerequisite for eliminating poverty and reducing inequalities. The provision of basic services, spanning from clean water provision to healthcare, depend on energy availability. Likewise, there cannot be development without the activities enabled by energy – such as, for instance, lighting, transport, heating, or telecommunication. For this reason, the United Nations (2015, p.7) included the achievement of 'universal access to affordable, reliable, sustainable and modern energy' among the Sustainable Development Goals at the core of its 2030 Agenda for Sustainable Development.

The IEA (2019f) defines modern energy access as 'the situation of a household having reliable and affordable access to clean cooking facilities and to a minimum level of electricity consumption which is increasing over time'. Ensuring modern energy access to all represents the great social and economic challenge of our times: in 2017, 840 million people across the world indeed continued to lack access to electricity, while 2.9 billion people continued to lack access to clean cooking facilities (IEA et al., 2019).

Thanks to substantial efforts across developing countries, the global electrification rate increased from 83 per cent in 2010 to 89 per cent in 2017. As illustrated by the IEA et al. (2019, p.4),

> [E]lectrification efforts have been particularly successful in Central and Southern Asia, where 91 per cent of the population had access to electricity in 2017. Access rates in Latin America and the Caribbean, as well as Eastern and South-eastern Asia, climbed to 98 per cent in 2017. Among the 20 countries with the largest populations lacking access to electricity, India, Bangladesh, Kenya, and Myanmar made the most significant progress since 2010. Sub-Saharan Africa remains the region with the largest access deficit: here, 573 million people – more than one in two – lack access to electricity.

Not by coincidence, Sub-Saharan Africa is home to fifteen out of the twenty world's countries with the lowest electrification rates (Figure 1.7). In particular, Burundi, Chad, Malawi, the Democratic Republic of Congo, and Niger are the five countries in the world with the lowest electrification rates.

According to the IEA et al. (2019, p.6), 'the share of global population with access to clean cooking fuels and technologies increased from 57 per cent in 2010 to 61 per cent in 2017. However, in 2017 almost 3 billion people continued to lack access to clean cooking across the world'. Central and Southern Asia, Eastern and South-eastern Asia, and sub-Saharan Africa account for the majority of the population lacking access (Figure 1.8).

In sub-Saharan Africa, the number of people without access to clean cooking keeps rising as a result of strong population growth outpacing clean cooking access progress. Across the continent, the population lacking access indeed increased from less than 750 million in 2010 to around 900 million in 2017 (IEA et al., 2019). In contrast, in the same period of time, Asia showed substantial progress relative to population growth. India and other developing countries in Asia have indeed made substantial progress in the field, employing different methods depending on the national context (e.g., liquefied petroleum gas in India; natural gas

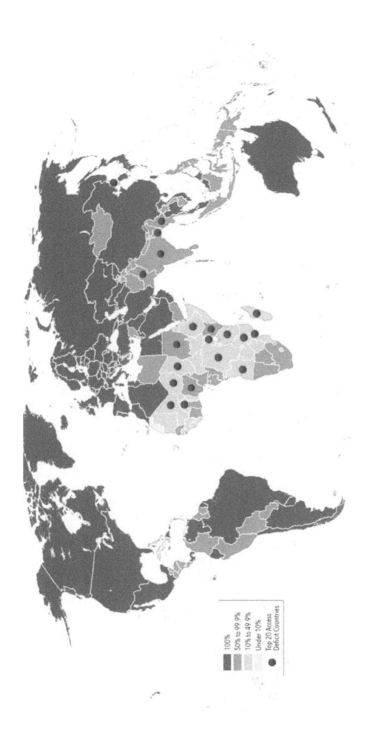

FIGURE 1.7 Share of population with access to electricity, 2017

Source: International Energy Agency et al., Tracking SDG 7: The Energy Progress Report 2019.

100%
50% to 99.9%
10% to 49.9%
Under 10%
Top 20 Access
Deficit Countries

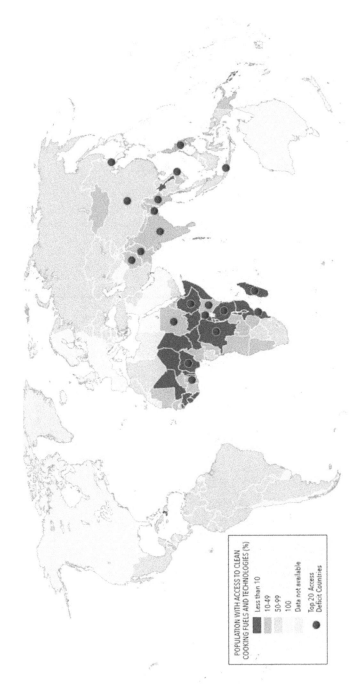

FIGURE 1.8 Share of population with access to clean cooking fuels and technologies, 2017
Source: International Energy Agency et al., Tracking SDG 7: The Energy Progress Report 2019. All rights reserved.

POPULATION WITH ACCESS TO CLEAN
COOKING FUELS AND TECHNOLOGIES (%)

Less than 10
10-49
50-99
100
Data not available

● Top 20 Access
Deficit Countries

grid expansion in China). It should be noted that, globally, a strong urban–rural divide exists in this field: the rate of access to clean cooking fuels and technologies remains at 83 per cent in urban areas, while it stands at only 34 per cent in rural areas (IEA et al., 2019).

Providing universal access to electricity and clean cooking would have great benefits for the living standards as well as for the economic prospects of the people currently lacking access. The case of electrification is illustrative of how the lack of energy access represents a major stumbling block for socio-economic development. Any developed country has required secure access to electricity to foster its economic development. In developing countries, electricity access is key to improve health conditions, increase productivity, enhance overall economic competitiveness, and ultimately promote economic growth and poverty reduction. Expanding electricity access indeed increases time spent in income-generating activities, especially outside the agricultural sector. Expanding access to electricity also increases the number of manufacturing firms, their productivity, and their revenues (Bonan et al., 2017).

The case of clean cooking is illustrative of the social character of energy access. In developing countries, women and children are often in charge of collecting firewood, an activity that is estimated to take on average an hour and half per day. This substantial amount of time could be rather used for education or for productive activities, boosting children's education as well as women's empowerment. Furthermore, each year across the globe, around 3.8 million people die prematurely from illness attributable to indoor air pollution generated from these cooking practices (WHO, 2018).[13] Given women and children the ones spending more time indoors, they are the first victims of this phenomenon. Expanding access to clean cooking would lower this morally unacceptable premature death toll, and enhance the living conditions of the most vulnerable.

---

[13] According to the WHO (2018), among these 3.8 million deaths: (i) 27 per cent are due to pneumonia; (ii) 18 per cent from stroke; (iii) 27 per cent from ischaemic heart disease; (iv) 20 per cent from chronic obstructive pulmonary disease; and (v) 8 per cent from lung cancer.

Solving these issues represents a fundamental prerequisite to unleash developing countries' economic potential. Given the order of magnitude of the challenge, only a joint effort of interested countries and of international public and private players could provide a comprehensive solution. This is already being demonstrated by a number of initiatives currently ongoing across the developing world, but in order to meet the United Nations' goal of ensuring universal access to modern energy to all by 2030, much stronger action is required.

I.5 ENERGY GEOPOLITICS

Energy has long shaped global geopolitics, determining great powers, alliances, and outcomes of wars. Every international order in modern history has been based on an energy resource: coal was the backdrop for the British Empire in the nineteenth century, oil has been at the core of the subsequent 'American Century', and today many expect China to become the twenty-first century's world renewable energy superpower (IRENA, 2019a).

Since World War I, oil has undoubtedly represented the cornerstone of global energy geopolitics. The decision of then-First Lord of the Admiralty Winston Churchill to shift the power source of the Royal Navy's ships from coal to oil in order to make the fleet faster than its German counterpart truly signaled the opening of a new era. The switch from the reliable coal supplies from Wales to the insecure oil supplies from what was then Persia, not only made the oil-rich Middle East a key epicentre of global geopolitics, but also turned oil into a key national security issue (Yergin, 1990).

Since the early twentieth century, control of oil resources played a central role in several wars. This was, for instance, the case of the 1967–70 Biafran War, the 1980–8 Iran–Iraq War, the 1990–1 Gulf War, the 2003–11 Iraq War, and of the conflict in the Niger Delta ongoing since 2004 (Yergin, 2011).

The second half of the twentieth century also saw increasing tensions between oil producing and consuming countries, which in two cases erupted in major oil crises. In September 1960, the

Organization of Petroleum Exporting Countries (OPEC) was established in Baghdad, with the participation of five member countries:
Saudi Arabia, Iraq, Iran, Kuwait, and Venezuela.[14] The original aim of
OPEC was to prevent its members from lowering the price of oil, by
coordinating their production and export policies. During the 1970s,
some of OPEC members also had the aim of nationalising their petroleum resources to preserve sovereignty.

OPEC's geopolitical role of became clear as the Arab–Israeli
War – also known as Yom Kippur War – erupted in October 1973.
Arab members of OPEC imposed an embargo against the United
States, the Netherlands, Portugal, and South Africa in retaliation of
their support to Israel. A ban of oil exports to the targeted countries, as
well as oil production cuts, were introduced by OPEC. This resulted in
a sharp rise in oil prices, and in severe oil shortages and spiralling
inflation across the West. As OPEC kept raising prices in the following
years, its geopolitical and economic power grew.

In the aftermath of the 1973 oil crisis, and upon proposal of then-
US Secretary of State Henry Kissinger, the IEA was established in
November 1974 as a platform for oil-importing countries in the West
to coordinate a shared response to major disruptions in the supply of
oil.[15] This also allowed the introduction of a requirement for all IEA
member countries to maintain strategic petroleum reserves equal to at
least ninety days of their previous year's net oil imports.[16]

---

[14] Other countries have since been added: Libya (1962), United Arab Emirates (1967),
Algeria (1969), Nigeria (1971), Ecuador (1973), Gabon (1975), Angola (2007), Equatorial
Guinea (2017), Democratic Republic of the Congo (2018). Indonesia, which joined in
1962, left the organisation in 2007. Qatar, which joined in 1961, left in 2019.

[15] The original founding members of the IEA in 1974 were Austria, Belgium, Canada,
Denmark, Germany, Ireland, Italy, Japan, Luxembourg, the Netherlands, Norway,
Spain, Sweden, Switzerland, Turkey, the United Kingdom, and the United States.
Joining in the following years were Greece (1976), New Zealand (1977), Australia
(1979), Portugal (1981), Finland (1992), France (1992), Hungary (1997), Czech
Republic (2001), Republic of Korea (2002), Slovak Republic (2007), Poland (2008),
Estonia (2014), and Mexico (2018).

[16] Interesting insights on the IEA's inception and early developments can be found in
Kissinger (2009).

A second oil crisis erupted in 1979, as a result of the Iranian revolution and the following 1980–8 war with Iraq, which brought the region into turmoil. By 1981, the price of oil stabilised at USD 32 per barrel, a level ten times higher than before the 1973 oil crisis (BP, 2018a).

In the following decades, other oil price shocks occurred, notably in relation to major geopolitical developments in the Middle East. For instance, in 1990, an oil price shock took place in the aftermath of the Iraqi invasion of Kuwait, with a doubling of oil price in a matter of a few months that contributed to the early 1990s recession in the United States.

But energy geopolitics is not limited to oil. Natural gas, nuclear energy, and even renewable energy sources such as wind and solar do have – more or less critical – geopolitical aspects.

In certain areas of the world natural gas is even considered to be more geopolitical than oil. This certainly is the case of Europe, where natural gas markets have been developed since the 1960s on the basis of large pipeline infrastructures connecting key suppliers such as Russia and Norway to European consumers. This situation has led to Europe's over-reliance on a few major suppliers. In 2017, natural gas imports from Russia still provided a third of Europe's total natural gas supply mix (EIA, 2018a).

For decades, this situation has not raised energy security concerns in Europe. During the 1970s and the 1980s, in the midst of the Cold War, Europe decisively pursued the construction of the long pipelines connecting the large Siberian natural gas fields and Europe, which still today represent the main avenues of Russian natural gas export. Europe pursued these projects notwithstanding the strong opposition of the Reagan Administration, which even sanctioned German and French companies engaged in the construction of the 'Brotherhood' pipeline, which still today represents the major natural gas supply route to Europe (European Parliament, 2016).

The (over-)reliance on Russian natural gas supplies started to be considered as a major geopolitical threat in Europe when, first in

January 2006 and then in January 2009, natural gas pricing disputes between Russia and Ukraine led to the halt of Russian natural gas supplies to Europe via Ukraine – its primary transit route. This caused economic damages to Europe, notably in Southeastern European countries heavily dependent on Russian natural gas for both electricity generation and residential heating. Europe responded to these natural gas crises by adopting an energy security strategy mainly focused on reducing its dependency on Russian natural gas supply. In the midst of the 2014 Ukraine crisis, concerns about a potential politically motivated disruption of all European natural gas supplies from Russia lifted this issue to the top of the European agenda again, leading to renewed efforts to lower the European dependency on Russian natural gas supply under the umbrella of the European Union (EU)'s 'Energy Union' initiative (Tagliapietra and Zachmann, 2016).

Nuclear energy presents both security and geopolitical concerns. Issues like safety of nuclear facilities and nuclear waste management represent serious security concerns. The concerns for nuclear safety have particularly amplified after the Chernobyl accident in 1986 and the Fukushima disaster of 2011. These events sparkled, particularly in Europe and in Japan, broad public debates on nuclear energy. In certain cases, these debates led to radical energy policy shifts. For instance, after the Chernobyl accident, Italy held a referendum on nuclear power, which resulted in the decision to close down all operating nuclear power plants in the country. More recently, after the Fukushima disaster, a surge of anti-nuclear protests in Germany pushed Chancellor Angela Merkel to announce the closure of around half of the operating reactors in the country and the complete phase-out of nuclear by 2022. These concerns have been most recently accompanied by the emergence of new risks concerning potential terrorist attacks at nuclear power plants.

From a geopolitical perspective, proliferation is the main risk associated with nuclear energy. Elements of the nuclear fuel cycle can in fact be used to develop nuclear weapons, either through uranium enrichment or through reprocessing (i.e., the separation of plutonium from the highly radioactive spent fuel). It was precisely the close link between the civil and military use of nuclear energy that led to the establishment in 1957 of the International Atomic Energy Agency (IAEA), a United Nations organisation tasked with promoting the peaceful use of nuclear energy. In 1968 (i.e., in the midst of the Cold War), the General Assembly of the United Nations also approved the Nuclear Non-Proliferation Treaty, aimed at the disarmament of countries with nuclear weapons, as well as at the prevention of nuclear weapons adoption by countries still without them.

Finally, it should be underlined that energy geopolitics is here to stay even in a low-carbon world. A radical transformation of the current global energy architecture would indeed have profound geopolitical implications. First of all, a large-scale shift to low-carbon energy would disrupt long-lasting socio-economic models, notably in oil and gas producing countries. For instance, producing countries in the Middle East and North Africa (MENA) are still overly reliant on the oil and gas rent. Notwithstanding the adoption of elaborate economic diversification strategies, countries in the region have struggled to diversify their economies, and this might represent an element of vulnerability in times of global energy transition (Tagliapietra, 2017a). Secondly, it is important to outline that the rapid development of wind and solar energy, alongside electric cars, has recently sparkled concerns over the potential security of supply risks related to the minerals underpinning the low-carbon transition. These concerns certainly echo the broader energy security risks associated to oil and gas resources, but they also reflect past experiences of mineral supply disruptions, such as the 1978 'Cobalt crisis'. As today, at the time, the Democratic Republic of the Congo (DRC, then named Zaire) was the world's leading producer of cobalt. In May 1978 a conflict broke out in the copper-cobalt–rich province of Katanga, as a separatist militia tried to force the province's secession from the regime of Mobutu Sese Seko. The political unrest caused a global cobalt supply shortage, leading international cobalt price to more than quintuple. Should something similar happen today, the consequences for the global supply chains for electric cars would be substantial. Cobalt is indeed a key component of electric cars' batteries, which are themselves the core components of electric cars. This is just an example of how the minerals underpinning the low-carbon transition (e.g., just to mention few of them, cobalt, lithium, graphite, nickel, rare earths) are likely to have their own geopolitical risks, exactly as oil and gas have had their own ones.

1.6   KEY TAKEAWAYS

Global Energy Trends

- Energy is a key prerequisite for modern life and is the lifeblood of modern societies.
- Global energy demand has more than doubled over the last fifty years.
- Led by China, global energy demand growth shifted from developed to developing countries.
- Coal, oil, and natural gas continue to provide 80 per cent of global energy supply.
- Wind and solar energy currently contribute to just 2 per cent of global energy supply.
- Energy supply mixes greatly differ among countries, also due to different resource endowments.
- Energy policy has three aims: security, cost-competitiveness, and environmental sustainability.

Energy and Climate Change

- Climate change: energy is responsible for about 70 per cent of global greenhouse-gas emissions.
- Until 2000, global emissions were driven by developed countries; after, by emerging countries.
- Among all fuels, coal is by far the worst offender as far as CO_2 emissions are concerned.
- The Paris Agreement aims at holding the increase in global temperature to well below 2 degrees Celsius.

- The world is currently not on track to meet the targets set under the Paris Agreement.

Energy Access

- Energy access is a key prerequisite for eliminating poverty and reducing inequalities.
- 840 million people lack access to electricity, notably in sub-Saharan Africa.
- A US refrigerator consumes ten times more electricity than a person in many African countries.
- 2.9 billion people lack access to clean cooking facilities, notably in Asia and Africa.
- 3.8 million people die prematurely every year due to indoor air pollution associated with cooking.

Energy Geopolitics

- Energy has long shaped global geopolitics, defining great powers, alliances, and wars.
- Oil has been at the centre of the twentieth-century international relations.
- In Europe, natural gas is viewed as being even more geopolitical than oil, notably due to Russia.
- Nuclear energy presents both security and geopolitical concerns, such as proliferation.

2 Oil

INTRODUCTION TO OIL

Oil is a fossil fuel, alongside coal and natural gas. Fossil fuels are the product of the remains of ancient plants and animals. During their lives, plants and animals accumulated energy coming from the Sun, and, after their deaths, they were buried for millions of years until they turned into fossil fuels. So, it can be said that what fossil fuels are giving us back today is the solar energy accumulated by prehistoric plants and animals in a very far-away past.

More precisely, as the EIA (2019b) puts it, 'oil is a mixture of hydrocarbons that formed from plants and animals that lived millions of years ago. Crude oil is a fossil fuel, and it exists in liquid form in underground pools or reservoirs, in tiny spaces within sedimentary rocks, and near the surface in tar (or oil) sands'. All existing hydrocarbon molecules consist of only two types of atoms: carbon atoms and hydrogen atoms. Depending on the quantity of carbon atoms present in the molecule, the hydrocarbons are gaseous (up to 4 atoms), liquid (from 5 to 16 atoms) or solid (over 16 atoms)[1]. Typically, about a third of the hydrocarbons in oil are present in the low-mass range, with fewer than 10 carbon atoms per molecule. A third fall in an intermediate range, with between 10 and about 18 carbon atoms per molecule. The heaviest components are represented by viscous, semi-solid compounds, as exemplified by asphalt. The key product of the early modern

---

[1] There are thousands of hydrocarbons with different molecular structures, but the same chemical composition. There are hydrocarbons with single bonds (like methane), double bonds (like propylene) or triple bonds (like acetylene). By treating heavier hydrocarbons through a process called cracking, it is possible to break these bonds and obtain lighter and more versatile molecules, with which the wide range of petrochemicals products is composed.

oil industry was kerosene, in wide demand in the pre-electric age for both domestic and public lighting. When combusted, kerosene decomposes into a number of molecular fragments that indeed radiate significant intensities of visible light. The molecules that make up kerosene are composed of 10–15 carbon atoms. Kerosene is slightly heavier and slightly less volatile than gasoline. Gasoline, which together with diesel would emerge as the most important product of the modern oil age, is composed of molecular species consisting of 8–12 carbon atoms. Diesel, less volatile than gasoline, is composed of 10–20 carbon atoms.

Oil has been the world's dominant source of energy since the mid-twentieth century. However, the roots of oil use extend deep into the past. Thanks to the ancient Greek historian Herodotus, we know that more than 4,000 years ago oil seeps were exploited to provide a source of asphalt and pitch that was used as mortar to construct the walls and towers of Babylon. In the first century AD, Persian scholar al-Rāzī described the method of oil distillation in his *Kitāb al-Asrār* (Book of Secrets), a method that, through Islamic Spain, would also have become available in Western Europe a hundred years later. Also in the first century AD, the Roman naturalist Pliny illustrated the pharmaceutical properties of oil and its ability to treat various maladies (Yergin, 1990). Since then, oil uses remained episodic and of little economic importance for many centuries, notably up to the second half of the nineteenth century.

The birth of the modern oil industry is usually attributed to the successful drilling of a well in Titusville, Pennsylvania, on 27 August 1859. The well, drilled by Edwin Drake, had a daily production of around 1,500 litres of oil, which were initially stored in whiskey barrels. The oil industry grew through the second part of the century, driven by the demand for kerosene and oil lamps. But the real game changer for the industry arrived towards the end of the nineteenth century, and on four wheels: the introduction of the motor car. In 1886, Karl Benz patented his Benz Patent-Motorwagen, marking the birth of the modern car. In 1908, the Ford Model T was launched, becoming one of the first cars to be accessible to the masses. Cars were rapidly adopted across the United States, and from that moment on oil demand increased sharply. By 1910, transportation had indeed already replaced lighting as the primary market for oil. In that context, early oil discoveries like those in Pennsylvania were not sufficient any more to satisfy demand. That led to 'oil booms' in several other regions, such as Ohio, Texas, Oklahoma, and California.

Those were the epic years that saw the irresistible rise of John D. Rockefeller, the founder of one of the largest oil companies that ever existed: Standard Oil. Thanks to a sustained policy of acquisitions, Standard Oil reached control of more than 60 per cent of the United States' oil market. In 1911, the Supreme Court ruled that Rockefeller's monopoly was illegal and ordered executives to divide the company into 34 independent companies, the biggest two being Standard Oil of New Jersey (which lately became Exxon) and Standard Oil of New York (which then became Mobil). Rockefeller owned a quarter of the shares of the resultant companies. As those share values mostly doubled after the break-up, Rockefeller turned out to be the world's richest man of his time, and among the richest men in history.

By 1910, significant oil reservoirs were discovered across the world, from the Dutch East Indies (1885) to Baku (1871), from Persia (1908) to Peru (1863), from Venezuela (1914) to Mexico (1914).[2] World War I kicked off a new oil era, which finally reached full steam after World War II as oil became the world's dominant source of energy that it still remains today.

---

[2]   The story of Persian oil is particularly remarkable. Oil exploration license was granted there in 1901 to the British businessman William D'Arcy. With no success by April 1908, the venture was close to collapse. Almost bankrupted, D'Arcy took the inevitable decision to abandon exploration activities in Persia. He sent a telegram to his chief of staff, ordering to end operations and go back home. Convinced of the proximity of a discovery, the chief of staff did not respect the order and delayed its follow-up. After few weeks, the venture found the large-scale Masjed Soleiman oil field. After the discovery, the Anglo-Persian Oil Company was founded. The company was renamed Anglo-Iranian Oil Company in 1935, and then British Petroleum Company in 1954 (one of the antecedents of today's BP). After the Islamic Revolution of 1979, its assets in Iran were nationalised and taken over by the National Iranian Oil Company.

2.2 OIL RESERVES, PRODUCTION, AND DEMAND

Oil resources can be either conventional or unconventional. Conventional oil resources consist of deposits for which the geological characteristics of the formations containing the crude oil and the physical properties of the fluid itself allow the crude oil to flow spontaneously to the extraction wells. In contrast, unconventional oil resources are those trapped in rocky deposits with low porosity and permeability or consisting of crude oil with high density (e.g., close to or greater than water density), the exploitation of which involves the application of specific recovery technologies, such as fracking and horizontal drilling. Conventional and unconventional oil resources thus do not differ in chemistry, but rather in the kind of reservoirs they are, as well as in the techniques required to extract them. All this also applies to natural gas (Figure 2.1).

While considering oil (and natural gas) reservoirs, it is important to pay particular attention to the terminology used. As illustrated by BP (2019, p.1),

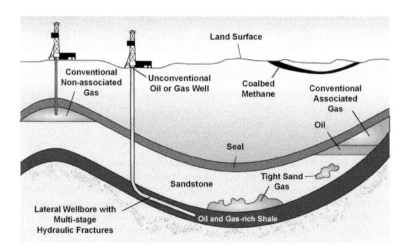

FIGURE 2.1 The geology of conventional and unconventional oil and gas reservoirs
Source: Energy Information Administration.

resources indicate the total amount of oil (or natural gas) in place in a reservoir, most of which typically can't be technically or economically recovered. Proved reserves indicate the portion of resources that is technically and economically recoverable. Proved reserves of a field are typically defined as having a better than 90 per cent chance of being produced over the life of the field. Proved reserves thus depend on both available technology and oil (or natural gas) prices. Probable reserves (called P50 reserves) indicate the reserves that are estimated to have a better than 50 per cent chance of being technically and economically producible. Possible reserves (called P10 or P20 reserves) indicate the reserves which, at present, cannot be regarded as probable, but which are estimated to have a significant, but less than 50 per cent chance of being technically and economically producible.

In 2017, proved oil reserves were estimated at 1,696.6 billion barrels (bbl) of oil (BP, 2018a), with approximately half of them being located in the Middle East (Figure 2.2).

In 2017, Venezuela owned the largest oil reserves in the world, with a considerably higher level than Saudi Arabia. Canada, Iran, and Iraq ranked third, fourth, and fifth, respectively. Further down in the top 10 emerged Russia, Kuwait, United Arab Emirates, United States, and Libya (Table 2.1).

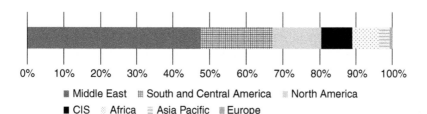

FIGURE 2.2 Share of proved oil reserves by world region, 2017
Source: author's elaboration on BP (2018a). Note: CIS indicates the Commonwealth of Independent States, which includes Russia and Armenia, Azerbaijan, Belarus, Moldova, Kazakhstan, Kyrgyzstan, Tajikistan, Turkmenistan, and Uzbekistan.

Table 2.1 *Proved oil reserves: Top-20 countries, 2017*

Country	Proved reserves (billion barrels)	Reserves-to-production ratio (years)
Venezuela	303.2	393.6
Saudi Arabia	266.2	61.0
Canada	168.9	95.8
Iran	157.2	86.5
Iraq	148.8	90.2
Russia	106.2	25.8
Kuwait	101.5	92.0
United Arab Emirates	97.8	68.1
United States	50.0	10.5
Libya	48.4	153.3
Nigeria	37.5	51.6
Kazakhstan	30.0	44.8
China	25.7	18.3
Qatar	25.2	36.1
Brazil	12.8	12.8
Algeria	12.2	21.7
Angola	9.5	15.6
Ecuador	8.3	42.7
Norway	7.9	11.0
Mexico	7.2	8.9

Source: author's elaboration on BP (2018a).

Being largely dependent on available technology and oil prices, proved oil reserves have significantly increased over time. As technology developed (making oil exploration and production easier) and oil prices grew (making a broader range of oil exploration and production activities economically viable), between 1997 and 2017 proved oil reserves sharply increased in Venezuela (from 74.9 to 303.2 bbl), Canada (from 48.8 to 168.9 bbl), and Iran (from 92.6 to 157.2 bbl). They increased slightly in Saudi Arabia (from 261.5 to 266.2 bbl) and Iraq (from 112.5 to 148.8 bbl) but decreased in Russia (from 113.1 to 106.2 bbl) (BP, 2018a).

In addition to the level of proved reserves, it is interesting to consider the reserves-to-production ratio (R/P), an indicator widely used in the sector to provide an idea of the amount of oil (or natural gas) reserves left, expressed in years.

R/P is an indicator utilised by both governments and companies to forecast the future availability of reserves. This is done for multiple purposes, such as determining a project's life and future income, or determining whether more exploration should be carried out to ensure continued supply. The R/P indicator is particularly important for companies, which generally try to keep it constant at around ten years to avoid scarcity risks.

But technological developments and changes in economic conditions can substantially alter the level of proved reserves, and therefore of the R/P indicator. In fact, the world's oil R/P level has constantly increased over the last decades.

For instance, in 1986, the world's oil R/P indicator signalled that the world would have run out of oil in forty years. After thirty years, the same ratio indicates that at current levels of proved reserves and production, the world could enjoy another fifty years of oil consumption without scarcity risk (BP, 2018a).

But how can oil reservoirs be exploited? Both onshore and offshore drilling techniques are utilised to extract oil from the earth. Onshore drilling currently represents about 70 per cent of global oil production. Various types of onshore drilling rigs exist, with different depth and mobility characteristics. The conventional land rigs typically employed in the industry cannot be moved as a whole unit, but mobile rigs (i.e., drilling systems that are mounted on wheeled trucks) also exist and are predominantly used in unconventional basins. Offshore drilling is more complex, and more expensive, than onshore drilling. The key element of offshore drilling is the platform, a structure which hosts the necessary facilities to explore, produce and process oil which lies in rocks beneath the seabed. Various types of platforms exist, also in order to respond to different situations (e.g., continental shelf, inland sea, lake). Depending on the context, a platform may be fixed to the ocean floor, may consist of an artificial island, or may float. Remote subsea wells may also be utilised to connect an oil field to a platform by flow lines. While remaining more expensive than onshore drilling, offshore drilling profitability rates have improved over time.

As outlined by Eni (2013),

> the production of oil is highly regulated and is subject to conditions imposed by governments throughout the world in matters such as the award of exploration and production interests, the imposition of specific drilling and other work obligations, income taxes and taxes on production, environmental protection measures, control over the development and abandonment of fields and installations, and restrictions on production.

Following major oil spills events (such as the Deepwater Horizon oil spill which occurred in the Gulf of Mexico in 2010, considered to be the largest marine oil spill in the history of the petroleum industry[3]) governments throughout the world have implemented stricter regulations on environmental protection and risk prevention.

Oil production operations represent the first step in the oil value chain, and are called upstream. The following steps in the oil value chain are the midstream and the downstream. The midstream sector entails the set of operational processes that includes procedures for the transport of oil (e.g., via pipeline, rail, oil tanker, truck) from the extraction site to the refining site, as well as its storage and the wholesale marketing of crude oil. The downstream sector involves the refining of crude oil, as well as the marketing and distribution of refined products. Refineries represent the core of the downstream sector.

The refining of petroleum is an industrial process that transforms crude oil into various finished products such as petrol, diesel, heavy fuel oil or naphtha. A heterogeneous mixture of various hydrocarbons (i.e., molecules composed of carbon and hydrogen atoms), crude oil is unusable in its natural state. Its components must be separated in order to obtain the final products that can be used directly. There are generally

[3]   See: Britannica (2019a).

two main types of oil products: (i) Energy products, such as petrol, diesel, jet fuel, heating oil, liquefied petroleum gas, natural gas; and (ii) Non-energy products, such as lubricants, bitumen, naphtha, asphalt, as well as hundreds of petrochemicals. Today, refining is no longer limited to the separation of the various hydrocarbons. Complex chemical processes are also used to optimise the final products. The various oil cuts can thus undergo transformations, improvements and blends to obtain market-able products and meet new environmental standards. Oil refineries have three basic steps:

(i) Distillation of crude oil to produce intermediate products. The distilla-tion of crude oil is carried out in two complementary steps. A first dis-tillation, called atmospheric distillation (i.e., carried out at atmospheric pressure), separates gases, gasoline and naphtha (i.e., light cuts), kerosene and diesel fuel (i.e., medium cuts) and heavy cuts. Atmospheric distilla-tion then consists of separating the different components of a liquid mixture according to their evaporation temperatures. The crude oil is injected into a large distillation tower, 60 metres high and about 8 metres wide, where it is heated to about 400 degrees Celsius. The various hydro-carbons contained in crude oil are vaporised: first the light ones, then the medium ones, and finally some of the heavy ones. The temperature decreases moving up in the tower, allowing each type of hydrocarbon to liquefy in order to be recovered. The lightest are recovered at the top, and the heaviest remain at the bottom of the tower.[4] The residues from the atmospheric distillation undergo a second distillation, called vacuum distillation (i.e., in a depressurised column), in order to recover additional average products with a commercial value (e.g., industrial lubricating oils, paraffins, heavy fuel oil, bitumen). Vacuum distillation takes place in a smaller, depressurised, column. The pressure drop makes it easier to recover heavy products with lower boiling temperatures.

---

[4]   From top to bottom: gases with between 1 and 4 carbon atoms, such as methane; naphtha, a liquid with 5 or 6 carbon atoms that will be used to make plastics; gasoline that contains between 7 and 11 carbon atoms; kerosene with up to 13 carbon atoms; and diesel, which has up to 25 carbon atoms. The residues are then treated under vacuum in a second distillation column.

(ii) The cracking of heavy hydrocarbons. After distillation, the proportion of heavy hydrocarbons generally remains high in view of the commercial demand for lighter products. The heavy molecules are therefore broken into several lighter molecules. This is called catalytic cracking. It usually takes place at about 500 degrees Celsius and in the presence of a catalyst. This operation is relatively energy consuming.

(iii) The manufacture of products. In general, products obtained from the first two stages require further processing before they can be marketed. Automotive fuels, for instance, must go through a stage of reducing their sulphur content to meet environmental standards. The operation takes place in a reactor at temperatures of around 400 degrees Celsius and a pressure of between 40 and 80 bar. Under these conditions, hydrogen injected into the mixture reacts with the sulphur atoms to form hydrogen sulphide, which can then be removed. Automotive fuels must also be treated to increase their octane rating to the level necessary for engines to properly work (i.e., 95–98). To do this, the product is injected into a catalytic reforming unit, in which chemical reactions occur, using platinum as a catalyst, at a temperature of 500 degrees Celsius and a pressure of around 15 bar. Paraffins and naphthenic hydrocarbons are then transformed into aromatic hydrocarbons with a higher octane rating.

To meet growing demand, global oil production tripled over the last fifty years, from a level of 31.8 million barrels per day (mbl/d) in 1965 to 92.6 mbl/d in 2017 (BP, 2018a). In terms of geographical distribution, over the last fifty years, the Middle East has become the first region by oil production, surpassing North America. Russia and other CIS countries approximately maintained their share, while Africa managed to slightly increase it. Driven by China, Asia Pacific's share in global oil production almost tripled, while that of South and Central America was significantly squeezed due to reduced production in Venezuela. Finally, while slightly increasing its share, Europe remained the smallest oil-producing region in the world (Figure 2.3).

In 2017, the United States led global oil production, followed by Saudi Arabia and Russia (Table 2.2). This is the result of the

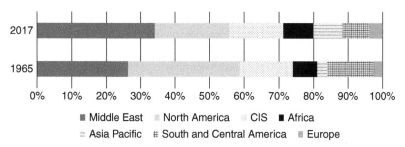

FIGURE 2.3 Global oil production share by world region, 2017 and 1965
Source: author's elaboration on BP (2018a).

impressive unconventional oil boom experienced by the United States since 2010. In fact, in 2010, the United States' oil production ranked third, after Russia and Saudi Arabia. Altogether, the United States, Saudi Arabia and Russia made up around 40 per cent of global oil production in 2017. It is remarkable to notice how many countries – from Saudi Arabia to Canada, from Iran to China – substantially scaled up their role in the global oil-production scene over the last fifty years. Back in 1965, the United States and the then-USSR alone indeed made-up around 40 per cent of global oil production.

Global oil demand grew over the last fifty years from 30.7 million barrels per day (mbl/d) in 1965 to 98.2 mbl/d in 2017 (BP, 2018a).[5] In regional distribution terms, the most visible dynamics in the last fifty years occurred since the mid-1980s, as the global oil demand epicentre progressively switched from North America to Asia Pacific. Meanwhile, the shares of Europe and CIS in global oil demand substantially reduced, while the share of the Middle East more than tripled and the share of Africa more than doubled (Figure 2.4).

The United States has traditionally been the first oil consuming country in the world, albeit its share in global oil demand fell from 37 per cent in 1965 to 20 per cent in 2017 as a result of the extraordinary growth in other countries around the world. In fact, while over the last

---

[5] As stated by BP (2018a, p.20), 'differences between these world consumption figures and world production statistics are accounted for by stock changes, consumption of non-petroleum additives and substitute fuels, and unavoidable disparities in the definition, measurement or conversion of oil supply and demand data'.

Table 2.2 *Global oil production: Top-20 countries, 2017 and 1965*

Country	2017 (thousand barrels per day)	1965 (thousand barrels per day)
United States	13,057	9,014
Saudi Arabia	11,951	2,219
Russia	11,257	4,858*
Iran	4,982	1,908
Canada	4,831	920
Iraq	4,520	1,313
United Arab Emirates	3,935	282
China	3,846	227
Kuwait	3,025	2,371
Brazil	2,734	96
Mexico	2,224	362
Venezuela	2,110	3,503
Nigeria	1,988	274
Norway	1,969	n/a
Qatar	1,916	233
Kazakhstan	1,835	n/a
Angola	1,674	13
Algeria	1,540	577
United Kingdom	999	2
Oman	971	n/a

Source: author's elaboration on BP (2018a) (* Indicative data, as it refers to USSR).

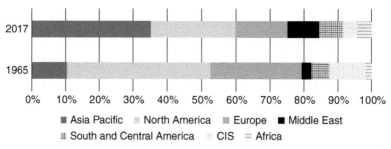

FIGURE 2.4 Global oil demand share by world region, 2017 and 1965
Source: author's elaboration on BP (2018a).

fifty years oil demand grew in the United States by a factor of 1.7, it grew by a factor of 60 in China, by a factor of 18 in India, and by a factor of 10 in both Saudi Arabia and Brazil. In other cases, like South Korea, it even grew by a factor of 110 (Table 2.3).

Oil demand is likely to keep growing strongly in emerging economies, given that their oil demand per capita remains far lower than in advanced economies. For instance, oil demand per capita in 2017 stood at around 1 barrel per year (b/y) in India, at 3 b/y in China, at 6 b/y in Brazil, 10 b/y in Germany, and 22 b/y in the United States (Eni, 2018a).

Table 2.3 *Global oil demand: Top-20 countries, 2017 and 1965*

Country	2017 (thousand barrels per day)	1965 (thousand barrels per day)	Increase 1965–2017
United States	19,880	11,522	73%
China	12,799	215	5,853%
India	4,690	252	1,761%
Japan	3,988	1,705	134%
Saudi Arabia	3,918	390	905%
Russia	3,224	3,314*	–3%
Brazil	3,017	306	886%
South Korea	2,796	25	11,084%
Germany	2,447	1,709	43%
Canada	2,428	1,108	119%
Mexico	1,910	316	504%
Iran	1,816	143	1,170%
Indonesia	1,652	122	1,254%
France	1,615	1,065	52%
United Kingdom	1,598	1,466	9%
Singapore	1,430	76	1,782%
Thailand	1,423	48	2,865%
Spain	1,293	268	382%
Italy	1,247	979	27%
Australia	1,079	313	245%

Source: author's elaboration on BP (2018a) (* Indicative data, as it refers to USSR).

By unpacking global oil demand into different product groups it is possible to see that 28 per cent of global oil demand in 2017 was represented by diesel, 26 per cent by gasoline, 7.8 per cent by fuel oil (i.e., including marine bunkers and crude oil used directly as fuel), 7.7 per cent by jet/kerosene, and the remaining 30.5 per cent by other products (e.g., refinery gas, liquefied petroleum gas, petroleum coke, lubricants and other refined products). It should be noted that regional oil products consumption patterns can widely differ. For instance, the United States uses more gasoline (47 per cent of total oil demand) than diesel (20 per cent), while, in contrast, the EU uses more diesel (45 per cent) than gasoline (14 per cent) (BP, 2018a). This difference is due to different transportation fuels patterns, as Americans mainly drive petrol cars, while Europeans drive mainly diesel cars[6].

Transport indeed represents the main oil-consuming sector, covering a share of 56 per cent of global demand in 2017 (Figure 2.5). The second largest oil-consuming sector is the one of petrochemicals (with a share of 12 per cent), which has become increasingly important also due to rising demand for plastics at the global level (IEA, 2018c).

Given the key role of transport – notably cars – in global oil demand, the issue of the potential impact of electric cars on the sector has started to emerge over the last few years, as electric car deployment has advanced across the globe.

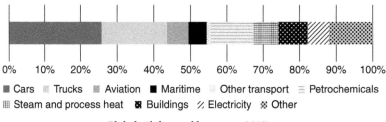

FIGURE 2.5 Global oil demand by sector, 2017
Source: author's elaboration on International Energy Agency (2018b).

---

[6]   As outlined by the EIA (2017a, p.17), 'several factors have contributed to diesel's high European market share – pro-diesel policies, including a lower at-pump fuel tax, high diesel vehicle make and model availability (on par with gasoline vehicles), and a high number of fuelling stations (on par with gasoline stations).'

First estimations indicate that in 2017 electric cars might have displaced about 0.38 mb/d of oil demand, corresponding to 0.39 per cent of global demand (IEA, 2018b). Assessing future potential impacts of course requires specific assumptions about the pace of electric car deployment across the world, which differs significantly among various organisations. But comparing different estimations is still interesting: according to the IEA (2018b), by 2040, electric cars might displace 3 mb/d of oil demand. According to Bloomberg New Energy Finance (2018), by 2040, electric cars might displace 7.3 mb/d of oil demand. Finally, according to BP (2018b), by 2040, electric cars might displace – also thanks to bans on diesel and gasoline cars across the world – 10 mb/d of oil demand. The potential long-term impact of electric cars on global oil demand is thus currently estimated to be limited, with a maximum projected displacement of global oil demand in 2040 of approximately 10 per cent of current oil demand.

2.3 OIL MARKET FUNCTIONING

Oil is a commodity operating in a largely open global market. This is also made possible by the fact that oil is relatively easy to transport, either in tankers or by pipeline. In 2017, 67.5 mbl/d of oil, in other words, 73 per cent of global oil production (BP, 2018a) were traded on global markets. The major oil importers were Europe, China, and the United States, followed by India and Japan. The major oil exporters were Saudi Arabia and other Middle Eastern oil producing countries, Russia, and Asia Pacific (excluding Japan), followed by the United States, West Africa, and Canada (Table 2.4).

While looking into the oil import portfolios of major importers, it is interesting to note two main features. First, all regions/countries have a well-diversified portfolio, with at least ten suppliers. Second, portfolios' composition widely differs, mainly as a result of geographical location. For instance, in 2017, 40 per cent of the United States' oil imports came from Canada, while 40 per cent of Japan's imports came from Saudi Arabia, and 33 per cent of Europe's imports came from Russia.

Table 2.4 *Oil trade movements, 2017*

	2017 (thousand barrels per day)	1980 (thousand barrels per day)
Imports		
Europe	14,060	12,244
China	10,241	n/a
United States	10,077	6,735
India	4,947	n/a
Japan	4,142	4,985
Rest of World	24,125	8,635
Total World	67,592	32,599
Exports		
Middle East (excl. Saudi Arabia)	15,680	8,155
Russia	8,611	2,040*
Saudi Arabia	8,238	9,630
Asia Pacific (excl. Japan)	7,641	2,099
United States	5,540	555
West Africa	4,470	2,475
Canada	4,201	445
South and Central America	3,993	3,010
Europe	3,281	n/a
North Africa	2,155	2,820
Mexico	1,279	875
Other CIS	1,974	n/a
Rest of World	528	495
Total World	67,592	32,599

Source: author's elaboration on BP (2018a) (* Indicative data, as it refers to USSR).

Looking into export portfolios of major oil exporters, is possible to denote that Russia, other CIS countries, and North African countries are predominantly focused on supply the European market. The United States have a considerable share of export to Canada, while West African exporters have a large share to China. On its side, Saudi

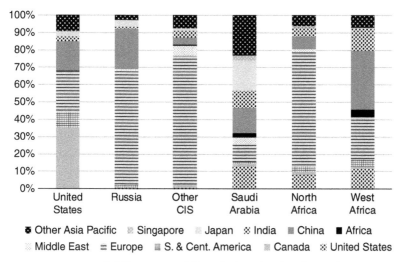

FIGURE 2.6 Oil export portfolios of selected regions/countries, 2017
Source: author's elaboration on BP (2018a).

Arabia shows a well-diversified portfolio, in which Asia plays an important role (Figure 2.6).

As more than half the world's oil production is moved on maritime routes, a major geopolitical risk for oil markets is represented by sea transit – due to world oil supply chokepoints. As outlined by the EIA (2014), 'blocking a chokepoint can lead to substantial increases in world oil prices. Chokepoints also leave oil tankers vulnerable to theft from pirates, terrorist attacks, political unrest and shipping accidents'. The Strait of Hormuz and the Strait of Malacca are the world's most important chokepoints, followed by the Bab el-Mandeb Strait and the Turkish Straits.

The Strait of Hormuz, situated between Oman and Iran, links the Persian Gulf with the Gulf of Oman and the Arabian Sea. With a daily oil flow of almost 17 mbl/d, it is the world's most important oil chokepoint. Flows through this strait indeed represent almost 20 per cent of oil traded worldwide (EIA, 2017b). This situation is further complicated by the lack of bypass options.

Linking the Indian Ocean and the Pacific Ocean, the Strait of Malacca is the shortest sea route between the Middle East and Asian markets. Almost a third of global oil and half of global LNG pass through this strait. Some 75 per cent of South Korea's energy supply, 60 per cent of Japan's energy supply, 80 per cent of China's oil imports go through here (EIA, 2017b).

Located between Yemen, Djibouti, and Eritrea, the Bab el-Mandeb Strait represents a key link between the Mediterranean Sea and the Indian Ocean. Most exports from the Persian Gulf that transit the Suez Canal and the Suez-Mediterranean Pipeline pass through this strait (EIA, 2017b).

The Turkish Straits – the Bosphorus and the Dardanelles – connect the Black Sea to the Aegean and Mediterranean Seas. They are a vital oil export route for Russian and Central Asian oil to European and global markets.

Let's now see how oil price is formed. The price of oil is based on quality of product (i.e., sour or sweet, light or heavy). The dominant benchmark used today is Brent. The basis for European and Middle East transactions, it is a high-quality crude, traded on the Intercontinental Exchange. In North America, the benchmark is the West Texas Intermediate (WTI), which has higher quality than Brent. This is the oldest of the exchanges, and is traded on the NYMEX. Brent and WTI can significantly diverge. Overabundance of WTI under the growing United States shale output has ensured a lower rate of ascent compared with Brent. Should more United States oil be exported to Asia – as a result of its more competitive price – the gap might close.

Oil price is highly volatile, as it depends on supply/demand trends as well as on geopolitical events. An additional factor increasing the volatility of oil price is financial speculation. In the world, there are indeed 'paper barrels' representing twenty-five to fifty times the total value of the oil upon which they are based. This is done for short-term hedging or for speculative purposes. Financial speculation can thus significantly contribute to oil price volatility.

High volatility has characterised global oil price over the past sixty years (Figure 2.7). Volatility notably exploded in the

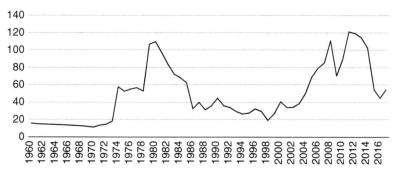

FIGURE 2.7 Oil prices, US dollar 2017 per barrel, average annual values,
1960–2017
Source: author's elaboration on BP (2018a).

1970s, as the two oil crises brought the level of oil price in 1981 to
a level ten times higher than in 1973. In the first decade of the
2000s, oil price skyrocketed again, due to many factors including
Middle East tensions (e.g., 2003–11 Iraq war), soaring demand from
China, the falling value of the US dollar, worries over peak oil,
and financial speculation. Since mid-2014, oil price stumbled,
similarly to 1985–6 (i.e., when OPEC countries decided to boost
production) and in 2008–9 (i.e., at the outset of the global financial
crisis). Key reasons of this drop have been slowing oil demand
growth in emerging markets, and most importantly in China;
major short-term drop in investment in oil exploration and production; and lack of response by OPEC countries, which failing to
reach agreement on production curbs in December 2014, further
exacerbated the price tumbling. After two years of low prices, in
December 2016, OPEC and non-OPEC producers reached an historical deal to curtail oil output jointly and ease the global glut,
a deal which led to a significant market rebalancing – albeit oil
price continued to remain at a far lower level than previous highs.

To conclude, it is important to stress that – given its strategic
importance – the oil market has traditionally been a playfield in which
governments and private companies closely interact. This is also reflected
by the various degrees of public ownership of oil companies. There are

indeed three main types of oil companies: (i) International oil companies (IOCs), entirely owned by investors, their aim is to increase shareholders value. Examples of IOCs are BP, Chevron, Eni, ExxonMobil, or Shell; (ii) National oil companies (NOCs), which operate as extensions of a government and have goals that can be determined politically. Examples of NOCs are the China National Petroleum Corporation or Saudi Aramco; and (iii) NOCs with strategic and operational autonomy, such as Equinor (formerly Statoil) or Petrobras.

2.4   THE INTERPLAY OF OIL, ECONOMICS, AND POLITICS IN MENA PRODUCING COUNTRIES

Endowed with half the world's known oil and gas reserves, the Middle East and North Africa (MENA)[7] region is a bedrock of the world's hydrocarbons supply.[8] In 2017, the region provided 37 per cent of global oil production, and 22 per cent of global gas production. As far as oil is concerned, Saudi Arabia dominates the regional oil landscape, followed by Iran, Iraq, the United Arab Emirates, and Kuwait. As far as gas is concerned, Iran leads regional production, followed by Qatar, Saudi Arabia, Algeria, and the United Arab Emirates (Table 2.5).

It should be noted that in most MENA hydrocarbon producers, activities in non-hydrocarbon and non-government sectors are also often linked to hydrocarbon and government activities. The main sources of manufacturing value-added indeed tend to include refinery, chemical, and other mining/extractive industries, while some non-hydrocarbon sectors, such as construction, depend heavily on government contacts (IMF, 2016).

In these countries, oil and gas are also the primary source of fiscal revenues. Just to provide a few examples, in 2017, oil and gas

[7]   MENA is here defined as including the North African countries (Morocco, Algeria, Tunisia, Libya, and Egypt), the Levant countries (Jordan, Israel, Lebanon, Syria, and Palestine), the Gulf Cooperation Council countries (Bahrain, Kuwait, Oman, Saudi Arabia, Qatar, and United Arab Emirates), Iraq, and Iran.

[8]   This section develops, enlarges, and updates a previous analysis carried out by the author: Tagliapietra (2017a).

Table 2.5 *Oil and gas rent (% of GDP)*

Country	2013	2014	2015	2016	2017
Algeria	28	24.4	15.9	12	14.5
Bahrain	9.3	8.6	5.1	3.2	3.5
Egypt	9.7	8.2	3.7	2.7	4.8
Iran	26.4	26.3	15.6	12.9	17
Iraq	45.6	45.6	35.1	31.4	38
Kuwait	58.4	55.2	38	32.1	37.1
Libya	52.7	42	28.5	22.3	38.4
Oman	44.9	39.6	23.8	19.7	23.4
Qatar	34.9	30.5	19.9	15.3	18
Saudi Arabia	45.5	41.2	24.2	19.9	23.7
United Arab Emirates	27.2	24.2	14	11.3	13.7
Oil price (USD/barrel)	*109*	*99*	*52*	*43*	*54*

Source: author's elaboration on World Bank, World Development Indicators database, accessed in June 2019 and BP (2018a).

revenue accounted for 67 per cent of fiscal revenues in Saudi Arabia.[9] In the same year, they accounted for 90 per cent of fiscal revenues in Kuwait (IEA, 2018h), 75 per cent of fiscal revenues in Qatar, and 60 per cent of fiscal revenues in Algeria (CIA, 2019).[10]

Likewise, oil and gas dominate these countries' exports. In 2018, oil and gas accounted for 80 per cent of Saudi Arabia's total exports, 90 per cent of Kuwait's total exports, 86 per cent of Qatar's total exports, and 95 per cent of Algeria's total exports (CIA, 2019).

In addition to GDP, fiscal revenues, and exports, hydrocarbons also heavily impact MENA hydrocarbon producers' labour markets. For instance, in Saudi Arabia, Iraq, and Kuwait, the public sector wage bill amounts to almost one-fifth of GDP, as 30 per cent of the Saudi and Iraqi workforces and 15 per cent of the Kuwait workforce are employed in the public sector (IEA, 2018h).

---

[9] Author's calculation on Kingdom of Saudi Arabia Ministry of Finance (2019, p.29).
[10] Author's calculation on Qatar Planning and Statistics Authority (2018, p.60).

This suggests that growth in the working-age population over the last two decades has not been matched in these countries by growth in private-sector job creation, but rather in public-sector employment. In Iraq, for instance, the public sector has grown from 1.2 million employees in 2003 to around 3 million in 2016. This places enormous strain on the state budget, costing over USD 30 billion in salaries in 2016, equivalent to 60 per cent of the country's net income from oil and gas that year (IEA, 2018h).

MENA hydrocarbon producers generally have seen relative declines in labour productivity, which suggests that many of the public sector jobs that have been created are not adding significantly to economically productive activity. The balance of employment across the private and public sectors is also shaped in many instances by a large gap in average wages, with public employment offering higher pay: across the Gulf Cooperation Council (GCC) countries, for example, the gap between average public and private wages is often between 150 per cent and 250 per cent (IMF, 2017). All this has contributed to lower the labour productivity of MENA hydrocarbon producers. This is one of the major barriers for economic diversification in MENA hydrocarbon producers, as it prevents the development of an internationally competitive private sector (Hertog, 2013).

It must be noted that public support schemes in these countries are not only based on oversized public sectors, but also on expensive and economically inefficient subsidy schemes, such as those for energy.

Iran's fossil fuel subsidies are the largest in the world, with an estimated value of USD 45 billion in 2017 (i.e., equivalent to 10 per cent of the country's GDP). In the same year, fossil fuel subsidies amounted, for instance, to USD 37 billion in Saudi Arabia, to USD 9 billion in the United Arab Emirates, and to around USD 7 billion in both Iraq and Kuwait (IEA, 2018h).

From an economic perspective, high fossil fuel subsidies generate significant economic losses, because oil resources are sold domestically at a fraction of their international market value. From an energy perspective, these subsidies distort the economics of energy and the price signals of energy resources, holding back the competitiveness of renewable energy sources. Furthermore, fossil-fuel subsidies lead to the inefficient allocation of resources and to market distortions, by encouraging rent-seeking behaviour and thus excessive production or consumption. Not by coincidence, MENA hydrocarbon producers are among the less energy-efficient countries in the world (IEA, 2018h).

Some progress has been made since 2014 in raising residential electricity prices in several MENA hydrocarbon producers, including in Saudi Arabia. But prices are still relatively low, with the average price for residential consumers in Saudi Arabia around 80 per cent lower than the global average in 2016 (IEA, 2018b). When Kuwait took steps to raise electricity prices significantly, including increases for the public sector by 500 per cent, it excluded residential electricity prices, which have been fixed at the same rate for more than fifty years (electricity prices are regulated by law in Kuwait and require parliamentary approval to modify). In many producer economies, electricity prices for residential consumers continue not to cover the cost of supply.

As a result of all these macroeconomic trends, it is not surprising that at present no MENA hydrocarbon producer economy ranks in the top-20 of the World Bank (2019) 'Ease of Doing Business' global rankings, a composite measure of indicators that reflect business sentiment.

A unique analytical framework to understand the interplay of oil, economics, and politics in MENA producing countries is represented by the Rentier State Theory (RST), which was first postulated by Hussein Mahdavy in 1970, in the context of a discussion on the evolution of economic development in the Middle East in general, and in Iran in particular. Mahdavy (1970) defined as rentier states those countries that receive on a regular basis substantial amounts of external rents, which have little to do with the production processes in their domestic economies.

Building on Mahdavy's seminal study, Hazem Beblawi and Giacomo Luciani in 1987 systematised the RST, and developed it into a widely accepted tool to interpret the MENA political economy and – more broadly – the political economies of all the world's oil-producing countries. According to the theoretical framework proposed by Beblawi (Beblawi and Luciani, 1987), a state is rentier when: (i) It relies on substantial external rent to sustain the economy, reducing the pressure to develop a strong productive domestic sector; (ii) It has a small proportion of the population engaged in the generation of the rent, while the majority of the population is only involved in the distribution or in the utilisation of it; and (iii) Its government is the principal recipient of the external rent.

MENA hydrocarbon exporters might then be considered as rentier states par excellence. But how does rentierism impact the political structures of these countries?

The conventional role of the state in providing public goods through taxation blurs in rentier states, as the role of the state becomes providing private favours through the ruler's benevolence. The fundamental principle of democracy, 'No taxation without representation', finds in rentier states its mirror image, 'No representation without taxation'. That is, untaxed citizens are less likely to demand political participation. Beblawi, recalling previous Mahdavy reflections, also highlighted that a rentier state economy creates a specific mentality – a rentier mentality – on which income is not related to work and risk bearing, but to chance or situation. This is also a reason why, according to Beblawi, rentier states tend to give rise to second-order rents, such as real estate and financial speculation.

Luciani (Beblawi and Luciani, 1987) expanded Beblawi's analysis, focusing on the key function of the state in rentier countries to understand the more profound interlinkages between oil, economics, and politics. Luciani outlined that rentier states might also be defined as allocation states because their key function is to allocate the income received from the rest of the world to their populations. This allocation function of rentier states profoundly differs from that of production states, which have to subtract – via taxation – resources from those that originally possess them, and reallocate them to others in the society on the basis of an asserted common interest, which ultimately requires democratic legitimation. Growth in the domestic economy is thus not a precondition for the existence and expansion of a rentier state, as long as the rent is guaranteed. That is, growth in the domestic economy becomes an essential precondition only in case a rentier state is forced to become a production state.

This mechanism is evident in MENA hydrocarbon producers. Historically, these countries have indeed put in place economic reform programmes aimed at increasing the diversification of their economies any time oil prices substantially dropped. However, as also outlined by Hvidt (2013), they regularly dismissed these strategies once oil prices recovered.

That is, MENA hydrocarbon producers showed in the past a tendency of easily giving up on their economic reform strategies designed under low-oil price pressure, and falling back on established ways of doing business, namely through patronage and the predominant role of the public sector.

The sharp drop in oil prices that began in 2014 created a major financial pressure on MENA hydrocarbon producers. For instance, in Saudi Arabia, foreign reserves peaked at over USD 730 billion in 2014, and then fell by some 30 per cent by 2017. Nearly USD 240 billion was used to cover a large budget deficit created by lower oil export revenues and to defend the currency peg. Despite efforts to consolidate spending, Saudi Arabia is still running a significant deficit, and it has turned to domestic and international bond issuances to help finance its budget (IEA, 2018b).

In this situation, all MENA hydrocarbon producers adopted economic diversification strategies (or, in some cases, reinforced already existing strategies), generally aimed at increasing the private sector's role in the economy, developing small and medium enterprises (SMEs), creating jobs, and investing in education and innovation (Table 2.6).

With their focus on the development of the non-hydrocarbon sectors of the economy, these strategies seem to go in the right direction: increasing the private sector's share of GDP is indeed an important way to promote higher labour productivity and to stimulate private sector investment and job creation. It should be noted that these strategies also reflect economic policy guidelines generally

Table 2.6 *MENA oil and gas producers' economic diversification strategies: Key targets*

Bahrain – Economic Vision 2030 *(Launched in 2008)*
- Stimulate growth by enhancing productivity and skills.
- Diversify and build the economy by focusing on existing high potential sectors.
- Transform the economy in the longer term by capturing emerging opportunities.

Algeria – New Economic Growth Model (2016–19) *(Launched in 2016)*
- Boost non-hydrocarbon exports to 9% of total exports by 2019, from less than 5% currently.

Iran – Sixth National Development Plan (2016–21) *(Launched in 2017)*
- 8% economic growth rate.
- Lower share of oil revenues in the budget to 22%.
- Increase power generation capacity by 25 gigawatts.
- Lower energy intensity by 15%.
- Lower unemployment to 8.9% and inflation rate to 7%.

Iraq – Private Sector Development Strategy (2014–30) *(Launched in 2014)*
- Increase the private sector up to a share of 60% of GDP by 2030.
- Improve the country's business environment, particularly for SMEs.
- Reduce the unemployment rate to 4% or less by 2030.

Kuwait – Kuwait Development Plan 2035 *(Launched in 2017)*
- Develop a prosperous and diversified economy to reduce the country's dependence on oil export.
- Increase the number of small businesses by 3,500.
- Increase investment by 11%.

Oman – Ninth Five-Year Development Plan (2016–20) *(Launched in 2016)*
- Reduce the contribution of oil in GDP at current prices from 44% in 8th five-year plan to 26% by 2020.
- Create more than 15 million jobs by 2020.
- Focus on the private sector and SMEs.

Qatar – National Vision 2030 *(Launched in 2008)*
- Increase and diversify the participation of Qataris in the workforce.
- Create a business climate capable of stimulating national and foreign investments.
- Manage the optimum exploitation of hydrocarbon resources.
- Expand industries and services with competitive advantages derived from hydrocarbon industries.

Table 2.6 (*cont.*)

- Create a knowledge-based economy characterised by innovation, entrepreneurship, and excellence.

Saudi Arabia – Vision 2030 *(Launched in 2016)*
- Increase the private sector's contribution from 40% to 65% of GDP by 2030.
- Increase SME contribution to GDP from 20% to 35% by 2030.
- Increase foreign direct investment from 3.8% to the level of 5.7% of GDP by 2030.
- Raise the share of non-oil exports in non-oil GDP from 16% to 50% by 2030.
- Increase non-oil government revenue from SAR 163 billion to SAR 1 trillion by 2030.

United Arab Emirates – Abu Dhabi Economic Vision 2030 *(Launched in 2018)*
- Reduce GDP volatility through diversification.
- Enlarge enterprise base.
- Equip the UAE youth to enter the workforce.
- Diversify fiscal revenue sources.

Source: author's elaboration on national plans, accessed in June 2019.

given to MENA hydrocarbon producers by international economic organisations (e.g., IMF, 2016; World Bank, 2016) as well as by academics (e.g., Luciani, 2012; Hvidt, 2013; Ben Ali, 2016).

Unlike in the past, this might well be the right time for MENA hydrocarbon producers to implement these long-awaited strategies. The reason is simple: if in the past the only argument for economic diversification was the risk of oil market volatility, today two additional arguments have emerged.

The first relates to the illustrated uncertainty regarding the speed of the global energy transition, and therefore the long-term sustainability of the hydrocarbons rent. This represents an important argument to domestically justify economic diversification reforms.

The second relates to the pressing need to create job opportunities for a large and youthful population. In the MENA region, population growth has averaged 2 per cent per year since 1990 (0.7 percentage points higher than the world average), leading to a population increase of 180 million over the last 25 years. This rate of increase made the MENA region among the youngest in the world: today, 60 per cent of the population is under the age of 25, and the median age is 22 (compared with a global average of 28).

With already challenging labour market conditions (Dadush and Demertzis, 2018; ILO, 2018), and with large numbers of young citizens set to further join their labour markets in the years ahead due to demographics, MENA hydrocarbon producers have a clear need to diversify their economies and create new productive jobs. Just to provide an idea of the order of magnitude of the challenge, 20 million young people are expected to join the MENA workforce by 2025 (WEF, 2019).

As rightly pointed by MENA hydrocarbon producers' economic diversification strategies, small and medium enterprises (SMEs) could play an instrumental role in tackling this challenge, given their potential to create jobs and foster innovation.

However, SMEs in the MENA region continue to face important obstacles, not least limited access to finance – an area where the region has the largest gap in the world. A recent World Bank/Union of Arab Banks survey of over 130 MENA banks shows that only 8 per cent of lending goes to SMEs across MENA, and even less in GCC countries (2 per cent). This is substantially lower when compared to the middle-income countries lending average of 18 per cent and high-income countries average of 22 per cent (IFC, 2017).

Solving SMEs' financing problem is therefore key for the implementation of economic diversification strategies in the region. The IMF (2019) estimates that solving this problem would indeed create more than 15 million new jobs in the region by 2025.

The first action to be taken to unlock financing for SMEs concerns the development of the financial sector. In several MENA hydrocarbon producers, banks are poorly capitalised, since the revenues from oil and gas flow directly from national oil companies to the government, bypassing the domestic banking system. As a result, the economy can be capital-rich and a net international saver in the hydrocarbons sector, but capital-poor and reliant on either foreign lending or family savings in the rest of the economy. A well-regulated and adequately capitalised banking system integrated into global financial markets would then play an important role with this regard. This also entails the development of financial regulatory and supervisory frameworks, with adequate incentives for SME financing (World Bank, IMF, and OECD, 2015).

Secondly, alternative channels of SME financing might be developed. As outlined by the IMF (2019, p.37), this includes 'i) The development of capital market instruments to mobilise savings and channel them to SMEs; ii) A large and diversified investor base and broader capital market development; iii) Adequate financial infrastructure and legal frameworks; and regulatory and supervisory frameworks that support the safe development and integrity of capital markets and fintech-supported SME financing'. An important alternative channel of SME financing might be represented by Sovereign Wealth Funds (SWFs).

MENA hydrocarbon producers own some of the largest SWFs in the world. These funds could be used to strategically invest in SMEs, instead of being used as tools to perpetuate the rent via financial or real estate speculation. Given their size, SWFs could well be the main driver of economic diversification in these countries, should their investment strategies be refocused on local production and on the expansion of SMEs.

Saudi Arabia has been a first mover in the area. A year after the launch of its 'Vision 2030', the country outlined the key role of the Public Investment Fund (PIF) in the implementation of its economic diversification strategy, and even defined the Fund as 'the engine behind economic diversity' in the country (PIF, 2017). In this context, the Fund – generally known for its multi-billion dollar investments in companies such as Tesla and Uber – set up a USD 1.1 billion 'fund of funds' to support the development of SMEs in the country (Reuters, 2017). Albeit it is still too early to assess the impact of this move, it seems to pave the way for a new utilisation of SWFs in the region, which should be further developed in the future.

To conclude, if in the past the only (insufficient) argument for economic diversification in MENA hydrocarbon producers was the risk of oil market volatility, today two additional arguments have emerged: the uncertainty regarding the speed of the global energy transition (and therefore the long-term sustainability of the hydrocarbons rent), and the pressing need to create job opportunities for a large and youthful population. The combination of these three arguments might well turn out to be decisive in firmly committing MENA hydrocarbon producers' leaderships in implementing their respective economic diversification strategies.

2.5   KEY TAKEAWAYS

Introduction to Oil

- More than 4,000 years ago, oil seeps were used as source of asphalt utilised to build Babylon.
- After centuries of marginal uses, the modern oil industry was born in 1859 in Pennsylvania.
- The 1886 invention of the motor car by Karl Benz marked the beginning of the oil era.
- Oil has been the world's dominant source of energy since the mid-20th century.

Oil Reserves, Production, and Demand

- Half of global oil reserves are located in the Middle East.
- Venezuela owns the largest oil reserves, followed by Saudi Arabia, Canada, Iran, and Iraq.
- Oil reserves have increased over time, being a function of available technology and oil price.
- Given current reserves, the world has fifty years of oil consumption without scarcity risk.
- To meet global demand, oil production tripled over the last fifty years.
- The United States is the number-one oil producer, followed by Saudi Arabia, Russia, and Iran.

- The United States is the number-one oil consuming country, followed by China, India, and Japan.
- Oil demand is set to keep growing in emerging countries, as demand per capita is still very low.
- Transport is the main world oil consuming sector, followed by petrochemicals.

Oil Market Functioning

- The major oil importers are Europe, China, the United States, India, and Japan.
- The major oil exporters are Saudi Arabia, other Middle Eastern countries, and Russia.
- Oil is mainly traded on maritime routes, making global chokepoints a geopolitical risk.
- Oil price is volatile as it depends on supply/demand, geopolitics, and financial speculation.
- Oil price volatility exploded during the 1970s and in the first decade of the 2000s.

The Interplay of Oil, Economics, and Politics in MENA Oil-Producing Countries

- Endowed with half the world's oil and gas reserves, the MENA is a cornerstone of global energy.
- Oil and gas profoundly impact MENA producers' economies and social contracts.
- MENA producers have made several attempts to diversify their economies, without success.
- Since the 2014 oil price drop, MENA producers adopted new economic diversification plans.
- Decarbonisation and the need to create jobs could today push these plans' implementation.
- Sovereign wealth funds could play a key role for the financing of private sector and SMEs.

3 Natural Gas

Fires caused by lightning strikes igniting natural gas naturally flaring from the earth's surface puzzled ancient civilisations, unleashing myth and superstition. Around 1,000 BC, on Mount Parnassus in Greece, a temple was built on one of these fires: the Oracle of Delphi. This temple housed the Pythia, a priestess who gave prophecies about the future she claimed were inspired by the flame. Similar situations occurred in India and Persia. Only around 500 BC was a first practical utilisation of natural gas invented in China, notably to boil seawater for desalinisation purposes. The modern natural gas industry was born in England at the end of the eighteenth century. At the time, natural gas was a side-product of coal, and was utilised to light houses and roads. Natural gas started to also be used for street lighting in the United States in 1816. For most of the nineteenth century, in absence of a reliable transport infrastructure, the use of natural gas remained limited to lighting. With the rise of electricity, natural gas producers started to explore new applications for their commodity, such as domestic heating and cooking. In 1891, the first natural gas pipeline was built to link gas production sites in central Indiana to Chicago. After World War II, technological improvements allowed the development of long natural gas pipeline systems. Between the 1950s and the 1960s, thousands of kilometres of pipelines were built in the United States, as well as in Europe. It was then in the second half of the twentieth century that natural gas acquired greater economic value, which led to the creation of the global natural gas markets we know today.

In geological terms, natural gas is a hydrocarbon mixture mainly consisting of methane (i.e., around 90 per cent), and small amounts of carbon dioxide (i.e., around 5 per cent), nitrogen, helium, butane, and ethane. Natural gas is found in deep underground rock formations or associated with other hydrocarbon reservoirs in coal beds and as methane clathrates. Natural gas is colourless and odourless. It is artificially odorised for safety reasons.

Natural gas resources can be found in either conventional or unconventional accumulations, exactly as in the case of oil (Figure 3.1). As illustrated by the EIA (2011), 'conventional natural gas accumulations occur when natural gas migrates from gas-rich shale into an overlying sandstone formation, and then becomes trapped by an overlying impermeable formation, called the seal. Associated natural gas accumulates in conjunction with oil, while non-associated natural gas does not accumulate with oil'.

Three types of unconventional gas accumulations exist: shale gas, tight sand gas, and coalbed methane. According to the EIA definitions (2011),

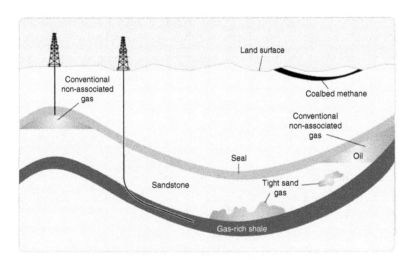

FIGURE 3.1 Geology of natural gas resources
Source: Energy Information Administration.

[G]as-rich shale is the source rock for many natural gas resources. Horizontal drilling and hydraulic fracturing have made shale gas an economically viable alternative to conventional natural gas resources. Tight sand gas accumulations occur in a variety of geologic settings where natural gas migrates from a source rock into a sandstone formation, but is limited in its ability to migrate upward due to reduced permeability in the sandstone. Coalbed methane does not migrate from shale, but is generated during the transformation of organic material to coal.

It is important to also outline the environmental aspects concerning natural gas. As stated by the EIA (2018a), 'natural gas is a relatively clean fuel if compared to other fossil fuels. Its combustion emits a level of CO_2 emissions (per unit of energy produced) that is around 40 per cent lower than coal and around 20 per cent lower than oil'. Natural gas production, transportation, and consumption entails significant methane emissions; this is an issue for natural gas, as uncertainty over the level of emissions raises questions about the extent of its real environmental benefits. It should also be outlined that, in comparison to other fossil fuels, natural gas has a lower impact on the local environment as it emits fewer pollutants when burned, including fine particulate matter, sulphur oxides, and nitrogen oxides (key drivers of air pollution). In a country's energy mix, a switch from most-pollutant coal to natural gas could therefore provide significant environmental benefits. For instance, as the United States massively switched from coal to natural gas since the shale gas revolution started, between 2006 and 2017 the country's power-sector CO_2 emissions fell by nearly 25 per cent (IEA, 2018c). As we will see, China and several other emerging countries are also pushing for a coal-to-gas switch in power generation, notably in order to reduce air pollution in cities. Due to its environmental profile, and to its flexibility in terms of dispatchability that makes it a perfect complement to variable renewable energy sources such as wind and solar, natural gas is often considered as a 'transition fuel' towards a low-carbon world.

3.2 NATURAL GAS RESERVES, PRODUCTION, AND DEMAND

In 2017, world's proved natural gas reserves[1] were estimated at 193.5 trillion cubic metres (tcm) (BP, 2018a), with approximately 40 per cent of them located in the Middle East and 30 per cent of them located in Russia and other CIS countries (Figure 3.2).

In 2017, Russia owned the largest natural gas reserves in the world, followed by Iran. Qatar, Turkmenistan, and the United States ranked third, fourth, and fifth, respectively. The top-10 list continued with Saudi Arabia, Venezuela, United Arab Emirates, China, and Nigeria (Table 3.1).

Proved natural gas reserves have significantly increased over the last two decades in various countries. An example of this is represented by the United States, where, due to new technologies allowing the

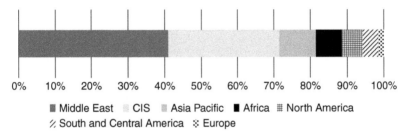

■ Middle East ▦ CIS ▨ Asia Pacific ■ Africa ▦ North America
▨ South and Central America ⋰ Europe

FIGURE 3.2 Proved natural gas reserves by world region, 2017
Source: author's elaboration on BP (2018a). Note: CIS indicates the Commonwealth of Independent States, which includes Russia and Armenia, Azerbaijan, Belarus, Moldova, Kazakhstan, Kyrgyzstan, Tajikistan, Turkmenistan, and Uzbekistan.

[1] As in the case of oil, it is also important to pay particular attention to the terminology used when dealing with natural gas reservoirs. As outlined by BP (2019), 'Resources indicate the total amount of natural gas in place in a reservoir, most of which typically can't be technically or economically recovered. Proved reserves indicate the portion of resources that is technically and economically recoverable. Probable reserves indicate the reserves that are estimated to have a better than 50 per cent chance of being technically and economically producible. Possible reserves indicate the reserves which, at present, cannot be regarded as probable, but which are estimated to have a significant, but less than 50 per cent chance of being technically and economically producible'.

Table 3.1 *Proved natural gas reserves: Top-20 countries, 2017*

Country	Proved reserves (trillion cubic metres)	Reserves-to-production ratio (years)
Russia	35.0	55
Iran	33.2	148
Qatar	24.9	142
Turkmenistan	19.5	314
United States	8.7	12
Saudi Arabia	8.0	72
Venezuela	6.4	170
United Arab Emirates	5.9	98
China	5.5	37
Nigeria	5.2	110
Algeria	4.3	47
Australia	3.6	32
Iraq	3.5	337
Indonesia	2.9	43
Malaysia	2.7	35
Canada	1.9	11
Egypt	1.8	36
Norway	1.7	14
Kuwait	1.7	97
Libya	1.4	124

Source: author's elaboration on BP (2018a).

exploitation of shale gas resources, proved natural gas reserves increased from 4.5 tcm in 1997 to 8.7 tcm in 2017. Another example is Turkmenistan, where, as a result of new geological assessments, proved natural gas reserves increased from 2.6 tcm in 1997 to 19.5 tcm in 2017. Other remarkable cases include Iran (from 22.7tcm in 1997 to 33.2 tcm in 2017) and Qatar (from 8.8 tcm in 1997 to 24.9 tcm in 2017) (BP, 2018a).

The R/P ratio indicates that the world has around fifty more years of natural gas consumption without scarcity risk (at current consumption levels). At current reserves and production levels, the

Middle East could keep producing natural gas for 120 years, CIS countries for 73 years, Africa for 60 years, South and Central America for 46 years, Asia Pacific for 32 years, Europe for 12 years, and North America for 11 years (BP, 2018a).

But how is natural gas explored and produced? Windgas (2019) offers a suggestive and insightful description of this process:

> In the search for natural gas deposits at land and on sea, geologists use a similar approach to that used to discover new oil fields. They begin by examining existing data, such as the results of previous explorations or geological databases. While scrutinising the data, they are looking for certain characteristics which indicate the presence of natural gas. It is often stored in basins which sit above a very thick layer of sedimentation, while porous sandstone and carbonates are also good indicators. Using advanced technology, the scientist can evaluate existing measurement data to create a model of what a promising basin full of natural gas looks like. Only when this extensive analysis indicates evidence of possible natural gas deposits will geologists begin their investigations. Sound waves play an important role in searching for new natural gas deposits. Geologists and physicists use sound waves to discover new reservoirs, even when the natural gas is under permafrost in Siberia or deep under the Atlantic. Using high-tech tools such as vibrator trucks or air cannons on ships to generate vibrations, they then measure the reflections of the sound from the rock strata with special microphones and then analyse the echo on computers which can calculate the structure of the potential reservoir. But the only way of being absolutely sure is to drill a test well. This extracts drill cores from underground which the scientists then analyse under the microscope. They have to persevere, as only one in every three or four test wells is successful in finding natural gas. Once discovered, a natural gas field can enter the production phase. Onshore natural gas production takes place in the following manner: the natural gas company drives a hole into the ground with a derrick, which is lined

with steel pipes and concrete and is sealed off with a 'Christmas tree' above ground to prevent natural gas from leaking from the borehole. If the natural gas lies under the sea bed (offshore), drilling platforms are usually necessary to access the natural gas. During production, the natural pressure of the natural gas in the reservoir makes sure the raw material flows to the surface, where it is then purified from unwanted elements such as steam or particulate matter. If the natural pressure falls too much because the reservoir is at an advanced stage of production, the technicians install compressors that suck the natural gas out of the ground, and maximise the yield from the reservoir. But it is not always so straightforward to extract the natural gas from the reservoirs. Tight gas and shale gas do not flow to the surface by themselves, because they are trapped in isolated pores within very dense rock, or, in the case of shale, the gas is still firmly embedded in in the layers of clay where it was formed. In order to extract this natural gas, water pressure has to be used to crack open the rock. Chemical additives are used in this process, as well as water and sand. This process is known as hydraulic fracturing, or 'fracking'.

Natural gas production operations represent the first step in the natural gas value chain, and are named upstream. The following steps in the natural gas value chain are, as in the case of oil, the midstream and the downstream.

The midstream sector involves the supply of natural gas, including the initial separation and the removal of impurities. Normally, when natural gas is produced it is treated immediately to remove these less valuable substances. It can then be added to the high-pressure transmission network and the end-market distribution networks. In most cases, the natural gas reserves are not located in the same areas as the refineries and areas of consumption, making distribution an important part of midstream activities. Transportation of natural gas from production sites to consumers takes place either via natural gas pipelines or via liquefied natural gas (LNG) carriers for longer distances.

The downstream sector relates to the deposit and storage of natural gas and LNG and the wholesale and retail of natural gas products. This portion of industry therefore includes natural gas distribution companies.

In order to meet growing global natural gas demand, production almost quadrupled over the last fifty years, from 975.8 billion cubic metres (bcm) in 1970 to 3,680.4 bcm in 2017 (BP, 2018a). In terms of geographical distribution, back in 1970 the world's natural gas production was centred on North America (65 per cent of the total), CIS countries (19 per cent), and Europe (11 per cent). As countries discovered natural gas resources and started to make use of them, global natural gas production became more globally widespread over time. In 2017, North America continued to lead global production (26 per cent of the total), followed by CIS countries (22 per cent), the Middle East (18 per cent), Asia Pacific (16 per cent), Europe (7 per cent), Africa (6 per cent), and South and Central America (5 per cent) (Figure 3.3).

In 2017, the United States were the first-ranked natural gas producing country in the world, followed by Russia and Iran (Table 3.2). This is the result of the impressive shale gas boom experienced by the United States since 2010. In fact, in 2010, the United States' natural gas production ranked second after Russia. Altogether, the United States, Russia, and Iran made up around 40 per cent of global natural production in 2017. It is remarkable to notice how many countries – from Iran

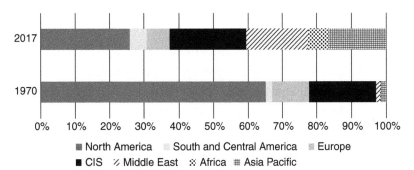

FIGURE 3.3 Global natural gas production share by world region, 2017 and 1970
Source: author's elaboration on BP (2018a).

Table 3.2 *Global natural gas production: Top-20 countries, 2017 and 1970*

Country	2017 (billion cubic metres)	1970 (billion cubic metres)
United States	734.5	571.5
Russia	635.6	187.5*
Iran	223.9	3.6
Canada	176.3	54.0
Qatar	175.7	1.0
China	149.2	2.9
Norway	123.2	0
Australia	113.5	1.7
Saudi Arabia	111.4	1.5
Algeria	91.2	2.4
Malaysia	78.4	0
Indonesia	68.0	1.3
Turkmenistan	62.0	0
United Arab Emirates	60.4	0.8
Uzbekistan	53.4	0
Egypt	49.0	0.1
Nigeria	47.2	0.1
United Kingdom	41.9	10.9
Mexico	40.7	0
Thailand	38.7	0

Source: author's elaboration on BP (2018a) (* Indicative data, as it refers to USSR).

to China, from Qatar to Turkmenistan – substantially entered or scaled-up their role in the global natural gas production scene over the last fifty years. Back in 1970, the United States and then-USSR alone indeed made-up around 80 per cent of global natural gas production.

In 2017, 78 per cent of global natural gas production originated from conventional resources, 13 per cent from shale gas, 7 per cent from tight gas, and 2 per cent from coalbed methane (IEA, 2018b).

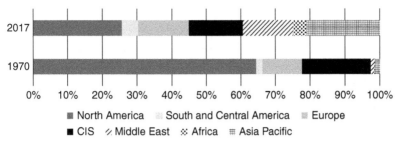

FIGURE 3.4 Global natural gas demand share by world region, 2017
and 1970
Source: author's elaboration on BP (2018a).

Global natural gas demand grew from 961.4 bcm in 1970 to
3,670 bcm in 2017 (BP, 2018a).[2] From a regional distribution perspective, it is possible to note that back in 1970 natural gas was mainly
consumed in North America, CIS countries, and Europe. Over time,
consumption became globally widespread, with Asia Pacific and the
Middle East surging as key natural gas demand regions (Figure 3.4).

The United States has always been the largest natural gas consuming country in the world, albeit its share in global natural gas
demand fell from 60 per cent in 1970 to 20 per cent in 2017 as
a result of growth in other countries around the world. In fact, while
over the last fifty years natural demand grew in the United States by
a factor of 1.2, it boomed – for instance – by a factor of 83 in China, by
a factor of 80 in Iran, and by a factor of 74 in Saudi Arabia (Table 3.3).

Natural gas demand is likely to keep growing in emerging economies, given that their demand per capita remains far lower than in
advanced economies. For instance, natural gas demand per capita
in 2017 stood at around 43 cubic metres (cm) in India, 161 cubic metres
in China, 621 in Mexico, 1,110 in Germany, and 2,326 in the United
States (Eni, 2018b). Natural gas demand is also set to grow in emerging
economies as a result of a coal-to-natural-gas switch in power generation,

[2]   Note: as explained by (BP, 2018a, p.29), 'the difference between these world consumption figures and the world production statistics is due to variations in stocks at storage
facilities and liquefaction plants, together with unavoidable disparities in the definition, measurement or conversion of gas supply and demand data'.

Table 3.3 *Global natural gas demand: Top-20 countries, 2017 and 1970*

Country	2017 (billion cubic metres)	1970 (billion cubic metres)
United States	739.5	574.9
Russia	424.8	189.0*
China	240.4	2.9
Iran	214.4	2.7
Japan	117.1	3.6
Canada	115.7	34.6
Saudi Arabia	111.4	1.5
Germany	90.2	16.0
Mexico	87.6	10.0
United Kingdom	78.8	11.8
United Arab Emirates	72.2	0.8
Italy	72.1	12.2
Egypt	56.0	0.1
India	54.2	0.6
Turkey	51.7	0
Thailand	50.1	0
South Korea	49.4	0
Argentina	48.5	5.9
Qatar	47.4	1.0
France	44.7	9.6

Source: author's elaboration on BP (2018a) (* Indicative data, as it refers to USSR).

driven by these countries' climate change mitigation strategies, as well as air pollution reduction strategies (IEA, 2018b).

Electricity generation represents the main natural gas consuming sector in the world (40 per cent of global demand in 2017), followed by industry (23 per cent), and buildings (21 per cent) (Figure 3.5). In industry, natural gas is mainly used in energy-intensive industries (i.e., which typically require high-temperature heat), while in buildings it is mainly used for heating and cooking.

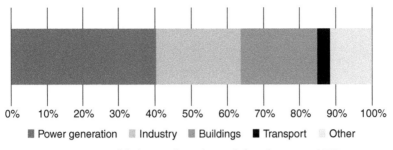

FIGURE 3.5 Global natural gas demand share by sector, 2017
Source: author's elaboration on International Energy Agency (2018b).

But how is electricity generated with natural gas? Two answers are the main types of natural gas-fired power plant: combined-cycle gas turbines (CCGTs) and simple-cycle gas turbines.

CCGTs use a gas turbine in tandem with a heat recovery steam generator (HRSG) (Figure 3.6). As illustrated by Sulzer (2019), in these power plants

> natural gas is combusted in a gas turbine burner which drives a generator to produce electricity. The hot exhaust gases coming from the gas turbine are sent to a HRSG to generate either subcritical or supercritical steam. The steam is directly sent to a turbine/generator unit to produce additional electricity, then passed through a condenser to convert it into demineralized water again.

In simple-cycle gas turbine plants (also known as open-cycle plants), there is no steam cycle. These plants are often installed as emergency or peaking capacity, because their thermal efficiency is substantially lower than in CCGTs. The high running cost per hour is offset by the low capital cost and the intention to run such units only a few hundred hours per year.

3.3   NATURAL GAS MARKETS FUNCTIONING

While discussing global natural gas trade, it is more appropriate to talk about 'markets' rather than 'market'. In fact, while oil represents

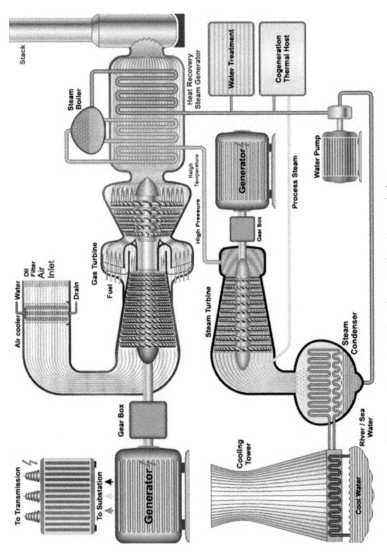

FIGURE 3.6 Scheme of a combined-cycle gas turbine (CCGT) plant
Source: Shutterstock.

a truly global market, natural gas still largely remains a regional fuel. In 2017, only 30 per cent of world natural gas consumption was traded internationally, while about 70 per cent of world oil consumption was so (BP, 2018a). This is due to the fact that natural gas is simply more difficult – and more expensive – to transport than oil.

The traditional regional dimension of global natural gas markets has also been the result of the several decades natural gas has been mainly transported via pipelines. Over the last two decades this situation has progressively changed, as LNG increased its share in total natural gas trade from 24 per cent in 2000 to 40 per cent in 2017 (IEA, 2018b). The scale-up of this technology has fostered a progressive globalisation of natural gas markets, pushing them to become more similar to the oil market, even if – as we will see hereafter – there is still a long way to go before a truly global natural gas market materialises.

Today, the global natural gas landscape continues to be characterised by three key regional markets – North America, Europe, and Asia/Pacific – each of which presents different demand/supply and pricing profiles.

North America is a self-sufficient market, which, thanks to the shale gas revolution, even became an exporter during the 2000s. In contrast, the European Union heavily relies on pipeline imports coming from Russia, Norway, and Algeria – plus a long list of other pipeline and LNG (notably Middle Eastern) suppliers. On its side, Asia/Pacific is a region characterised by a strong reliance on LNG imports (Figure 3.7).

Traditionally centred on Japan and Korea, natural gas demand in this region is currently growing due to China (Table 3.4), where strong policies have been put in place by the government to promote a coal-to-gas switch, notably to fight air pollution. For instance, the country's 'Blue Skies' policy, launched in 2017, aims at fighting air pollution by restricting the use of small coal boilers for industrial and residential use. Other new important contributors to natural gas demand growth in this region are India, Bangladesh, and Pakistan (IEA, 2018d).

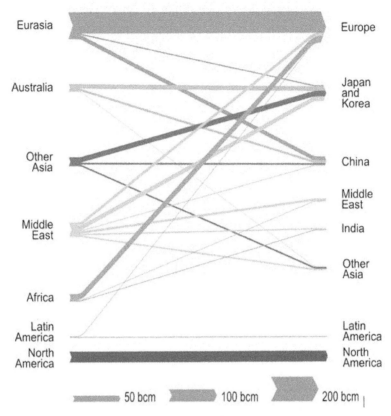

FIGURE 3.7 Global natural gas trade movements, 2017
Source: International Energy Agency, Gas 2018.

The three markets also differ in terms of natural gas pricing mechanisms. North America has the most highly liquid and transparent natural gas market in the world. The United States liberalised its natural gas market during the second half of the 1980s, making natural gas price entirely a function of demand/supply on the market. Since then, both the United States and Canada are characterised by fully liquid trading markets. As noted by the Energy Charter (2007, p.119), 'the United States' natural gas market has developed around a number of hubs where pipeline interconnections bring natural gas flows together from different sources and re-distribute it to different market regions'. One of the most important distribution hubs on the country's

Table 3.4 *Natural gas trade movements in selected regions/*
countries, 2017 and 2000

	2017 (billion cubic metres)	2000 (billion cubic metres)
Net importers		
European Union	349	221
China	106	1
Japan and Korea	162	97
India	26	0
Net exporters		
Russia	234	185
Middle East	119	24
North America	7	37
Australia	60	10
Caspian countries	78	36
Sub-Saharan Africa	33	6
North Africa	37	62
South and Central America	9	5

Source: author's elaboration on IEA (2018b).

natural gas pipeline system is located in Erath, Louisiana: Henry Hub.
This hub interconnects with nine interstate and four intrastate pipelines. Because of its crucial importance for the United States' natural
gas pipeline system, the Henry Hub has become the centrepiece of
North America's natural gas pricing system.

The natural gas pricing situation of the European Union is far
more complex than North America, and to fully understand it an
historical overview is necessary. Natural gas in Europe started to be
utilised in the 1960s, after the 1959 discovery of the Groningen field in
the Netherlands, which was followed few years later by the first
discoveries in the British sector of the North Sea. A number of pipelines delivering natural gas from the Dutch field to the consumption
centres in the Netherlands, Belgium, France, Germany, and Italy were

thus developed. While very small quantities of Russian gas have been exported to Poland since the late 1940s, the idea of large-scale imports into Western Europe effectively took place only in the 1960s, with the construction of the vast pipeline system that still today represents the key route to evacuating Russian gas to Europe. With regard to the Mediterranean quadrant, the Trans-Mediterranean Gas Pipeline (also known as Enrico Mattei Pipeline) from Algeria through Tunisia to Sicily started flowing gas to mainland Italy in 1983 and the Maghreb-Europe Gas Pipeline (also known as Pedro Duran Farell Pipeline) from Algeria through Morocco to Spain and Portugal was completed only in the 1996. A pipeline connecting Libya with Italy was also inaugurated in 2004. The construction of these international natural gas pipelines was subject to the conclusion of long-term contracts, aimed at guaranteeing the effective delivery of natural gas to the buyer and at guaranteeing the effective sale of the gas at the agreed price to the producer. With the long-term contracts, the risks associated to the construction of the infrastructure were thus distributed between the two parties.

As illustrated by Hafner and Tagliapietra (2013, pp.10–11),

> These contracts guaranteed source of revenue to companies that made enormous investments in exploration and in the development of infrastructure for the production and transportation of natural gas. Otherwise, it would have been commercially impossible to undertake large projects without having a buyer for the gas committed to a long-term purchase of large volumes. For all these reasons, long term contracts have played a crucial role in the European natural gas markets since their early stage. Two key features have always been associated with this kind of contracts: the take-or-pay clause and the oil-indexed price. Take-or-pay contracts formed the commercial basis on which the European natural gas industry was built, and still remain today in common use for large-scale, long-term gas supply contracts. These contracts force the buyer to pay for a minimum volume of gas regardless of

whether it is actually taken in delivery – both on a daily and yearly basis. This clause has been considered both as an incentive mechanism to seek compliance in the execution of the contract as well as a means to spread risk. The clause must provide an incentive to the buyer to take all the natural gas it can absorb when use of this gas is economically efficient, while curtailing the risk to the producer of making this gas available upstream. Consequently, the take-or-pay contracts have act both as an insurance mechanism upstream and as an incentive to efficient use of gas downstream. Most commonly, the natural gas price has been tied to that of gas oil/heating oil, although indexation to crude oil and fuel oil prices also has occurred. The original rationale was that end-users had a real choice between burning gas and oil products, and would switch to the latter if given a price incentive to do so. The first country to introduce this idea has been the Netherlands. In fact, in 1962 the Dutch Minister of Economic Affairs de Pous, introduced the basic principles of the Dutch natural gas policy. In order to generate maximum revenue for the state, the market value or replacement value principle was introduced as the basis for natural gas marketing. The price of natural gas was linked to the price of alternative fuels likely to be substituted by the different types of consumers – for instance, gas oil for small-scale users and fuel oil for large-scale users. On the one hand, the introduction of the market value principle meant that consumers would not have to pay more for natural gas than for alternative fuels. On the other hand, they would not pay much less. The market value approach enabled natural gas producers and the Dutch government to obtain much higher revenues than by pricing based on the low production costs of natural gas from the Groningen field. These are the reasons why, at its dawn, European markets were based on a netback market pricing mechanism based on the alternative fuel.

However, as Stern and Rogers (2017, pp.362–3) outlined,

In the major European national gas markets the rationale for continued linkage of long-term contract natural gas prices to those of oil products began to weaken during the 1990s, as a result of a combination of different factors: i) the virtual elimination of oil products from many stationary energy sectors in these markets; ii) the cost and inconvenience of maintaining oil-burning equipment and substantial stocks of oil products; iii) the emergence of modern natural gas-burning equipment in which the use of oil products means a substantial loss of efficiency; iv) tightening environmental standards in relation to pollutant emissions'.

Nevertheless, traditional oil product-linked pricing in long-term gas contracts remained largely unchallenged in Europe until the early 2000s. This situation completely changed since 2008, as a result of a perfect storm which radically reshaped European natural gas markets. The economic crisis severely hit the European Union's natural gas demand, which fell from 517 bcm in 2008 to 484 bcm in 2009. In the meantime, global LNG supply surged, offering Europe natural gas supplies far more competitive than oil-linked long-term contracts, as their prices in the meantime surged with oil prices rising beyond USD 100/bbl. This situation put unprecedented pressure on European natural gas buyers, who started not only to endorse hub pricing as the future price formation mechanism, but also to renegotiate long-term contract prices with traditional suppliers such as Russia, Norway, and Algeria to include a proportion of hub price indexation in the pricing terms or even a move to 100 per cent hub price indexation – many of which required international arbitration proceedings to resolve. As a result of this trend, European natural gas pricing mechanisms started to quickly move away from oil-indexation to hubs. If, back in 2005, only 15 per cent of natural gas sold in Europe was priced at hubs, this level rose to 70 per cent in 2017. Correspondingly, the share of natural gas priced in relation to oil shrank from nearly 80 per cent in 2005 to less than 30 per cent in 2017. However, as IGU (2018, p.14) noted, 'the change in price formation mechanisms in Europe was not universal across the region. Northwest Europe has seen the most dramatic change in price formation mechanism, followed by Central Europe where significant changes also occurred'. On the contrary, much less change occurred in Southern Europe. Just to provide an example, in Northwest Europe, the share of oil-linked pricing fell below 10 per cent in 2017, while in Southern Europe it remained at around 60 per cent.

Asia and Pacific markets are predominantly supplied with LNG under long-term contracts with oil-linked prices. It should be noted that China also receives substantial volumes of natural gas via pipeline from Turkmenistan (as well as smaller amounts from Kazakhstan, Uzbekistan, and Myanmar), always under oil-linked pricing schemes. In 2017, the share of oil-indexed prices stood at around 60 per cent in the region. The region still has to develop a competitive wholesale natural gas market. Doing so requires, first of all, a price that reacts to changes in the supply–demand balance, which is not the case if prices follow fluctuations in the oil market. Then, it requires the existence of various sources of natural gas supply that can actually compete in a market and the possibility for buyers to re-sell and ship the natural gas within their market to other buyers. LNG, which is inherently more flexible than a bilateral pipeline, can stimulate competition, but this needs to be complemented in natural gas-importing markets by natural gas market liberalisation and the development of liquid and transparent pricing points – which still lack in several regional markets.

These profound demand/supply and pricing schemes differences among the three key world's natural gas markets result in significantly different price levels (Figure 3.7). The United States' natural gas price substantially decoupled from other international prices since the shale gas revolution, with Henry Hub prices stabilising at a level of USD 3 per million British thermal units (mbtu). Assuming the German average import price as an approximate indicator of the European price level (which, of course, widely differs internally), it is possible to see that this level remains at around

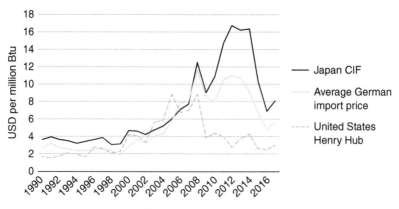

FIGURE 3.8 Natural gas prices, 1960–2017
Source: author's elaboration on BP (2018a).

USD 6/mbtu (i.e., double the Henry Hub price). Assuming the Japanese price as a benchmark for Asia/Pacific prices, it is possible to see that here prices stay at a level of USD 8–10/mbtu (i.e., triple the Henry Hub price), albeit the enormous gap experienced since the 2011 Fukushima accident (when Japan's nuclear capacity had to be replaced overnight by LNG) has been largely reduced. Globally, this results in a three-tier natural gas market with considerable scope for arbitration.

Low-cost natural gas has boosted the United States' industrial and economic competitiveness and greatly contributed to the post-2008 economic recovery. This has also been illustrated by econometric models Bilgili et al. (2016). On the contrary, higher energy prices in Europe and some Asian countries have had a negative impact on their energy-intensive industries. Given that natural gas plays a relevant role in electricity generation, natural gas price differentials have contributed to substantial variation in electricity prices across regions, too. In Europe, Japan, and China, industrial electricity prices remain roughly twice as high as in the United States. To enhance energy competitiveness, and to mitigate the impact of energy price disparities, Europe and Asia are pressured to improve energy competitiveness, starting by improving energy efficiency.

As the globalisation process of natural gas markets unfolds with the increasing share of LNG in global trade, increasing price convergence among the three markets is to be expected. Of course, convergence is due to happen first amongst countries with market-related pricing schemes and with a high degree of interconnection with global markets.

3.4 KEY TAKEAWAYS

Introduction to Natural Gas

- Gas is a hydrocarbon gas mixture primarily consisting of methane (90 per cent).
- Gas is found in deep underground rock formations, or associated with other hydrocarbons.
- Gas resources can be conventional or unconventional.
- Gas combustion emits 40 per cent less CO_2 than coal, and 20 per cent less than oil.
- Gas combustion emits fewer air pollutants than coal, a significant environmental benefit.

Natural Gas Reserves, Production, and Demand

- Some 40 per cent of global gas reserves are in the Middle East, and 30 per cent in Russia/CIS.
- Russia has the largest reserves in the world, followed by Iran and Qatar.
- To meet global demand, gas production quadrupled over the last 50 years.
- The United States is the first-ranked producer, followed by Russia and Iran.
- The United States is also the first-ranked consumer, followed by Russia and China.
- Power generation is the main gas-consuming sector, followed by industry and buildings.
- Gas demand is likely to keep growing, driven by China and other Asian countries.

Natural Gas Market Functioning

- Gas largely remains a regional fuel, as its transport is more difficult and expensive than oil.

- Global gas markets are globalising, mainly due to the strongly increasing role of LNG.
- Three key gas markets currently are North America, the European Union, and Asia/Pacific.
- Since the shale gas revolution, North America has become a self-sufficient market.
- The European Union largely relies on pipeline imports from Russia, Norway, and Algeria.
- North America has the most liquid and transparent gas market, with low prices.
- European markets are moving from oil indexation to spot pricing, but prices remain high.
- Asia highly relies on oil-linked LNG, with prices three times higher than in the United States.
- As the globalisation process of gas markets unfolds, global price convergence will increase.

4 Coal

4.1 INTRODUCTION TO COAL

Coal is a fossil fuel like oil and natural gas, and it is formed from the remains of plants that lived hundreds of millions of years ago in swampy forests, the structure and form of which, albeit modified, can still be observed with a microscope. Layers of dirt and rock covered the plants over millions of years. The resulting pressure and heat turned, over millions of years, the plants into coal. The combustion of coal thus frees the energy of the sun stored in plants through photosynthesis millions of years ago.

Coal is mostly composed of carbon, with variable amounts of hydrogen, sulphur, oxygen, and nitrogen. The are four major types (or ranks) of coal. As illustrated by the US Geological Survey (2019),

> [R]ank refers to steps in a slow, natural process called 'coalification', during which buried plant matter changes into an ever denser, drier, more carbon rich, and harder material. The rank of a coal deposit is determined by the amount of pressure and heat that acted on the plants over time. The four ranks are: i) Anthracite: it is highest rank of coal. It is a hard, brittle, and black lustrous coal, often referred to as hard coal, containing a high percentage of fixed carbon and a low percentage of volatile matter; ii) Bituminous: it is a middle rank coal between subbituminous and anthracite. Bituminous usually has a high heating value; iii) Subbituminous: it is black in color and dull, and has a higher heating value than lignite; iv) Lignite: also known as brown coal, it is the lowest grade coal with the least concentration of carbon.

Anthracite is mainly used by the steel industry, which uses it to smelt iron ore into iron to make steel. Bituminous coal is mainly used in electricity generation and in iron and steel industries. Subbituminous coal and lignite are mainly used in electricity generation.

Coal has been known since ancient times. Archaeological evidence indicates that the use of coal as a source of energy dates back to the Bronze Age, in China (Dodson et al., 2014). Around 300 BC, the Greek scientist Theophrastus made the first reference to the use of coal for the manufacture of iron (Swank, 1892). The Romans widely exploited coal and also created a lively trade of the commodity, which they predominantly used to heat public baths and the villas of wealthy individuals. The modern coal industry saw its inception at the end of the eighteenth century, with the Industrial Revolution – and most notably with the invention of the steam engine. Being cheaper and more efficient than wood fuel in most steam engines, coal demand indeed rapidly surged. Coal powered not only factories, but also trains and ships, which led to a rapid expansion of international trade, and therefore to a rapid acceleration in the process of globalisation. Since then, coal has had a central role in the global energy system, and still today it accounts for around one fourth of the global energy mix (BP, 2018a).

Coal indeed presents some important advantages compared to oil and natural gas. Coal resources are abundant and widely distributed across the globe, making it a natural option for countries seeking a cheap and secure source of energy. Coal is indeed far cheaper than other fossil fuels, and its price is also less exposed on geopolitical risks.

But coal also has a huge disadvantage: it is, by far, the most polluting fossil fuel. Its combustion indeed emits the highest levels of CO_2, as well as of sulphur dioxide (which contributes to acid rain and respiratory illnesses), nitrogen oxides (which contribute to smog and respiratory illnesses), and particulates (which contribute to smog, haze, and respiratory illnesses and lung disease). This makes coal a leading cause of both climate change and air pollution. This is the reason why, given the current lack of technologies to make coal cleaner in an economically viable manner, an increasing number of countries – from Germany to China – are trying to significantly reduce its utilisation – or even to phase it out – for both climate change mitigation and air pollution reduction reasons.

4.2 COAL RESERVES, PRODUCTION, DEMAND, AND TRADE

In 2017, world proved coal reserves were estimated at 1,035,011 million tonnes (mt), with approximately 40 per cent of them being located in Asia Pacific, 25 per cent in North America, and 22 per cent in CIS countries (BP, 2018a) (Figure 4.1).

In 2017, the United States owned the largest coal reserves in the world, followed by Russia, Australia, China, India, Germany, Ukraine, Poland, Kazakhstan, and Indonesia (Table 4.1).

The reserves-to-production ratio indicates that the world has around 130 more years of coal consumption without scarcity risk. At current reserves and production levels, Asia Pacific could keep producing coal for around 80 years, North America for 330 years, CIS countries for 397 years, Europe for 160 years (BP, 2018a).

Depending on the nature of the deposit, coal can be extracted in the open air or underground through wells and tunnels. The first case applies when the layer of soil covering the deposit and which must be

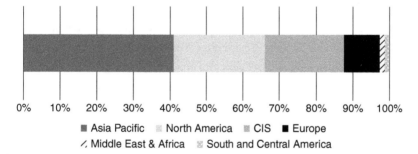

FIGURE 4.1 Proved coal reserves by world region, 2017
Source: author's elaboration on BP (2018a). Note: CIS indicates the Commonwealth of Independent States, which includes Russia and Armenia, Azerbaijan, Belarus, Moldova, Kazakhstan, Kyrgyzstan, Tajikistan, Turkmenistan, and Uzbekistan.

Table 4.1 *Proved coal reserves: Top-20 countries, 2017*

Country	Proved reserves (million tonnes)	Reserves-to-production ratio (years)
United States	250,916	357
Russia	160,364	391
Australia	144,818	301
China	138,819	39
India	97,728	126
Germany	36,108	206
Ukraine	34,375	> 500
Poland	25,811	200
Kazakhstan	25,605	230
Indonesia	22,598	49
Turkey	11,353	115
South Africa	9,893	39
New Zealand	7,575	> 500
Serbia	7,514	188
Brazil	6,596	> 500
Canada	6,582	111
Colombia	4,881	55
Czech Republic	3,640	81
Vietnam	3,360	88
Pakistan	3,064	> 500

Source: author's elaboration on BP (2018a).

removed to discover coal is not too high in relation to the thickness and extent of the deposit. The removal of the surface layer is usually carried out with mobile dredgers and coal is recovered by mechanical means. The open-air system, when possible, allows significant savings and high productivity. It is widely applied in different locations, from South Africa to the United States, from Germany to Australia. If the deposit is deep, it is reached through wells and the cultivation of the layer is carried out with cutting machines and mechanical transport following short forehead, or preferably long forehead systems, as the latter allows high productivity and reduces costs, but requires heavy capital investment. After being extracted, coal is moved to processing plants – typically located in proximity to the mine – where it is cleaned and duly processed in order to remove rocks, dirt, and any other unwanted material.

Coal can then be transported to consumers, either via rail, truck, or ship. Transportation is often coal's main cost item, being typically higher than the mining cost itself. In order to abate transportation costs, coal-fired power plants tend to be located, where possible, in proximity of a coal mine.

Global coal production doubled over the last four decades, from 3,900 mt in 1981 to 7,700 mt in 2017 (BP, 2018a). The geography of coal production substantially changed during the period. Back in 1981, world coal production was indeed fairly spread between Europe (30 per cent of the total), Asia Pacific (25 per cent), CIS (20 per cent), and North America (20 per cent). In 2017, it was predominantly centred on Asia Pacific (69 per cent), with only marginal shares in North America (10 per cent), Europe (10 per cent), CIS (7 per cent), and other regions (Figure 4.2).

China has led global coal production since 1985, and, in 2017, it accounted for half of it, followed by India, the United States, Australia, Russia, and South Africa. Two European countries, Germany and Poland, also ranked among the top-10 global producers, before Kazakhstan and Canada. It is interesting to note how, over the last

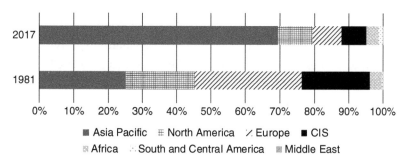

FIGURE 4.2 Global coal production by world region, 2017 and 1981
Source: author's elaboration on BP (2018a).

Table 4.2 *Global coal production: Top-10 countries, 2017 and 1981*

Country	2017 (million tonnes)	1981 (million tonnes)
China	3,523.2	621.6
India	716.0	130.1
United States	702.3	747.3
Australia	481.3	128.5
Russia	411.2	778.1*
South Africa	252.3	130.4
Germany	175.1	492.8
Poland	127.1	198.6
Kazakhstan	111.1	n/a
Canada	59.5	40.1

Source: author's elaboration on BP (2018a) (* Indicative data, as it refers to USSR).

four decades, China and India increased their coal production by a factor of six, while the United States, Germany, and Poland substantially decreased their production over time (Table 4.2).

China and India have indeed made increasing use of coal over the last decades in order to meet their booming energy demand in a cheap and secure manner. In 2017, China and India were the bulk of global coal demand, respectively accounting for 51 per cent and 11 per cent of global demand (BP, 2018a) (Figure 4.3). In the same year, China's coal-based electricity sector represented the largest coal-consuming sector globally by far, as approximately one of every four tonnes of coal consumed in the world was used in China to generate electricity (IEA, 2018e). Meanwhile, as natural gas prices substantially lowered in the country as a result of the shale gas revolution, the United States precipitated coal-to-gas switching in the electricity sector, which led to a sharp decrease in coal consumption in the country.

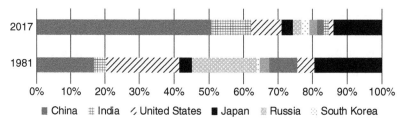

FIGURE 4.3 Global coal demand by country, 2017 and 1981
Source: author's elaboration on BP (2018a).

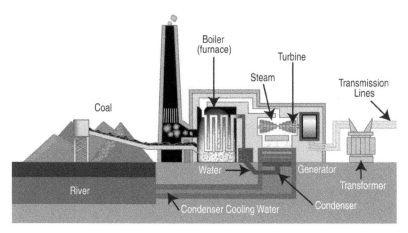

FIGURE 4.4 Scheme of a coal-fired power plant
Source: Shutterstock.

Coal is predominantly used for electricity generation and heat. In 2017, 65 per cent of global coal demand was indeed due to these purposes (BP, 2018a). The conversion of coal into electricity is a multifaceted process (Figure 4.4). A coal-fired power plant is mainly composed of a boiler (or furnace), a turbine, a generator, a transformer, and a cooling system. After having been pulverised, the coal is burned in a boiler to generate heat. This heat is then convoyed to pipelines containing high-pressure water, which boils to steam. This steam passes through a turbine, which converts thermal energy into mechanical energy. The turbine is connected to a generator, the rotation of which transforms the mechanical energy into electricity. Meanwhile, the steam is discharged under vacuum into a condenser, and the resulting water is then pumped again into the cycle. Since substantial volumes of water are required in this cycle, coal-fired power plants are generally located in proximity of water (e.g., river, sea, or lake).

From a regional perspective, it should be noted that in developed economies the share of electricity and heat produced from coal fell to 27 per cent in 2017, from 44.4 per cent in 1985. Meanwhile, in emerging economies in 2017, electricity production from coal contributed to 46.5 per cent of total electricity production (IEA, 2018e). Coal is also essential for the iron and steel industry and its use there has increased substantially during the last forty years, driven primarily by increased production in China. Emerging economies account for 83 per cent of the total global consumption of coal within the iron and steel sector.

As far as trade is concerned, in 2017, Indonesia led global exports, followed by Australia and Russia. These exports primarily targeted Asian countries, as China led global coal imports, together with India, Japan, and Korea (Table 4.3).

Table 4.3 *Global coal trade, 2017*

Major coal exporters	(million tonnes)	Major coal importers	(million tonnes)
Indonesia	390.6	China	271.1
Australia	378.9	India	208.3
Russia	189.7	Japan	187.5
United States	88.0	Korea	148.2
Colombia	86.1	Chinese Taipei	67.6
South Africa	71.0	Germany	48.0
Mongolia	33.4	Netherlands	40.3
Canada	31.1	Turkey	38.3
Kazakhstan	27.1	Malaysia	31.5
Netherlands	24.4	Russia	29.0

Source: author's elaboration on IEA (2018e).

4.3 ENVIRONMENTAL AND SOCIAL ASPECTS OF COAL

As previously mentioned, coal has a huge disadvantage: its environmental impact. Having the highest carbon content among fossil fuels, coal emits the highest amount of CO_2 per unit of energy output while burned. The EIA (2018b) estimates anthracite's emissions to 228.6 pounds of CO_2 per million British thermal units (pCO_2/mbtu), bituminous coal's emissions to 205.7 pCO_2/mbtu, lignite's emissions to 215.4 pCO_2/mbtu, and subbituminous coal's emissions to 214.3 pCO_2/mbtu. To have a comparison, diesel fuel's emissions are estimated at 161.3 pCO_2/mbtu, while natural gas emissions' are estimated at 117 pCO_2/mbtu.

This characteristic makes coal the most important single contributor to global CO_2 emissions, and therefore to climate change. In 2016, while contributing to 27 per cent of the global energy mix, coal indeed generated 44 per cent of global CO_2 emissions from fuel combustion. And it should be considered that CO_2 emissions from fuel combustion represent over two thirds of total GHG emissions. In comparison, while contributing to 32 per cent of the global energy mix, oil was responsible for 35 per cent of CO_2 emissions from fuel combustion. Meanwhile, natural gas contributed to 22 per cent of the global energy mix, and to 20 per cent of emissions (IEA, 2018a).

In 2016, with shares of electricity from coal of 69 per cent and 75 per cent respectively, China and India together produced 40 per cent of the global emissions from electricity generation, while the United States, Europe, Russia, and Japan – with a greater role of natural gas in their electricity generation mixes – contributed altogether to 32 per cent (IEA, 2018a).

To generate the same amount of electricity, a coal-fired power plant indeed emits 40 per cent more CO_2 than a natural gas-fired power plant and 20 per cent more than an oil-fired power plant. For instance, to produce enough electricity for an average European household for one year, five tonnes of CO_2 would be emitted if the electricity was generated from coal, three tonnes if generated from natural gas and zero tonnes if generated from wind and solar. As a result of this, in 2017, coal generated around 80 per cent of the CO_2 emissions from the European electricity generation mix, to which it only contributed 25 per cent (Tagliapietra, 2017b).

There are limited ways to improve the efficiency of coal and to make it cleaner. New more efficient, or 'ultra-supercritical', coal power stations still produce substantially more CO_2 than natural gas power stations. Meanwhile, carbon capture and storage technology remains unproven as a fully integrated process. Effective capture technology has not been developed and safe long-term storage at the scale necessary has not been demonstrated. Therefore, it is hard to see how carbon capture and storage for coal would ever be able to compete on price with renewables, the costs of which are rapidly falling (Tagliapietra, 2017b).

The persistent role of coal in the global energy mix represents a problem for the climate, but also for the environment and for human health.

Coal-fired power plants are responsible for the largest volumes of sulphur dioxide, nitrogen oxides, and particulate matter released into the air. Sulphur dioxide and nitrogen oxides are key contributors to the phenomenon of acid rain. As the acidified precipitation falls to the surface, it percolates into the ground, triggering decomposition of a variety of naturally occurring minerals in the soil. Included in the elements mobilised in this manner are calcium and magnesium, which are essential for healthy plant growth, and toxic species such as aluminium, which, when transported to rivers and lakes, can seriously impact the health and even the very survival of fish communities. Acid precipitation has been implicated also in the dieback of forests, especially in regions where the chemical composition of soils is incapable of neutralising the added acid. These particles, typically small in size, have an additional consequential impact on human health. Respired by humans, they can indeed penetrate into the lungs, triggering a variety of serious, potentially life-threatening consequences for impacted communities. Mercury in particulate and oxidised form is removed relatively rapidly from the atmosphere either by incorporation in rain or through contact with surface materials (what atmospheric chemists refer to as dry deposition). In elemental form, though, mercury can survive for a year or more as a gas in the atmosphere. The impact in this case can extend to global scale, in contrast to the more localised impact of the element in its shorter-lived chemical expressions. A significant fraction of the mercury emitted by burning mercury-rich coal ends up in aquatic systems. Once there, it can be converted to methyl mercury, the chemical form in which it is most toxic to organisms. Ingested by fish, methyl mercury can be concentrated in the tissue of these organisms. The problem that results is particularly serious for human populations for which mercury-exposed fish constitutes an important fraction of their diet. Babies born to mothers who have ingested excessive quantities of methyl mercury when pregnant can suffer from a range of disabilities, including difficulties in learning to speak, in processing information, and in coordinating visual and motor functions.

In addition to the range of negative environmental impacts associated with the combustion of coal, it is worth noting the variety of problems associated with its production: the lives that have been lost due to accidents in coal mines; the deaths of coal miners that ensued as a result of black lung and other respiratory diseases; the destruction caused by the removal of entire mountain tops to facilitate more efficient extraction of the resource; the collapse of slag heaps that buried neighbouring communities; and the pollution of rivers and ground waters from the disposal of coal ash. That is, coal may have fuelled the success of industrial economies around the world for more than a century, but the benefits have been achieved at significant cost both to human communities and to the environment on which they depend for their health and support.

Given its environmental impacts, governments have taken aggressive steps in recent years to limit – or even terminate – their consumption of coal.

For instance, in 2013, China adopted an air pollution action plan, which included air quality targets for key regions including Beijing to be met mainly through the closing of coal-fired power plants and through the ban on burning coal for heat. As a result of this policy, between 2013 and 2017 air pollution levels in Beijing dropped by more than 30 per cent. In 2018, China adopted a new three-year plan for cleaner air – named 'Winning the Battle for Blue Skies'. The plan further scaled up previous efforts, mandating to a wider spectrum of regions and cities to reduce air pollution levels by at least 18 per cent by 2020 from 2015 levels, and to ensure that the rate of days with good air quality reaches 80 per cent annually. As indicated by the IEA (2018e, p.12), 'The main target of the policy action is to reduce direct coal use and small boilers in residential heating, as well as in the commercial and industrial sectors'. But cement, steel, and small power producers are also targeted in China's air-quality campaign. Natural gas use for heating and industry, and renewables for power generation, are considered as key elements to replace coal in these sectors (State Council of The People's Republic of China, 2018).

In 2017, the governments of Canada and the United Kingdom launched the 'Powering Past Coal Alliance', an initiative aimed at promoting the end of unabated coal power generation by 2030.[1] Based on the recognition that shifting away from unabated coal power generation is essential for a clean and healthy environment as well as for meeting the Paris Agreement's targets, the Alliance was initially endorsed by 27 national, provincial, state, and city governments. Since 2017, the initiative has continuously expanded, adding to its supporters a long list of national governments, sub-national governments, as well as business and organisations[2]. However, major coal producing and consuming countries have not joined the Alliance, since those countries are unable to envisage the end of coal

[1] Unabated coal power generation refers to the use of coal without any technologies to substantially reduce its CO_2 emissions, such as carbon capture and storage.

[2] For the full list, please refer to: https://poweringpastcoal.org/.

power generation for at least three reasons: energy security, energy competitiveness, and job losses.

For several coal producing countries, job losses and wider economic repercussions for coal-mining regions indeed represent a key challenge for coal phase-out. This problem has led to the development of the concept of 'just transition'. This concept was initially developed by North American unions in the 1990s, with a focus on support for workers who lost their jobs as a result of environmental protection policies. The concept broadened over time, becoming a deliberate effort to plan for and invest in the transition to environmentally and socially sustainable jobs, sectors, and economies. As the understanding of climate change grew, unions began to tie the 'just transition' concept to action on climate change. They also began campaigning to insert 'just transition' into international regimes, including UNFCCC negotiations. As a result of this, in 2015 the concept of 'just transition' was inserted into the preamble of the Paris Agreement.

A 'just transition' for coal-mining regions is possible, and lessons from past coal mine closure programs demonstrate it (World Bank, 2018a)[3]. An example of policy solutions that could be applied in the area is offered by the European experience with the coal-mining transformation of the 1950s – a time when mechanisation deeply dented jobs in the sector. To face that challenge, Europe set-up a transition mechanism for coal-mining regions, called 'European Coal and Steel Community Fund for the Retraining and Resettlement of Workers'. The fund was created to facilitate re-employment opportunities for those coal and steel workers who lost their jobs as a result of the introduction of new technical processes or new equipment. The fund proved to be successful, and represented the first step in the creation of a European social and regional policy. With the 1957 Treaty of Rome, the fund was transformed into the 'European Social Fund', which in its early stages was indeed used to support workers who lost their jobs in sectors that were modernising, such as coal mining.

[3] These examples are taken from: Tagliapietra (2017b).

More recently, a number of 'just transition' initiatives have emerged across the world. In the United States, the 'Partnerships for Opportunity and Workforce and Economic Revitalisation' was started by President Obama in 2015, and the 'Assistance to Coal Communities', was launched by the Trump administration in 2017. In Canada, the government – which decided in 2016 to phase out the use of coal-fired electricity by 2030 – committed to working with provincial governments and unions to ensure workers affected by the accelerated coal phase-out are involved in a successful transition; in this context, in 2017, the government of Alberta launched the 'Coal Community Transition Fund', aimed at assisting regional communities impacted by coal phase-out. In 2017, the EU utilised its 'European Globalisation Adjustment Fund' to provide support to a coal mining region in Spain during the phase-out. The fund, established in 2006, supports workers who lose their jobs as a result of major structural changes in world trade patterns resulting from globalisation, by helping workers who have been made redundant find another job or set up their own business. In Germany, in 2019, an expert commission appointed by the government to study a potential phase-out of coal in the country recommended the shutdown of all coal-fired power plants by 2038 and the set-up of a EUR 40 billion fund to support regions affected by the phase-out.

To conclude, it should be noted that in the run-up to the 2015 Paris Agreement and since then, the international financial community has also begun to reposition itself vis-à-vis the coal sector. The move is partially driven by climate and environmental responsibility, but mainly by a purely financial consideration: to stop investing in an industry that could become obsolete in few decades as a result of global climate policy and renewable energy developments – an issue that in financial jargon is defined as 'stranded assets'.

Between 2015 and 2019, around sixty leading international banks have decided to stop financing coal-fired power plants, and/or stop financing coal mining companies – albeit some of them with caveats, such as geographical limitation to developed countries only.

Multilateral development banks have also started to adopt such an approach. In 2013, the European Investment Bank introduced an emissions performance standard of $550gCO_2/kWh$ as an assessment criterion for lending to energy projects, therefore ruling out any further lending to regular coal-fired power plants. In 2013, the World Bank decided to limit financing of coal-fired power plants to rare circumstances. In 2018, the European Bank for Reconstruction and Development announced a new energy strategy centred on eliminating funding for thermal coal mining and coal-fired power plants, to focus on renewable energy sources. Again in 2018, the Asian Development Bank declared its intention to stop financing coal-fired power plants, no longer considering them a viable option to meet electricity demand of developing countries.

4.4 KEY TAKEAWAYS

Introduction to Coal

- Coal is a fossil fuel formed from plants that lived hundreds of millions of years ago.
- Coal has four ranks: anthracite, bituminous, subbituminous, and lignite.
- Coal has been a cornerstone of the global energy system since the Industrial Revolution.
- Coal is abundant, widely distributed across the globe, and cheap in comparison to oil and gas.
- Coal is the most polluting fossil, fuel, both in terms of CO_2 emissions and air pollutants.

Coal Reserves, Production, Demand, and Trade

- Global coal reserves are abundant, and mainly located in Asia, North America, and CIS.
- Global coal production doubled over the last four decades, with a huge increment in Asia.
- China drives global coal demand since 1985, and today accounts for half of it.
- One of every four tonnes of coal consumed globally is used in China's electricity sector.

- Coal is mainly used in electricity generation and heat, as well as in iron and steel industries.
- Indonesia, Australia, and Russia are main exporters, while China and India main importers.

Environmental and Social Aspects of Coal

- Coal contributes to 27 per cent of global energy mix, but to 44 per cent of global CO_2 emissions.
- To generate the same amount of electricity, coal emits 40 per cent more CO_2 than natural gas.
- There are limited ways to improve coal efficiency and to make it cleaner.
- Coal combustion also emits high levels of air pollutants, which endanger human life.
- From China to Europe, countries are scaling up policies to limit coal use due to air pollution.
- China's 'Blue skies' strategy aims at reducing coal use in electricity and heat to clean up the air.
- Canada and the UK have launched a 'Powering Past Coal Alliance' to move beyond coal.
- Ensuring a 'just transition' in coal-mining regions is key to fostering coal phase-out.

5   Nuclear Energy

5.1   INTRODUCTION TO NUCLEAR ENERGY

Nuclear energy is contained in nuclei of atoms, which can be released using two different physical processes: nuclear fission and nuclear fusion. Nuclear fission entails splitting atoms in a reactor, then collecting the heat to vaporise water into steam, turn a turbine and generate electricity; this is a well-established technology that has been in use for decades. Nuclear fusion is the process where two atomic nuclei unite to form a common nucleus, hereby releasing a high amount of energy. Nuclear fusion is the source of energy of the sun and of the stars. Research into developing controlled nuclear fusion for civil purposes began in the 1940s and still continues today, but whether or not it will become a commercially viable technology is not yet clear. Major hurdles remain, including the high temperatures (several million Celsius degrees) that need to be reached and maintained.

Nuclear energy is used in both military and civil fields. The first nuclear reactors were built during World War II. They were not used to supply electricity but, on the model of the first chain reaction battery built by Enrico Fermi in Chicago, to obtain technical information on the parameters that regulate nuclear reactions and to analyse the principles of operation, experiment with different reactor models, and produce material for bombs. Nuclear bombs can be built in two ways: by enriching the uranium to produce uncontrolled fission in a pure quantity of uranium, along the path leading to the launch of the atomic bomb on Hiroshima; or through the use of reactors to produce plutonium.

Each reactor operating on uranium fuel creates plutonium as a by-product. Once the fuel used is taken from a reactor, plutonium can be extracted through a specific chemical process. In the huge reactors built during World War II in the United States for the Manhattan project[1], the energy produced by fission was treated simply as waste. The energy released by these reactors warmed the waters of the adjacent Columbia River, which served as a coolant, while the recovered plutonium was used in the first nuclear explosion (the Trinity test) and for the construction of the bomb dropped on Nagasaki.

After 1945, research into the development of reactors continued as part of the plutonium production process. As it became clear that, in many ways, it was the best way to produce bombs, nations with nuclear ambitions in the military field – such as the Soviet Union, the United Kingdom, and France – allocated substantial government funds for research programmes on the reactors in competition with the United States. Once the hydrogen bomb based on nuclear fusion was built, the reactors continued to be used as neutron sources for the production of tritium, which was necessary for the operation of the bomb itself.

Between the end of the 1940s and the beginning of the 1950s, the first nuclear engineers, trained on site, began to design more advanced projects than those conceived under the pressure of war. They modified the structural arrangements of the reactors, experimented with different neutron moderators and studied the possibility of using plutonium or enriched uranium as alternative nuclear fuels. The new nuclear specialists also worked to exploit the thermal energy that would otherwise have been lost. The idea of using reactors to power airplanes, ships, and submarines aroused strong military interest; such vehicles could travel long distances with a compact source of energy and with modest supply needs. The military outlook also went hand in hand with expectations of innovations for civilian use that could be achieved through nuclear science: the supply of electricity in areas far from natural resources, the implementation of intensive

---

[1]   A research project undertaken in the United States (with the collaboration of the United Kingdom and Canada) during World War II to produce the first nuclear weapon.

energy processes such as desalination of sea water to irrigate deserts, the raising of the standard of living in the world, and the entry into an era of material well-being.

The civil nuclear energy sector originates from these post-war projects. Research and development programmes were launched in the 1950s in most industrialised countries and later in some industrialising countries. The American initiative 'Atoms for Peace', presented in 1953, shows the passion with which the new possibilities offered by nuclear science were announced in the choice of the name. In the United States, however, there was no progress in the exploitation of nuclear energy for civil purposes, due to the strong emphasis placed on its use in the military field, because in that country, but also elsewhere, planning was stimulated mainly by geopolitical and commercial reasons. The focus on energy production was accompanied by the desire to achieve national industrial independence, as well as an interest in the marketing and installation of power plants, which included a large export market.

Although several power plants are competing for primacy, the small Obninsk reactor, which began generating electricity in 1954 in a secret nuclear site of the Soviet Union, is generally considered the first nuclear power generator. The Calder Hall power plant in the United Kingdom, connected to the electricity grid in 1956, made it possible to demonstrate that – alongside the production of plutonium to be used for nuclear weapons – it was also possible to produce electricity on an industrial scale.

In many countries that built their own reactors, projects implemented for civilian use still retain the concrete echo of previous military interests. This is particularly the case when they originated under governments that had a national interest in both plutonium production and electricity generation (e.g., France), or that developed specific technologies for military propulsion (e.g., the United States, attracted by the idea of carrying out submarine nuclear projects). Countries focusing from the outset on energy production, such as Canada, Germany, and Japan, represented an exception.

In the 1950s and the 1970s, the global nuclear industry was characterised by a wide variety of nuclear reactor models. The United Kingdom developed Magnox, a reactor designed to run on natural uranium with graphite as the moderator and carbon dioxide gas as the heat exchange coolant. In total, only a few dozen reactors of this type were constructed, most of them in the country, with very few exported to other countries. France independently developed a similar kind of reactor to meet similar requirements of simultaneous production of electric power and plutonium, the UNGG (Uranium Naturel Graphite Gaz). Also in this case, only a few dozen reactors were constructed, and mostly domestically. Canada developed the CANDU (Canadian deuterium uranium) reactor, with unenriched uranium and heavy water moderator. The United States developed the pressurised water reactor (PWR) and the boiling water reactor (BWR). Both used enriched uranium, which was then much more readily available in the country than elsewhere, to compensate for the disadvantages of using moderate, ordinary water-cooled reactors. PWR and BWR were licensed by two major industries, Westinghouse and General Electric. The Soviet Union developed two main types of reactors: the RBMK (reaktor bol'šoj moščnosti kanal'nyi), with graphite-moderate pressure channels, and the VVER (vodo-vodjanoj energetičeskij reaktor), with water under pressure. Other types of reactors were also tested in Sweden, Switzerland, and then-Western Germany.

The initial wide variety of nuclear reactor types progressively reduced over time. Since the 1970s, the global nuclear landscape started to get more polarised. In line with the overall Cold War context, Western countries increasingly adopted reactors developed by the United States, while Soviet and Eastern European countries adopted reactors developed by the Soviet Union.

The development of the nuclear industry led to substantial investments and involved national training programmes for engineers, scientists, and technicians. In many countries, such initiatives were supported by a wider shift in post-war cultural policy towards greater emphasis on science and technology. The new experts could

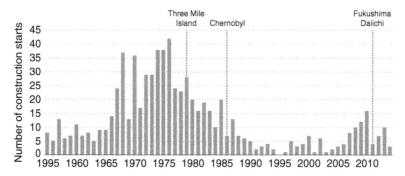

FIGURE 5.1 Historic timeline of nuclear reactors' construction starting
Source: International Energy Agency, Technology Roadmap. Nuclear
Energy 2015.

deal with the different phases of the overall fuel cycle, from uranium mining and processing to the construction of uranium plants and the disposal of nuclear waste.

In the 1960s and 1970s, the construction of nuclear power plants increased sharply across the world, notably in the United States, Europe, Japan, and the Soviet Union (Figure 5.1). This was possible also because until the 1970s public concern about nuclear energy was limited. In many countries, the oil shock of 1973 also proved fundamental in strengthening governmental commitment to nuclear energy. Since the mid-1970s, however, numerous technical, economic and political difficulties have led to a considerable slowdown in this development. In some developed countries, emerging public scepticism about the actual scientific and technological progress related to nuclear energy has fuelled widespread anti-nuclear movements, while in industrialising economies, national political commitment to nuclear energy has instead been maintained, or even expanded.

In many cases, nuclear energy has become a strong element of political division and public debates on its future have in some cases led to rapid changes in countries' nuclear energy policies. These debates notably intensified in the aftermath of nuclear power plant accidents.

A first accident occurred in 1979 in the United States, at the Three Mile Island nuclear power plant in Pennsylvania. The events that triggered the disaster, in short, were as follows: a valve that was supposed to close remained open; the refrigerant circuit controlled by the valve itself began to empty, and the reactor core overheated. The operators, unaware of the malfunctioning of the valve, which the system indicated as closed, worsened the situation by reducing the flow of refrigerant from the emergency systems. This led to further overheating and finally to a partial melt-down of the core. Much of the damage was confined, the protective systems of reactor 2 remained intact (managing to contain much of the radioactive material) and after few hours of convulsions, the cooling system had also been restored. But two days later, the news of the release of radioactive material came as a source of fear. The alarm forced the Governor of Pennsylvania to suggest the precautionary evacuation of the most sensitive population living around the plant, such as pregnant women and children. The announcement caused panic among the locals, and only the arrival of President Jimmy Carter at the power plant two days later was able to partly reassure the population. The accident's repercussions on health were limited, with no deaths or injuries directly related to it. However, the incident catalysed public opinion against nuclear energy, and contributed to the decline of a new nuclear reactor construction program in the country, which was already slowing down due to economic reasons.

Much more devastating was the explosion in 1986 of one of the RBMK reactors in Chernobyl, in the Soviet Union (now Ukraine). The type of reactor, combined with negligence in the operation and administration of the plant, led to a situation where the chain reaction occurred completely out of control. The core temperature increased to such an extent that the fuel broke down and the cooling water turned into steam as it escaped from the reactor. A second explosion and a strong fire in the graphite moderator released some of the melted fuel and fission products into a large radioactive cloud. Thirty-one people were the immediate victims of the accident. Many more were exposed to the radioactive material, a large number of whom later developed cancer. In Europe, and notably in Scandinavia, radiation control monitors picked up the radioactive rain, causing an international sensation. The incident polarised world public opinion and in several countries, such as Italy, it steered national nuclear policies towards a new course.

More recently, on March 11, 2011, following a violent earthquake with an underwater epicentre, the nuclear power plant of Fukushima Daiichi, in Japan, was hit by a tsunami that severely damaged its three reactors, causing ecological damage of enormous proportions, comparable to those of the 1986 Chernobyl disaster. Since 2011, losses of radioactive water from the reservoirs of the plant have continued to occur with alarming frequency, at a level inducing the Japanese president to seek assistance from foreign countries to solve the issue in October 2013. This serious incident has prompted governments of many industrialised countries, such as Germany and Switzerland, to review their energy policies and to reduce or even eliminate nuclear from their energy mixes.

Another critical issue linked to nuclear energy is the one of proliferation. More recently, the two main global proliferation risks have been represented by Iran and North Korea. As far as Iran is concerned, after the 2005 presidential election of Mahmoud Ahmadinejad, the IAEA reported that the country resumed uranium conversion. In 2006, the IAEA reported Iran to the United Nations Security Council – which voted for sanctions and gave Iran sixty days to suspend enrichment. In 2007, the Security Council unanimously approved further financial and weapons sanctions to Iran. In the same year, China, France, Russia, the United Kingdom, the United States, and Germany (the so-called 'P5+1') agreed to push tougher sanctions. Five years after, the 'P5+1' and Iran started to negotiate on the Iranian nuclear weapons programme. After the 2013 presidential election of Hassan Rouhani, negotiations between Iran and the 'P5+1' advanced, and in 2015 the parties signed a nuclear deal, formally known as the Joint Comprehensive Plan of Action (JCPOA). The deal ended twelve years of nuclear standoff between Iran and Western powers. In exchange for Iran giving up its nuclear weapons programme, international sanctions were lifted – giving a relief to the struggling Iranian economy. But in 2018, US President Donald Trump announced the US withdrawal from the Iran nuclear deal, opening a new phase of uncertainty and tensions.

As far as North Korea is concerned, the most recent developments started in 2016, when the US Geological Survey detected a magnitude 5.1 seismic disturbance in Korea. North Korea claimed the realisation of a test involving a hydrogen bomb. In reaction to this, the United Nations Security Council promptly decided to impose additional sanctions against North Korea. As a response, North Korea announced in 2017 the realisation of a new hydrogen bomb test – this time also accompanied by several intercontinental ballistic missiles launches, allegedly able to carry super-heavy nuclear warheads. North Korea's President Kim Jong Un announced these developments stating that North Korea had finally realised the great historic cause of completing the state nuclear force. Tensions subsequently de-escalated in 2018, after Kim Jong Un launched a message of appeasement by signalling his desire to send athletes to the 2018 Olympics to be held in South Korea. This appeasement also paved the way for the first-ever meeting between the Presidents of North Korea and the United States in 2018, in Singapore. The result of the meeting was the signature of a joint statement, with which the two Presidents agreed to security guarantees for North Korea, new peaceful relations, and the denuclearisation of the Korean Peninsula.

5.2   NUCLEAR ENERGY PRODUCTION

The scientific basis of the current nuclear power plants is nuclear fission, the process – discovered in 1938 – in which the nucleus of an atom splits into smaller, lighter nuclei. A nuclear reactor is a facility that uses the principle of nuclear fission to produce electricity. In a nuclear reactor, uranium nuclei basically replace fossil fuels used in thermal power plants. When a neutron hits a uranium nucleus, it breaks down by releasing other neutrons and energy in the form of heat. The released neutrons will hit other uranium nuclei and so on:

the reaction is self-sustaining, and it is defined as a chain reaction. The heat released during the chain reaction is used to produce water vapour. In the same way as in thermal power plants, it is this steam that drives a turbine and its generator to produce electricity. The remaining vapour is then condensed in a condenser, which is a heat exchanger connected to a secondary side such as a river, the sea, or a cooling tower. The water is then pumped back into the steam generator and the cycle starts again (Figure 5.2).

This operation is based on three independent circuits filled with water that operate through heat exchange. The primary circuit is a closed circuit that transfers the heat released in the reactor core (i.e., where the fuel is located and the chain reaction takes place) to the steam generators that convert this heat into steam. The secondary circuit is a closed circuit that brings the steam produced in the steam generators to the turbine of the turbo-alternator group that produces the electricity. Then the steam is transformed back into water in the condenser. Finally, the cooling circuit supplies cold water to the condenser. This water can be drawn from a river or from the sea.

Depending on the reactor model, the water can then be released at the source at a slightly higher temperature (i.e., reactor without air cooler) or cooled in an air cooler and then fed back into the cooling system (i.e., reactor with air cooler).

The cooling tower, which people tend to identify as main element of a nuclear power plant, is a hollow tower, at the centre of which a stream of air naturally enters at the bottom and exits at the top. As it passes, this air stream takes the heat contained in the water in the cooling system and disperses it into the atmosphere in the form of a cloud of water vapour. To replace this volume of water vapour dispersed in the atmosphere, an equivalent sample is taken from a nearby river or from the nearby sea. This operation is constantly reproduced. It should be noted that only the water in the primary circuit is radioactive, while the water in the secondary circuit and the water in the cooling circuit are never in contact with the nuclear fuel.

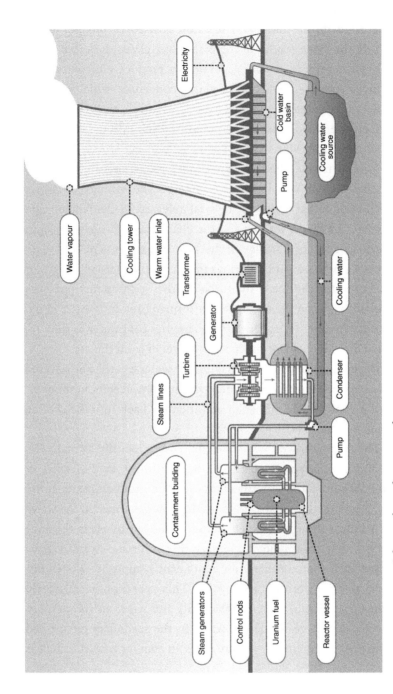

FIGURE 5.2 Scheme of a nuclear power plant
Source: Shutterstock.

To ensure the operational safety of a nuclear reactor, it is essential to maintain three safety functions at all times: (i) The control of the chain reaction; (ii) The cooling of nuclear fuel. When the reactor is in operation, the heat from the nuclear fuel must be continuously removed. When the reactor is shut down, the residual heat remaining after the end of the chain reaction must also be removed; and (iii) The containment of radioactivity. The aim is to prevent the dispersion of radioactive substances in the environment, and to ensure the protection of people and the environment from radiation.

The technological evolution of nuclear reactors has been categorised into four generations (IAEA, 2015). Generation I reactors were built between the 1950s and 1960s, and have now been all decommissioned. Generation II reactors – also known as pressurised water reactors (PWRs) – were built between the 1970s and the mid-1990s. Used to generate electricity as well as to propel nuclear submarines and naval vessels, PWRs make use of light water (i.e., ordinary water, as opposed to heavy water) as their coolant and neutron moderator. PWRs were originally designed for the US Navy, however, they quickly grew to become the most widely used reactor in nuclear power plants. Of the 449 nuclear reactors operational in the world in 2019, 298 were PWRs (IAEA, 2019).

Generation III reactors were built between 1995 and 2010 with a more advanced design and increased safety levels. After the 2011 Fukushima nuclear accident, nuclear safety authorities of various countries mandated new standards to allow reactors to withstand, without core melting, external conditions such as earthquakes, floods, and extreme weather conditions, as well as acts of terrorism and cyberattacks. This led to the development of Generation III+ reactors, which have significantly higher safety levels than Generation III reactors. These reactors are intended to function as a bridge towards the future deployment of Generation IV reactors.

In the developmental stage since 2010, Generation IV reactors are not expected to be operational before 2030–40. These reactors will feature higher safety levels than those of Generation III+ and better performance in terms of both efficiency and cost. Particularly interesting are the 'fast' closed-cycle reactors (uranium-plutonium cycle refrigerated with sodium, lead, or helium) for the simple fact – already scientifically proven – that with them the percentage of energy extracted from uranium would rise to 70 per cent, from 0.6–0.8 per cent in Generation II, III, and III+ reactors (IAEA, 2019). This means multiplying by 100 the energy that can be exploited from the same natural uranium resources. There is another great advantage: with Generation IV reactors, the amount of minor actinides (e.g. americium, curium, and neptunium) having very long radioactive lives and great activity could be reduced by 100 times. This means reducing by 100 times the space needed in the deep geological deposits that today are indispensable for the irradiated fuels coming from the open cycles of the current thermal water reactors of the II and III generation.

The United States have historically been the leaders of nuclear energy production, accounting for around a quarter of the world's nuclear power generation between 1965 and 2017. In the same period, France has also played a major role, as well as Japan up to the 2011 Fukushima accident, which led to the abrupt shut-down of the country's nuclear reactors. Countries such as Russia, South Korea, Canada, and Germany have also traditionally been important players in the field. It is also interesting to outline the brisk expansion of China's nuclear power generation, which rose rapidly from 16 TWh in 2000 to 248 TWh in 2017, placing the country in the top-3 of global nuclear power generation (Figure 5.3).

Nuclear power generation in China is set to further expand by the mid-2020s, as in 2019 the country had under construction eleven new reactors, with a total installed capacity of 11 GW. India, Russia, South Korea, and the United Arab Emirates also had substantial nuclear power plants under construction in 2019 (Figure 5.4).

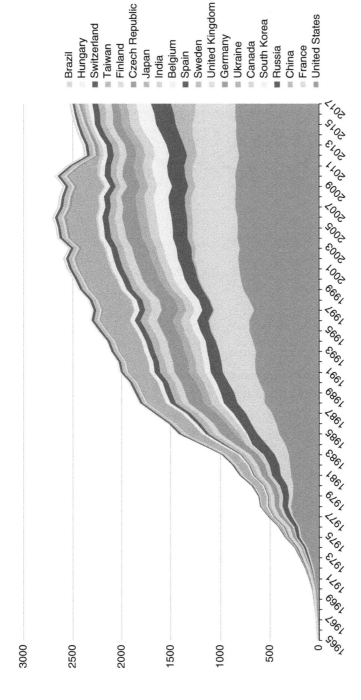

FIGURE 5.3 Top-20 countries by nuclear power generation, TWh, 1965–2017
Source: author's elaboration on BP (2018a).

Brazil
Hungary
Switzerland
Taiwan
Finland
Czech Republic
Japan
India
Belgium
Spain
Sweden
United Kingdom
Germany
Ukraine
Canada
South Korea
Russia
China
France
United States

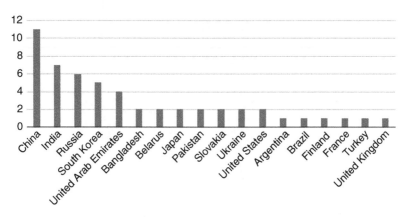

FIGURE 5.4 Number of nuclear power plants under construction by country, 2019
Source: author's elaboration on IAEA, Power Reactor Information System database, accessed in June 2019.

5.3 ONGOING DEVELOPMENTS IN NUCLEAR ENERGY TECHNOLOGY

Since the early 2010s, interest has increased for the potential development of small-scale nuclear power plants, the so-called small modular reactors (SMRs). This interest is driven by attempts to reduce capital costs of nuclear power plants, as well as to provide an alternative supply source for decentralised mini-grid solutions – which could play an important role in fostering electrification in remote areas of developing countries.

The typical power output of a SMR module would stand at 300 MW per unit, which compares to 1,000 MW average power output of a traditional nuclear reactor. To date, the economics of SMRs (i.e., capital costs, operation and maintenance costs, fuel costs) is not yet known, as the first prototypes of SMRs are under development.

According to the Nuclear Energy Agency (2016, p.10),

> SMRs could present several competitive advantages vis-à-vis traditional nuclear reactors, such as: i) Lower upfront investment requirements; ii) Better flexibility for utilities operating in markets with high shares of variable renewable energy sources; iii) Smaller

transmission infrastructure requirements; iv) Easier deployment due to adaptability to various locations; v) Avoidance of long outage periods due to multi-unit configuration; vi) Easier decommissioning. If these competitive advantages are realised, SMRs might well have lower absolute and per kW total construction costs than traditional nuclear power plants. But this would only be possible if SMRs were produced in large numbers, through optimised supply chains and with smaller financing costs.

To conclude, nuclear fusion should also be discussed. Nuclear fusion is the process in which two atomic nuclei join together to form a heavier nucleus. This reaction underpins the Sun as well as most of the stars in the Universe. Since the 1940s, extensive research has been carried out to develop controlled nuclear fusion for civil purposes, but so far there has been no breakthrough. The difficulty in carrying out nuclear fusion processes stems from the electrostatic repulsion – that is, coulomb repulsion – between the nuclei, which all have positive electrical charge. This repulsive force, with a long range of action, prevails on the nuclear forces, having a short range of action, except at very small distances, of the order of the nuclear dimensions. Nuclear fusion reactions can be realised and maintained only if the raw material for such reactions is confined to a density and a temperature sufficient to allow the kinetic energy of the elementary constituents to be sufficient to overcome the coulomb repulsion. In the case of thermonuclear explosions, this is achieved by means of a nuclear fission explosion that produces nuclear radiation in such a way as to compress and heat the mass of material that then gives rise to the fusion. In the case of stars, compression is caused by gravitational force. The controlled nuclear fusion model that appears most promising for the commercial production of electricity is based on the confinement by magnetic fields of a plasma consisting of atoms of deuterium and tritium, at very high temperature.

In southern France, thirty-four countries[2] are collaborating since 1985 to build the International Thermonuclear Experimental

---

[2]   China, EU countries, India, Japan, Korea, Russia, and the United States.

Reactor (ITER), the world's largest tokamak. First invented in the 1950s, a tokamak is an experimental machine designed to harness the energy of fusion using powerful magnets to confine the plasma. As illustrated by ITER (2019), 'inside a tokamak, the energy produced through the fusion of atoms is absorbed as heat in the walls of the vessel. Just like a conventional power plant, a fusion power plant will use this heat to produce steam and then electricity by way of turbines and generators'. Thousands of engineers and scientists have contributed to the design of ITER, which aims to be the first fusion device to test the integrated technologies, materials, and physics regimes necessary for the commercial production of fusion-based electricity. To date, the world record for fusion power is held by the European tokamak Joint European Torus (JET), based at the Culham Centre for Fusion Energy in the United Kingdom. This is, so far, the largest and most successful fusion experiment in the world, which also serves as a small-scale prototype for ITER. According to ITER (2019), 'in 1997, JET produced 16 MW of fusion power from a total input heating power of 24 MW. ITER is designed to produce a ten-fold return on energy, or 500 MW of fusion power from 50 MW of input heating power'. It should be noted that ITER does not aim at capturing the energy it produces as electricity, but rather at paving the way for a machine that can do so. So far, a convincing demonstration of its feasibility has yet to be given, as 'the first act of ITER's multi-decade operational program – the first magnetic confinement plasma physics experiment – is scheduled for 2025, with full deuterium–tritium fusion experiments starting in 2035' (ITER, 2019). Should these landmarks be successfully achieved, ITER would then be succeed by the DEMOnstration power plant (DEMO), which would represent the world's first nuclear fusion reactor to produce electricity in an experimental environment.

Various countries are simultaneously advancing research in the field. As the IAEA (2018) shows,

China has a program called China Fusion Engineering Test Reactor (CFETR) that aims at bridging the gaps between ITER and

DEMO by 2030. The European Union and Japan are jointly building a powerful tokamak called JT-60SA in Naka, Japan, as a complement to ITER and as a preparation for the engineering design and construction of DEMO. India has announced plans to begin building a device called SST-2 to develop components for a DEMO around 2027, and then start construction of a DEMO in 2037. South Korea initiated a conceptual design study for a K-DEMO in 2012 targeting the construction by 2037 with potential for electricity generation starting in 2050. Russia plans the development of a fusion-fission hybrid facility called DEMO fusion neutron source (FNS), a reactor that would harvest the fusion-produced neutrons to turn uranium into nuclear fuel and destroy radioactive waste. The DEMO-FNS is planned to be built by 2023, and is part of Russia's fast-track strategy to a fusion power plant by 2050. The United States is considering an intermediate step called Fusion Nuclear Science Facility (FNSF) to be used for the development and testing of fusion materials and components for a DEMO-type reactor. Plans call for operation to start after 2030, and construction of a DEMO after 2050.

In any case, nuclear fusion is expected to eventually (i.e., should research finally bring positive results, which have not been accomplished so far) become a commercially viable solution only after 2050.

5.4 KEY TAKEAWAYS

Introduction to Nuclear Energy

- Nuclear energy is contained in nuclei of particles, which can be released either through fission or fusion.
- Fission harnesses nuclear energy released in the splitting of atoms; it is a well-established technology.
- Fusion is when two atomic nuclei unite to form a common nucleus; it is not yet viable.
- The civil nuclear energy sector originates from post–World War II military projects.

- Construction of nuclear energy plants boomed globally between the 1960s and the 1970s.
- Three incidents (Three Mile Island, Chernobyl, and Fukushima) impacted the development of nuclear energy.
- Concerns about proliferation of weapons also cast doubts on the development of nuclear energy.
- The International Atomic Energy Agency was created in 1957 to promote peaceful use of nuclear energy.
- The Nuclear Non-Proliferation Treaty was signed in 1968 to prevent nuclear weapons.

Nuclear Energy Production

- Fission takes place inside a reactor, at the centre of which is the core containing uranium fuel.
- There have been four generations of nuclear reactors with increasingly higher efficiency and safety standards.
- The United States leads global nuclear power production, accounting for a quarter of the total.
- France and Japan (up to the 2011 Fukushima incident) have also been key nuclear producers.
- China is rapidly expanding its nuclear power production, with a high number of new reactors.
- India, Russia, South Korea, and the United Arab Emirates are also building several new reactors.

Ongoing Developments in Nuclear Energy Technology

- Interest is rising for small modular reactors, which could have lower costs and more flexibility.
- Commercial viability of small modular reactors still needs to be proven.
- Since the 1940s, extensive research has been done in the field of nuclear fusion.
- ITER, the world's largest fusion experiment, started in 1985 and might be completed by 2035.
- ITER is not aimed at producing power; for that, the DEMO power plant will have to be developed.
- China, the EU, Japan, India, Russia, and the United States are all advancing parallel research in the field.

6 Renewable Energy: Introduction and Established Sources

Renewable energy is derived from natural processes that are replenished constantly. Bioenergy (e.g., wood, animal waste, municipal solid waste, biofuels, biogas), hydropower, wind energy, solar energy, geothermal energy, and ocean energy (e.g., wave energy, tidal energy) are all renewable energy sources.

Renewable energy has accompanied humankind since its appearance. From prehistory and all the way up to the mid-nineteenth century, nearly all energy used worldwide was indeed renewable.

The first proven use of renewable energy, entailing the utilisation of wood to fuel fires, dates back to about 400,000 years ago. Since then, other forms of renewable energy have progressively been utilised. Just to mention some examples, archaeologists discovered that humans harnessed wind to drive ships on the Nile already 7,000 years ago. Likewise, there is evidence of the use of geothermal energy released by hot springs for bathing purposes at least since the Palaeolithic times, while it took until the ancient Romans to make use of geothermal energy also for space heating. Around 2,500 years ago, watermills started to be employed in Syria and Asia Minor, while windmills only started to be developed in Europe during the fourteenth century to mill grain.

After the emergence of coal in the mid-nineteenth century and after the oil boom began in the mid-twentieth century, the role of renewable energy in the global energy system became more marginal – contributing to roughly a tenth of global energy supply. In 1971, bioenergy contributed for 11 per cent of global energy supply, while

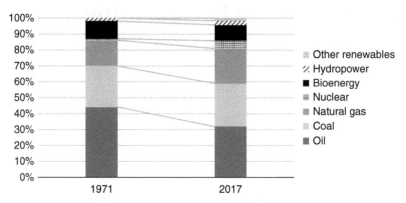

FIGURE 6.1 Contribution of renewable energy to global energy supply, 1971 and 2016
Source: author's elaboration on IEA (2018b).

hydropower contributed for 2 per cent. In 2017, bioenergy contributed for 10 per cent, hydropower for 2.5 per cent, and other renewables (i.e., wind, solar, geothermal, and ocean) for another 1.8 per cent (Figure 6.1).

While the share of renewable energy in global energy supply only slightly increased between 1971 and 2017, its internal composition substantially changed over time – most notably since the early 2000s. In 2000, half of the global renewable energy mix was composed of solid biomass – for example, wood, charcoal, agricultural residues, and animal dung. This was used for cooking and heating purposes by low-income households, mainly in emerging and developing countries, using old cookstoves with highly negative impacts on health – due to indoor smoke pollution – and the environment.

Since 2000, the share of solid biomass in the global renewable energy mix substantially decreased, while the share of modern bioenergy increased. As mentioned by IRENA (2019b), 'modern bioenergy solutions include liquid biofuels produced from plants; bio-refineries; biogas produced through anaerobic digestion of residues; wood pellet heating systems; and other technologies'. In the meantime, between 2000 and 2017, the share of hydropower remained stable, while the share of other renewables – notably wind and solar – in the global renewable energy mix more than doubled (Figure 6.2).

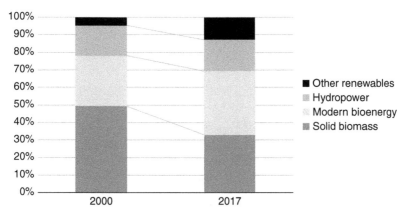

FIGURE 6.2 Global renewable energy supply mix, 2000 and 2017
Source: author's elaboration on IEA (2018b).

This illustrates the dynamism of the global renewable energy sector, which is due to both rapid renewable energy technology cost decrease and strong government policy support.

As far as renewable energy technology cost decrease is concerned, between 2009 and 2018, the cost of wind and solar energy technologies dramatically declined. Over the period, the mean levelized cost of electricity (LCOE)[1] for utility-scale wind indeed decreased by 69 per cent, while the one of solar photovoltaic decreased by 88 per cent (Figure 6.3).

The sharp drop in wind and solar photovoltaic cost was due to several factors, such as decreasing supply-chain costs, improving technology efficiency, and increased competition at global scale. These cost developments have made the two technologies increasingly competitive with coal and natural gas-based electricity generation in a growing number of countries across the world.

---

[1] As defined by the EIA (2019a), 'Levelized cost of electricity (LCOE) represents the average revenue per unit of electricity generated that would be required to recover the costs of building and operating a generating plant during an assumed financial life and duty cycle. 4 LCOE is often cited as a convenient summary measure of the overall competitiveness of different generating technologies. Key inputs to calculating LCOE include capital costs, fuel costs, fixed and variable operations and maintenance (O&M) costs, financing costs, and an assumed utilization rate for each plant type'.

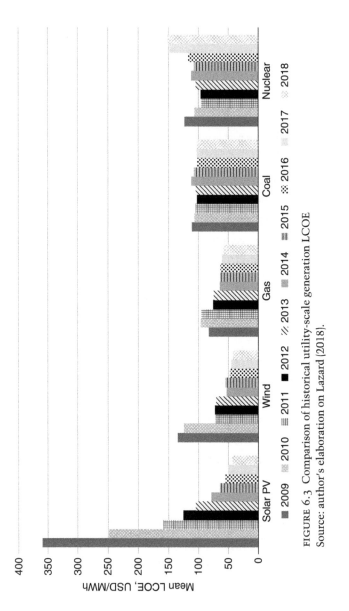

FIGURE 6.3 Comparison of historical utility-scale generation LCOE

Source: author's elaboration on Lazard (2018).

Government policies have had a very important impact on renewable energy technology development, deployment, and overall cost reduction. The number of countries with renewable energy targets and regulatory policies in the electricity generation sector increased from 40 in 2004 to 128 in 2017 (REN21, 2018). Drivers behind renewable energy policy support span from climate change mitigation to air pollution reduction; from energy security (i.e., through the replacement of fossil fuels import with domestic renewable energy sources) to industrial policy aimed at fostering clean technologies.

Climate action has undoubtedly been a key driving force behind the efforts to increase the role of renewables in the global energy system. Under the Paris Agreement, more than 140 countries referred to renewable energy action to mitigate and adapt to climate change, and around 100 of them also included quantified renewable energy targets (UNFCCC, 2019).

Air pollution reduction in urban areas is rapidly becoming another important driver of renewable energy policy, particularly considering the severe impact of air pollution on health. At the global level, the WHO (2019) estimates '4.2 million deaths every year as a result of exposure to ambient (outdoor) air pollution'. Renewable energy represents a sensible solution to this problem, and several countries, such as China, have scaled-up renewable energy investments with the primary aim of closing down coal-fired power plants in major cities to reduce air pollution.

By lowering reliance on fossil fuels import, renewable energy also increases a country's energy security while reducing its overall energy import bill. This represents an important driver for several oil and gas importing countries.

In developing countries, renewable energy truly represents a game-changer in view of fostering access to electricity and clean cooking solutions. Renewable energy can bring electricity to rural areas not reached by the power grid, either through stand-alone or mini-grid solutions. Similarly, renewable energy can provide a sensible contribution to fostering access to clean cooking.

As outlined by IRENA et al. (2018, p.19),

> Public and private actors alike are increasingly seeing renewable energy as a good investment that can provide higher revenues than other fuels. In several countries, renewables are or are becoming cost-competitive with other sources, even when not considering the negative externalities of fossil fuels and nuclear energy. Some countries pursue renewables deployment as a means of promoting local economic value and job creation, as it offers the potential to lower energy spending, increase incomes, and enhance welfare and industrial development.

Several countries across the world have put in place fiscal incentives and other public finance schemes to support the deployment of renewable energy in the electricity sector. For instance, in 2017 alone, countries across the globe devoted around USD 140 billion to subsidise renewables-based electricity (IEA, 2018b). Europe has traditionally been the world's region that subsidised renewables-based electricity the most, namely in the form of feed-in tariffs. Between 2008 and 2017, around 15 per cent of the electricity price paid by European households was indeed devoted to renewable energy subsidies (European Commission, 2019). While these subsidies started to fall in 2016, the share of renewables in several European countries' electricity generation mixes continued to grow, suggesting that – as a result of falling technology cost – renewable energy technologies might have reached maturity and cost competitiveness.

According to REN21 (2018), policy support for renewable energy deployment in other sectors – such as heat and transport – has been much more limited. For instance, in 2017 the number of countries with renewable energy targets and regulatory policies in heat and transport indeed only stood at 29 and 70, respectively.

As government policy support is key to fostering renewable energy deployment, it is not surprising that – as a result of these policy trends – global investment in renewables-based electricity generation stood at USD 298 billion in 2017, while investment in renewables-based heat stood at USD 109 billion and investment in transport biofuels stood at USD 2 billion only (IEA, 2018b).

Consequently, the global contribution of renewable energy to both heat and transport has remained much lower than in electricity. In this context, modern renewables continue to have the largest penetration in electricity, where they accounted for 24 per cent of global electricity consumption in 2017. Yet electricity is responsible for only one-fifth of the world's total final energy consumption. Therefore, despite gains in the electricity sector, the share of renewables in overall final consumption stood at 10 per cent, due to lower shares and less progress in other sectors. Heat and transport indeed account for over 80 per cent of final energy consumption and their renewables shares (10 per cent in heat and 3 per cent in transport) remained substantially lower than for electricity – albeit opportunities for renewables in these sectors are vast (Figure 6.4).

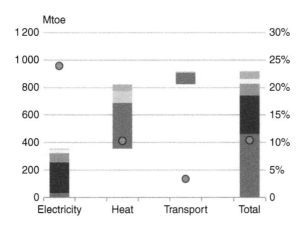

FIGURE 6.4 Modern renewable energy total consumption, 2017
Source: International Energy Agency, Renewables 2018. All rights reserved.

6.2 BIOENERGY

The vegetation that covers our planet can be seen as a natural storehouse of solar energy. Biomasses are indeed produced through the process of photosynthesis, during which – thanks to solar energy – atmospheric CO_2 and soil water combine to produce the sugars needed for life. In the chemical bonds of these substances is stored the same solar energy that activated photosynthesis. Photosynthesis is very important, as it nourishes life on earth and removes substantial amounts of CO_2 from the atmosphere. When biomass is burned, atmospheric oxygen combines with the carbon they contain; CO_2 and water are then released and heat is produced. The CO_2 then goes back into the atmosphere, where it is again available to be reintroduced into the process of photosynthesis to produce new biomass. This is the reason why biomass is a renewable resource. And this is also the reason why burning biomass is damaging for the climate as well as for the air.

Biomass has accompanied humankind since the dawn of civilisation. Fire, perhaps the most important invention in human history, was discovered thanks to the accidental combustion of wood. Once man understood how to master it, fire became the fundamental element to nourish, heat, illuminate, and protect. For thousands of years, wood represented the cornerstone of global energy use. Today, it continues to play an important role, notably in developing countries with limited access to modern energy solutions.

The IEA and FAO (2017, p.7) define biomass as 'any organic matter, i.e., biological material, available on a renewable basis – including feedstock derived from animals or plants, such as wood and agricultural crops, and organic waste from municipal and industrial source'.

Modern technologies have introduced new ways to convert biomass into solid, liquid, and gaseous products that can more efficiently meet today's energy needs – and this is called bioenergy. As illustrated by Concawe (2019),

A wide range of biomass feedstocks can be used as sources of bioenergy. These include: wet organic wastes, such as sewage sludge, animal wastes and organic liquid effluents, and the organic fraction of municipal solid waste (MSW); residues and co-products from agroindustries and the timber industry; crops grown for energy, including food crops such as corn, wheat, sugar and vegetable oils produced from palm, rapeseed and other raw materials; and non-food crops such as perennial lignocellulosic plants (e.g., grasses such as miscanthus and trees such as short-rotation willow and eucalyptus) and oil-bearing plants (e.g., jatropha and camelina)'.

Many processes are available to turn these feedstocks into a product that can be used for electricity, heat, or transport (Figure 6.5).

To date, the most common pathways have been: the production of heat and electricity from wood, agricultural residues and the biogenic fraction of wastes; maize and sugarcane to ethanol; and rapeseed, soybean, and oil crops to biodiesel.

As shown by the IEA (2017a, pp.11–12),

Each of these bioenergy pathways consists of several steps, which include biomass production, collection or harvesting, processing to improve the physical characteristics of the fuel, pre-treatment to alter chemical properties, and finally conversion of the biomass to useful energy. The number of these steps may differ depending on the type, location and source of biomass, and the technology used to provide the relevant final energy use.

As previously illustrated, modern bioenergy and solid biomass dominate the global renewable energy supply mix, with a share of 40 per cent and 30 per cent respectively (IEA, 2018b).

Modern bioenergy is the largest source of renewable energy owing to its widespread use in heat and transport, sectors in which other renewables currently make a far smaller contribution. Modern bioenergy is predominantly used in the heating sector, although both bioenergy for electricity generation and transport biofuels have been

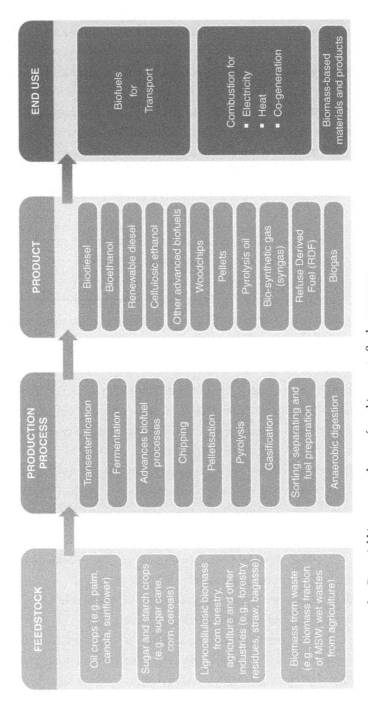

FIGURE 6.5 Potential bioenergy pathways: from biomass to final energy use

FEEDSTOCK

Oil crops (e.g., palm, canola, sunflower)

Sugar and starch crops (e.g.: sugar cane, corn, cereals)

Lignocellulosic biomass from forestry, agriculture and other industries (e.g.: forestry residues, straw, bagasse)

Biomass from waste (e.g., biomass fraction of MSW, wet wastes from agriculture)

PRODUCTION PROCESS

Transesterification

Fermentation

Advances biofuel processes

Chipping

Pelletisation

Pyrolysis

Gasification

Sorting, separating and fuel preparation

Anaerobic digestion

PRODUCT

Biodiesel

Bioethanol

Renewable diesel

Cellulosic ethanol

Other advanced biofuels

Woodchips

Pellets

Pyrolysis oil

Bio-synthetic gas (syngas)

Refuse Derived Fuel (RDF)

Biogas

END USE

Biofuels for Transport

Combustion for
■ Electricity
■ Heat
■ Co-generation

Biomass-based materials and products

growing faster since the early 2000s, on the basis of higher levels of policy support. As far as the heat sector is concerned, industry was the largest end user of modern bioenergy in 2017 (63 per cent), followed by buildings (34 per cent), and agriculture (3 per cent) (IEA, 2018b).

Bioenergy can play a significant role in the industrial sector, as it meets temperature, pressure, and quantity of heat and steam required by many processes. This is particularly the case of industries that produce biomass waste during their processes, such as the paper industry.

In the residential sector, modern bioenergy can be used for heating purposes, albeit several non-economic barriers exist (e.g., building suitability, households' inertia). Based on strong policy support and public finance support, bioenergy in the heating sector has, for instance, been well developed in Europe. This has not only entailed the promotion of modern stoves and boilers using wood logs, woodchips, and pellets, but also district heating networks. These solutions have notably been developed in Nordic and Baltic countries, due to a convergence of several factors spanning from excellent forestry resources availability to a strong commitment to reduce dependency on imported fossil fuels.

In the electricity sector, various modern bioenergy solutions can be adopted on the basis of the specific national context. For instance, in China the sector is being mainly developed on energy-from-waste and agriculture straw solutions, while in Europe and in the United States it is mainly being developed on the basis of forestry residues. According to the IEA (2019g), 'in most markets, solid biomass and wastes are the main contributors, accounting for over two-thirds of bioenergy electricity capacity in developed countries. Bioenergy supplied around 500 TWh of electricity in 2017, accounting for 2 per cent of global electricity production'. Bioenergy electricity generation has the important benefits of being dispatchable and of being a good solution to enhance waste management. However, major barriers to the development of bioenergy in the sector relate to the high generation costs and to the low efficiency of plants that operate in a simple cycle (i.e., without recovering the waste heat produced to enhance efficiency). In 2017, bioenergy contributed to 8 per cent of global renewable electricity generation (IEA, 2018b).

In the transport sector, the global production of conventional biofuels increased from 37 mtoe in 2007 to 84 mtoe in 2017, accounting for around 5 per cent of world's road transport fuel (BP, 2018a). The role of transport biofuels is concentrated in a limited number of markets. In 2017, the United States accounted for 42 per cent of world's biofuels production, followed by Brazil (21 per cent), and the European Union (17 per cent) (BP, 2018a). Biofuels are categorised into four generations.

First-generation biofuels use agricultural crops as feedstocks. Food crops are thus explicitly grown for fuel production. The sugar, starch, or vegetable oil obtained from the crops is converted into biodiesel or ethanol either through transesterification or yeast fermentation. A clear trade-off exists between these biofuels and food production, as cultivating agricultural crops for such use displaces food production on existing agricultural land.

Second-generation biofuels use lignocellulosic feedstocks like woody crops, agricultural residues, or waste plant material. As outlined by IRENA (2016b, p.8), 'some of these feedstocks can have high yields, sequester carbon, and grow on land poorly suited for food crops. They are converted to biofuels using biochemical and thermochemical technologies that are now in a pilot or demonstration phase'.

Third-generation biofuels entail the use of oil-rich algae to create ethanol. As outlined by IRENA (2016b, p.8), 'they are at an early stage of development and are not yet cost-effective. But they could grow on much less land while producing a variety of useful co-products. Because of their technical, economic and environmental promise, they are focus of intense research and development in several countries'.

Fourth-generation biofuels, also in the early experimental phase, entails the development of electrofuels – also known as synthetic fuels. As illustrated by Bosch (2019), 'synthetic fuels capture CO_2 in the manufacturing process. In this way, CO_2 becomes a raw material, from which gasoline, diesel, and substitute natural gas can be produced with the help of electricity from renewable sources'. With synthetic fuels, current internal combustion engine cars could then continue to be used, exactly as the established petrol filling-station network.

Biofuels development currently remains largely policy-driven. In 2017, global biofuel production remained almost entirely based on first-generation biofuels, with sugar- and starch-based ethanol leading production in the United States and Brazil, and oil-crop biodiesel leading production in the European Union and the rest of the world. Production of advanced biofuels from non-food-crop feedstocks remained limited in 2017, with biodiesel and hydrotreated vegetable oil from waste oil and animal fat feedstocks contributing to only 7 per cent of all biofuel output (BP, 2018a).

After this review of modern bioenergy, traditional biomass use can be discussed. IEA and FAO (2017) define traditional biomass use as 'the use of solid biomass such as wood, charcoal, agricultural residues and animal dung converted with basic techniques, such as a three-stone fire, for heating and cooking in the residential sector. It tends to have very low conversion efficiency (10 per cent to 20 per cent) and often relies upon an unsustainable biomass supply'. Traditional biomass is mainly used by low-income households who do not have access to modern cooking and heating fuels or technologies. This entails several negative consequences. First, burning wood or other solid biomasses in old stoves or domestic open fires generate high particulate matter emissions and other air pollutants which, combined with poor indoor ventilation, lead to a number of health problems. According to the WHO (2018), 'Exposure to smoke from polluting fuels from cooking contributes to approximately 4 million premature deaths each year – more than malaria, HIV, and tuberculosis combined – of which 54 per cent are of women and children'. Second, the use of traditional biomass entails substantial social impacts. Across developing countries, the collection of biomass often requires a few hours per day, and this task is generally the responsibility of women and children, limiting their available time for productive and empowering activities. The use of traditional biomass also has environmental consequences. As noted by the IEA et al. (2019, p.117), 'while the use of solid biomass is not the leading cause of deforestation, wood is exhaustible unless stocks are managed sustainably. The overall extent of forested areas continues to decline, while the global population depending on biomass for cooking continues to rise'.

Assessing the global use of traditional biomass is difficult, given its unregulated nature. However, the IEA et al. (2019) estimated that in 2017, around 3 billion people were still relying on polluting fuels and technology for cooking. The transition away from traditional use of solid biomass to more modern and efficient heating and cooking solutions can be achieved through renewable energy solutions as well as through fossil fuels, such as liquefied petroleum gas. More advanced biomass stoves and biogas systems are also available to offer improved efficiency and lower pollutant emissions, reducing health impacts and biomass resource demand.

6.3   HYDROPOWER

The mechanical power of falling or flowing water has been used for hundreds of thousands of years in many parts of the world. Ancient Greeks and Romans used the power of water to operate water mills to grind grain. In the Middle Ages, mechanical hydropower was used extensively for milling and pumping. As recalled by the US Bureau of Reclamation (2019),

> Its coupling with the electrical generator in the late 19th century gave birth to hydropower, the main source of electricity at the dawn of the 20th century – e.g., generating 40 per cent of the electricity produced in the United States by 1920. With many towns, cities and industries located near rivers, hydropower was able to supply electricity from plants close to the load centres.

Since then, hydropower has become a reliable and competitive source of electricity generation worldwide.

Hydropower plays an important role in the global electricity generation mix, contributing, in 2017, to more than 17 per cent of electricity generation worldwide and about 80 per cent of global renewable electricity (IEA, 2018b). In addition to electricity generation itself, it should be noted that, as illustrated by the IEA (2012, p.9),

> The fast response capabilities of large reservoir and pumped storage plants provide critical energy services to networks, helping to match fluctuations in electricity demand and supply from less flexible electricity sources. The contribution of hydropower to the energy mix is thus twofold: the primary benefit is its clean, renewable electricity. The secondary benefit is its role as enabler for a greater contribution of other renewables – notably variable and non-dispatchable wind and solar – into the grid.

In 2017, hydropower was particularly relevant in the electricity generation mix of South and Central America (55 per cent), while in North America, Europe, CIS, Africa, and Asia Pacific its contribution averaged at 15 per cent (BP, 2018a).

In 2017, China led – by far – global hydropower generation, followed by Canada, Brazil, the United States, and Russia (Table 6.1).

Hydropower is not a variable renewable energy source as are wind or solar energy, due to both its storage capabilities and greater predictability. However, it certainly has an element of long-term variability, being dependent on precipitation and water run-off.

Various types of hydropower plants exist, with diverse sizes, types of generating unit, heights of the water fall ('head'), and – in some cases – even with diverse functions (e.g., electricity generation, capacity or multipurpose). Hydropower plants are strictly related to their local context, but they can be categorised in three groups: run-of-river plants, reservoir (or storage) plants, and pumped storage plants. Run-of-river and reservoir hydropower plants can be combined in

Table 6.1 *Global hydropower generation: Top-20 countries, 2017 and 1965*

Country	2017 (Terawatt-hours)	1965 (Terawatt-hours)
China	1,155.8	22.1
Canada	396.9	117.1
Brazil	369.5	24.0
United States	296.5	199.0
Russia	183.3	85.0*
Norway	141.4	49.4
India	135.6	19.2
Japan	79.2	70.0
Venezuela	76.7	1.4
Vietnam	70.2	0.3
Eastern Africa	66.5	6.1
Sweden	64.7	46.5
Turkey	58.4	2.2
Colombia	57.3	3.5
France	49.2	46.9
Argentina	41.6	1.2
Austria	39.1	16.1
Italy	36.3	42.6
Switzerland	32.0	24.1
Mexico	31.7	8.9

Source: author's elaboration on BP (2018a) (* Indicative data, as it refers to USSR).

cascading river systems and pumped storage plants can utilise the water storage of two or several reservoir hydropower plants.

A run-of-river hydropower plant exploits the natural flow of a watercourse, placed on two different levels. The water is drawn from and fed into a reservoir and through a system of pipelines reaches the hydroelectric power station, after which the water is discharged through a discharge channel and returned to the stream. The output of the flowing water power plants therefore depends on the flow rate of the watercourse. As outlined by the IEA (2012, p.12),

> These plants may include short-term storage or 'pondage', allowing for some hourly or daily flexibility in adapting to the load demand profile, albeit the generation profile is mostly driven by natural river flow conditions or releases from any upstream reservoir hydropower plant. In the absence of such upstream reservoir plant, generation depends on precipitation and runoff, and normally has substantial daily, monthly, seasonal and yearly variations.

A reservoir hydropower plant uses a reservoir, which can be either of natural origin – as a lake – or artificial. Sometimes this involves the creation of a dam, which is used to increase the flow of natural reservoirs. Depending on the position of the hydropower plant in relation to the reservoir from which the water is drawn, this is referred to as: (i) Hydropower plant against the dam, if the power plant is at the same level as the reservoir; or (ii) High-fall hydropower plant, if the power plant is located at a higher level than the reservoir. The water is conveyed through penstocks, from the dam to the hydraulic turbines that generate electricity as they rotate. Unlike run-of-river systems, reservoir systems allow operators to control the flow of water, and thus to manage it according to the needs of a certain day or of a certain time of the year. As the IEA (2012, pp.12–13) outlined,

> Storing water in a reservoir provides the flexibility to generate electricity on demand, and reduces dependence on the variability of inflows. Very large reservoirs can retain months or even years of average inflows and can also provide flood protection and irrigation services. However, it should be noted that – according to their location – they might have negative impacts on the local environment as well as on local communities. In general, most reservoir schemes serve various purposes. The hydropower plant design and provision of these services is very much dependent on the environment and social needs of the region and local project conditions. Reservoir hydropower

plants are characterised by their size and electrical capacity. If the capacity is small compared to the generation potential and if the reservoir size allows, the plant might be used for base load, round the clock and in all seasons. Conversely, larger turbines would more rapidly exhaust the potential; generation in this case would preferably take place during hours of peak demand.

Pumped storage plants are structured on two reservoirs located at different heights, one upstream and one downstream, connected with a conducting tube equipped with a pump turbine. When electricity demand is lower, the water is pumped from the valley reservoir to the upper reservoir, in order to allow operators to safely meet electricity demand when needed (i.e., in this case, water is released from the upper reservoir towards the valley reservoir, passing through turbines to generate electricity). As illustrated by the IEA (2012, pp.13–14),

> Both reservoir hydropower plants and pumped storage plants store potential energy as elevated water for generating on demand. The difference is that pumped storage plants take energy from the grid to lift the water up, then return most of it later (round-trip efficiency being 70 to 85 per cent), so pumped storage plant is a net consumer of electricity but provides for effective electricity storage. Most pumped storage plants are 'open-loop' systems developed from an existing hydropower plant system by addition of either an upper or a lower reservoir. They are usually 'off-stream'. The off-stream configuration consists of a lower reservoir on a stream, river or other water source, and a reservoir located off-stream usually at a higher elevation (although it is possible to have the off-stream reservoir at a lower elevation such as an abandoned mine or underground cavern). Another type is the 'pump-back' project using two reservoirs in series: a conventional hydro project with a pumped storage cycle imposed on the normal hydropower operations. Pumping from the downstream reservoir during low-load periods makes additional water available to use for generation at high demand periods. Finally, closed-loop systems are completely independent from existing water streams – both reservoirs are off-stream.

Pumped storage represented 99 per cent of global on-grid electricity storage in 2017 (IEA 2018b).

Hydropower plants can be classified by their hydraulic head. This classification thus refers to the difference between the upstream and the downstream water levels. According to the IEA (2012, p.14),

> The classifications of 'high head' (e.g., above 300 m) and 'low head' (e.g., less than 30 m) technologies vary widely from country to country, and there are no generally accepted scales. Head determines the water pressure on the turbines. Together, head and discharge[2] are the most important parameters for deciding the type of hydraulic turbine to be used.

Three are the main types of hydraulic turbine: Pelton, Francis, and Kaplan turbines.

Pelton turbines are used for high heads (i.e., from 50 to 1300 metres) with small water flows. This is generally the case of mountain areas, where natural waterfalls are exploited for power generation. These turbines can be equipped with one or more (i.e., up to six) injection nozzles. They must be adequately protected from load detachment, which could lead the turbine to destructive escape speeds. They are equipped with a diverting tile for the purpose. At the outlet of the blade the speed of the water is almost zero, so the case containing the wheel and injector nozzles must not withstand any particular pressure and can therefore be of light construction.

Francis turbines are used for medium heads (i.e., from 20 to 700 metres) with small to very large flows. These turbines have a broad rate capacity and outstanding hydraulic efficiency. Francis turbines are in fact jet turbines, where the water moves like in a pressure pipe. The adjustable blade distributor (spiral case) conveys the water to the fixed blade impeller. The spiral case is very large compared to the impeller. In this type of turbine, the power supply is almost always radial while the discharge is axial.

---

[2]   Hydroelectric discharge is the volume of water that passes through a hydroelectric power plant per unit time.

Kaplan turbines are used for small heads (i.e., up to 50 metres) and large flows. They are generally employed in run-of-river systems, which can be characterised by a flow of water that can reach hundreds of cubic metres per second (Figure 6.6). Kaplan turbines are axial-flow jet turbines. The blades of the wheel in Kaplan turbines are adjustable, while those of the distributor can be either fixed or adjustable.

Hydropower plants can also be classified by their size. This classification notably refers to the installed capacity of the plant, and has led to concepts such as 'small hydro' and 'large hydro', but there is no worldwide consensus on size categories. As outlined by the IEA (2012, p.15),

> Different countries or groups of countries define small hydro
> differently (from below 1.5 MW in Sweden to below 50 MW in
> China), so small-scale hydro spans a very wide range of plants. This
> broad spectrum relates to countries' local energy and resource
> management needs. Some have even used terms such as 'mini-
> hydro', 'micro-hydro' and 'pico-hydro', but again with no widely
> accepted definitions. Indeed, hydropower plant capacities range from

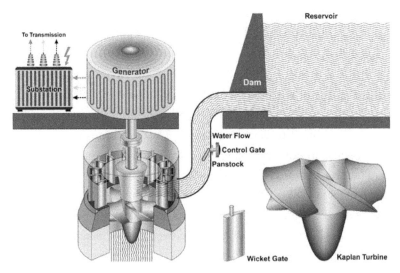

FIGURE 6.6 Example of hydropower generation: a Kaplan turbine system scheme
Source: Shutterstock.

several watts for the smallest individual installations, to tens of GW for the largest. Hydropower plants of capacity lower than 10 MW are estimated to represent about 10 per cent of the global hydropower plant capacity. While most small-scale hydropower plants seem to be run-of-river, there are also quite large run-of-river plants.

It has been mentioned that, in addition to renewable electricity, hydropower plants also provide – thanks to the fast response capabilities of both large reservoir hydropower plants and pumped storage plants – important services to the electricity system, notably contributing to match fluctuations in electricity demand and supply from less flexible electricity sources such as wind and solar energy.

Hydropower does represent a sustainable energy solution. However, like any other significant change within natural settings, it does presents risks for the environment, as well as for population settlement. The risk of dam failure should also be mentioned. Just to provide some examples, in 1963, the Vajont Dam in Italy experienced a water overtopping due to a landslide caused by instability of the rock around it, causing 1,917 deaths. In 1975, the Banqiao Reservoir Dam in China failed after extraordinary rains, resulting in flooding that caused as many as 230,000 deaths. In 1979, the Machhu Dam in India collapsed, killing thousands of people.[3]

Careful planning and implementation are needed to avoid, minimise, mitigate, or compensate all the risks related to hydropower. As outlined by the IEA (2012),

> Particular attention should be paid to the energy-water nexus. Many and varied are the demands on the world's water resources. The need for potable water supply and irrigation have to be fulfilled along with its use for hydropower, industry, cooling of thermal power plants, navigation, fisheries and recreation, all within the context of ecosystem integrity and water resource and flood management. Thus, the future of hydropower development has to

---

[3] Estimates range between 1,800 and 25,000 people killed.

be balanced with social and environmental responsibility, integrated resource management and sound business practice. Water and energy are closely linked, particularly in hydropower, where the generation of electricity is an integral part of water management.

Considerations driving the energy-water nexus are also tied to sustainable development. For hydropower they include: (i) Rapid population growth in many regions of the world and associated economic development is increasing demand for electricity and pressure on freshwater resources; (ii) Multipurpose hydropower schemes, providing irrigation and flood control as well as other non-energy benefits, can enhance regional development; (iii) Hydropower development can be integrated with water supply and agriculture; (iv) Hydropower generation is usually a domestic source of energy, and with its reliance on water can combine energy security and water security; and (v) In some regions, rivers cross borders and water resource management requires transnational co-operation.

In the future, increasing attention should also be paid to the relations between hydropower and climate change. Depending on the region, climate change can have either a positive or a negative impact on water availability. However, climate change–induced extreme weather events can pose substantial water supply reliability issues. This problem is particularly relevant in countries with high shares of hydropower in the electricity generation mix. As outlined by Falchetta et al. (2019), an example of this is represented by sub-Saharan Africa, where 160 million grid-connected people live in countries where hydropower covers more than 50 per cent of total electricity supply. Resiliency of hydropower plants, as well as of the overall electricity system, should be increased in such countries, for instance by adopting a strategic energy plan combining hydropower and variable renewables such as wind and solar in a synergetic manner.

6.4 GEOTHERMAL ENERGY

While the use of geothermal hot springs dates back to prehistoric times, historians have identified in the Etruscan civilisation the first structured utilisation of geothermal resources. Etruscans indeed had the habit of building their settlements and cities in proximity of hydrothermal springs, also to make extensive use of geothermal products (e.g., alabaster, travertine, iron oxides, thermal muds) for various purposes – such as the construction of buildings. The know-how developed by the Etruscans was then absorbed and perfected by ancient Romans, who also made extensive use of geothermal heated spas. In the nineteenth century, also thanks to the rapid development of thermodynamics, scientists learned how to convert the steam into mechanical energy and then into electricity through turbines and generators. In this context, a first small geothermal power generator able to light five light bulbs was built in 1904 in Lardarello, a locality in Tuscany renewed for its geothermal productivity. Towards the end of the nineteenth century, a first geothermal district heating system was built in the United States, and Iceland followed in the 1920s. In 1911, again in the area of Larderello, the world's first geothermal power plant was finally built.

Since then, installed geothermal electricity capacity has increased to 13 GW in 2017, that is, 0.5 per cent of global renewable electricity generation capacity (IEA, 2018f). Geothermal thus provides a marginal contribution to global electricity production, albeit it provides a significant role in specific countries (i.e., Iceland, El Salvador, New Zealand, Kenya, and the Philippines).

Geothermal energy is stored in rock and in trapped vapour or liquids, such as water or brines; these geothermal resources can be used for providing heat (and cooling) and for generating electricity. Some geothermal systems use the earth's temperatures near the surface (in this case, they are classified as low enthalpy[4] systems), while others require up to 5 km drilling into the earth (in this case, they are classified

---

[4] Enthalpy is the measure of energy contained in water or steam.

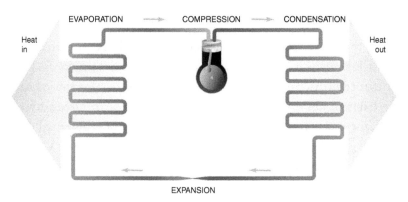

FIGURE 6.7 Heat pump functioning scheme
Source: Shutterstock.

as high enthalpy systems). Low-enthalpy deposits are defined by a relatively low temperature, while high-enthalpy deposits have high temperatures, allowing electricity to be generated using turbines.

In the heating (and cooling) sector, the most utilised geothermal technology is the ground source heat pump (Figure 6.7). As illustrated by the IEA (2011, p.7),

> Ground source heat pumps make use of the stable temperature of the ground (e.g., 10 to 15 degrees Celsius) in moderate climates, at a few meters depth in case of horizontal heat exchanger systems and depths of up to 150 metres for heat pumps using vertical heat exchange boreholes. Ground source heat pumps are mainly used in buildings for space heating, cooling and sometimes domestic hot water supply. Heat pumps allow transformation of heat from a lower temperature level to a higher one by using external energy (e.g., to drive a compressor). The amount of this external energy input, be it electric power or heat, has to be kept as low as possible to make the heat pump environmentally and economically desirable. In contrast to other heat pumps, such as air-to-air heat pumps, ground source heat pumps can store extracted heat in summer and make this heat useful again in the heating mode in winter.

Another relevant geothermal heat application is district heating. First used in France in the fourteenth century, this solution allows the use of the earth's thermal energy to heat a group of buildings. Adequate locations for this solution are found in proximity to geothermal springs with temperatures ranging between 40 and 150 degrees Celsius.

In the electricity sector, as illustrated by the IEA (2011, p.14),

> Whereas fossil-fuel plants burn coal, oil or gas to boil water, many existing geothermal power plants use steam produced by 'flashing' (i.e., reducing the pressure of) the geothermal fluid produced from the reservoir. Geothermal power plants today can use water in the vapour phase, a combination of vapour and liquid phases, or liquid phase only. The choice of plant depends on the depth of the reservoir and the temperature, pressure and nature of the entire geothermal resource.

The three main types of geothermal plant are flash steam, dry steam, and binary plant. Flash steam plants turn deep and high-pressure boiling water into colder and low-pressure water. The separated steam is piped to a turbine to generate electricity and the remaining hot water may be flashed again two or three times at progressively lower pressures and temperatures, to obtain more steam. Flash steam plants made up about two-thirds of geothermal electricity installed capacity in 2017 (IEA, 2018f). Dry steam plants, the oldest geothermal technology extracts steam from soil fractures and uses it directly to drive a turbine. Dry steam plants made up about a quarter of global geothermal capacity in 2017 (IEA, 2018f). Binary plants see boiling water running next to a second fluid, that with a low boiling point; this causes – through heat exchanges – the latter fluid to turn into steam, which is then used to drive a turbine.

The main advantages of geothermal electricity generation relate to the fact that it does not depend on weather conditions and that is has very high capacity factors (e.g., up to 95 per cent). This makes geothermal both an adequate technology for baseload electricity generation, as well as for peak electricity generation, notably through the use of submersible pumps tuned to reduce fluid extraction when demand falls.

To conclude, it is important to summarise geothermal's main benefits and challenges. As noted by the IEA (2011, p.7),

> Although geothermal energy has considerable benefits and also significant technical potential across the world, its exploitation is hampered by costs and distances of resource from energy demand centres. So far, geothermal technology development has focused on extracting naturally heated steam or hot water from natural hydrothermal reservoirs. However, geothermal energy could have the potential to make a more significant contribution on a global scale through the development of the advanced technologies, especially the exploiting of hot rock resources using enhanced geothermal systems techniques that would enable energy recovery from a much larger fraction of the accessible thermal energy in the earth's crust.

6.5   KEY TAKEAWAYS

Introduction to Renewable Energy

- Renewable energy contributes to around 14 per cent of global energy supply.
- Bioenergy contributes to 10 per cent, hydropower to 2.5 per cent, and wind/solar to 1.8 per cent.
- Since 2000, a substantial share of solid biomass has been replaced by modern biomass.
- Between 2009 and 2018, wind costs decreased by 69 per cent, and solar costs by 88 per cent.
- Government policies have had a key impact on renewables development and deployment.
- Countries with renewable electricity targets/policies increased from 40 in 2004 to 128 in 2017.
- In contrast to electricity, renewables' contribution to heat and transport remains limited.

Bioenergy

- Bioenergy includes both traditional uses of solid biomass and modern technologies.
- Modern bioenergy is the predominant renewable energy source.
- In heat, industry is the main end user of modern bioenergy.
- In electricity, modern bioenergy is based on either biomass, waste, or liquid or gaseous fuels.
- In transport, biofuels account for 5 per cent of global road transport fuel.

Hydropower

- Hydropower contributes to 17 per cent of global electricity generation.
- Hydropower provides renewable electricity, as well as key energy services to networks.
- China leads global hydropower generation, followed by Canada, Brazil, and the United States.
- Run-of-river, reservoir, and pumped storage and the key types of hydropower plants.
- Hydropower projects could entail a number of environmental and socio-economic impacts.

Geothermal Energy

- Geothermal resources can be used for providing heating and cooling, and generating electricity.
- In heating and cooling, heat pumps are the most utilised technology.
- In electricity, flash plants, dry steam plants, and binary plants can be used.
- Geothermal does not depend on weather conditions and has very high efficiency.

7 Renewable Energy: New Sources

This chapter looks at the new sources of renewable energy: wind, solar, and marine energy. This categorisation relates to the fact that even if these sources have been utilised over centuries for different purposes, they only started to significantly enter the modern energy system – notably through electricity – in the early 2000s. Let's start with wind.

People have utilised wind energy for a very long time. Wind propelled boats along the Nile River as early as 5,000 BC, and helped Persians pump water and grind grain already as early as 500 BC. Ancient also is the technology of the mill, in which the motion of rotation of the blades is used to obtain mechanical energy in agriculture, crafts, and industry, as well as the wind pump, still used today for the extraction of water from the subsoil. With the Industrial Revolution, the importance of wind declined, as windmills were progressively replaced by steam mills and internal combustion engines. The first windmill used for electricity generation was built in Scotland in 1887 by James Blyth, a professor of natural philosophy at the Anderson's College in Glasgow, who used it to light his holiday cottage. However, as mentioned by the British Library (2017), 'its lack of a braking mechanism meant it was prone to damage in strong winds'. A few months after Blyth's first wind generator was built, the first automatically operated wind turbine – with a rotor 17 metres in diameter mounted on an 18-metre tower – was built by the American inventor Charles Brush. The connected dynamo was used to light up to 100 incandescent light bulbs as well as to power various machineries in Brush's laboratory. Furthermore, the design of Brush's machine also allowed it to be shut down manually to protect it from wind damage (Righter, 1996).

Throughout the first half of the twentieth century, small wind stations were developed to provide electricity to farms as well as to houses in remote areas not connected to the grid. In certain cases, larger utility-scale wind generators were also developed, notably to provide some electricity to a local utility network. But interest in wind turbines only really materialised after the oil shocks of the 1970s, as energy-security concerns in the United States and Europe skyrocketed – alongside oil prices.[1] This led several countries to develop wind-energy research programmes, though, efforts were subsequently reduced since the mid-1980s as the price of oil fell. However, the knowledge acquired during that period was sufficient to start the development of large wind turbines. Since the late-1990s, increasing attention to the issue of climate change led to several countries being willing to increase the share of wind energy in the energy mix. In comparison to other renewable energy sources, wind energy requires lower investments and uses a resource – wind – that is generally available across the world, although its variability can be a major concern in some contexts (World Bank, 2018b).

In 1990, global wind power generation amounted to only 3.6 TWh, corresponding to 0.03 per cent of total electricity generation. Wind output continued to remain marginal throughout the 1990s, reaching 31.4 TWh in 2000, or 0.2 per cent of total generation. Only during the 2000s was wind's contribution to global electricity generation finally scaled up, reaching a level of 1,122 TWh in 2017, or 4 per cent of total generation. China, the United States, and the European Union drove this trend, being collectively responsible for 80 per cent of the world's total wind electricity generation in 2017 (Figure 7.1).

[1] For instance, in 1978, the US Congress passed the *Public Utility Regulatory Policies Act*, which required electric utilities to buy a certain amount of electricity from renewable energy sources, including wind.

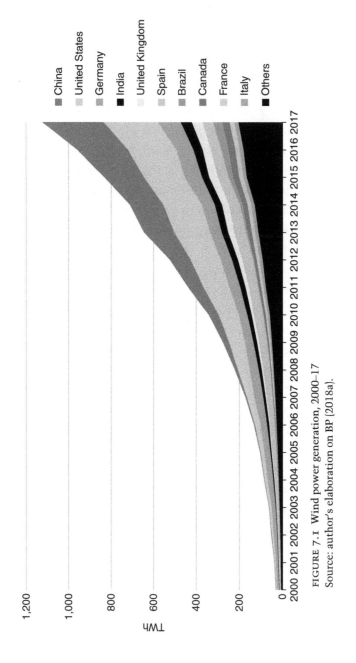

FIGURE 7.1 Wind power generation, 2000–17
Source: author's elaboration on BP (2018a).

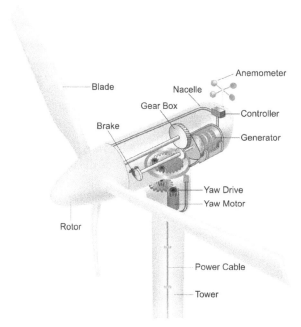

FIGURE 7.2 Wind turbine scheme
Source: Shutterstock.

Wind turbines use blades to harness the kinetic energy of wind, which is proportionate with wind speed.[2] Wind flows over the blades creating lift, which causes the blades to turn. Blades are indeed shaped such that the interaction with wind results in a difference in pressure between the top and bottom of the blades. It is this difference in pressure that causes the blades to rotate (Figure 7.2). As illustrated by the US Department of Energy (2014),

> A series of gears increase the rotation of the rotor from about 18
> revolutions a minute to roughly 1,800 revolutions per minute –
> a speed that allows the turbine's generator to produce electricity.

[2] The two main types of wind turbines are the horizontal-axis turbines and the vertical-axis turbines. We here only describe the functioning of horizontal-axis turbines, as nearly all of the wind turbines in use globally are of this type. Vertical-axis turbines – featuring blades that are attached to the top and the bottom of a vertical rotor – are indeed not utilised, as they do not perform as well as horizontal-axis turbines.

A streamlined enclosure called a nacelle houses key turbine components – usually including the gears, rotor and generator – are found within a housing called the nacelle. Sitting atop the turbine tower, some nacelles are large enough for a helicopter to land on. Another key component is the turbine's controller, that keeps the rotor speeds from exceeding 12 and 17 metres per second (m/s), to avoid damage by high winds. An anemometer continuously measures wind speed and transmits the data to the controller. A brake, also housed in the nacelle, stops the rotor mechanically, electrically or hydraulically in emergencies.

The electricity output of a wind turbine depends on a number of factors, notably the wind speed and the area swept out by the blades. As illustrated by a typical wind turbine power curve (Figure 7.3), a turbine's blades start to turn with a wind speed – technically called cut-in speed – of around 3.5 m/s. As the wind speed rises above the cut-in speed, the level of electricity output rises rapidly. As noted by Singh (2012, p.653),

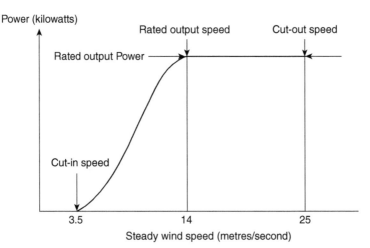

Typical wind turbine power output with steady wind speed.

FIGURE 7.3 Typical wind turbine power curve
Source: author's elaboration.

Somewhere between 12 and 17 m/s, the electricity output reaches the limit that the electrical generator is capable of. This limit to the generator output is called the rated power output and the wind speed at which it is reached is called the rated output wind speed. At higher wind speeds, the design of the turbine is arranged to limit the power to this maximum level and there is no further rise in the output power. How this is done varies from design to design but typically with large turbines, it is done by adjusting the blade angles so as to keep the power at the constant level. As the speed increases above the rate output wind speed, the forces on the turbine structure continue to rise and, at some point, there is a risk of damage to the rotor. As a result, a braking system is employed to bring the rotor to a standstill. This is called the cut-out speed and is typically around 25 m/s.

The rotor is connected to a transmission shaft, which rotates inside the nacelle. Thanks to an electric generator, the rotational (i.e., mechanical) energy of the transmission shaft is transformed into electrical energy. The electricity produced is conveyed into the cables that run inside the tower and that distribute it to the users or to the electricity grid. The rotor and the electric generator can be directly connected or associated with a speed multiplier. Indispensable in large wind turbines, the speed multiplier ensures that the slow rotation of the blades still allows a proper power supply of the electric generator. Smaller wind turbines with high blade rotation speeds can also do without the speed multiplier. Most wind turbines, whether isolated or connected to the grid, are also equipped with an inverter. The inverter converts direct current into 220 Volt alternating current, making it suitable for feeding into the grid or for self-consumption. Only in the case of small, isolated consumers that are directly supplied by the direct current, is it possible to dispense with the inverter. As the wind speed increases, the instantaneous power delivered by the machine gradually increases until the rated wind speed is reached; that is, the wind speed at which the generator reaches its rated power.

The peak power output remains constant up to the maximum threshold of wind speed tolerated by the machine (i.e., the cut-out speed). Beyond this threshold, the generator stops producing energy and makes itself safe, using active or passive protection systems, in order to avoid damage to the mechanical components.

From a theoretical perspective, the maximum efficiency of a wind turbine corresponds to the maximum amount of power that a wind turbine can harness from the wind. This is called the Betz limit, as it was first calculated in 1919 by the German physicist Albert Betz. He concluded that this value is 59.3 per cent, implying that at most 59.3 per cent of the kinetic energy from wind can be used to spin the turbine and generate electricity. But even with this limit, wind turbines can be considered as very efficient. To ensure optimal efficiency, wind turbines are preferably installed on tops of hills, open plains, open sea, and mountain gaps that funnel and intensify wind. When considering a site for the installation of a wind turbine, it is essential to assess the true extent of the wind resource. A weather station is then installed at the site for several months to monitor wind speed and direction and turbulence levels at different altitudes. The recorded data allow the evaluation of both future energy production and the economic feasibility of the project. Normally, wind turbines are placed in groups – called 'wind farms' – so as to exploit areas with particularly favourable conditions and constitute appreciable nuclei of electricity production to be connected to the distribution network. It should be noted that turbines in a wind farm are spaced to minimise interference in the airflow between neighbouring turbines. A right balance should then be found between the objective of maximising the electricity generated per turbine and the objective of optimising the number of turbines sited on the available land.

Wind turbine capacity has increased over time, as a result of increasing height of the tower and increasing length of the blades. In 1990, the most powerful wind turbine had a capacity of 0.5 MW, and a tip height equal to a five-floor building. In 2000, the most powerful turbine had a capacity of 2 MW, and a tip height of 80 metres. In 2017, the most powerful turbine had a capacity of 9.5 MW and a tip height of 220 metres.

To date, wind energy has almost entirely been developed onshore. In 2017, 95 per cent of global wind generation indeed occurred onshore, while only 5 per cent occurred offshore. However, the deployment of offshore wind has more than quintupled between 2010 and 2017 (IEA, 2018g). This trend has been due to a concerted series of public–private initiatives undertaken by countries bordering the North Sea in Europe. According to the IEA (2018g, pp.17–18),

> More than 80 per cent of global offshore wind capacity in 2017 was indeed located in Europe[3]. Beyond Europe, only China had large-scale offshore wind capacity, while smaller offshore wind facilities are located in the United States, Korea and Japan. Although it uses a fundamentally similar technology to onshore wind, offshore wind enjoys some distinctive advantages: the main ones are that offshore installations are able to tap more consistent and higher winds speeds, and there are fewer restrictions on ground area and height. As a result, project sizes and turbines are typically larger and performance indicators for offshore wind farms are higher. Already during the period from 2011 to 2015 in Denmark, Germany and the Netherlands, offshore wind delivered about 1.5 to 2 times the average capacity factor of onshore wind. Higher capacity factors and lower variability make offshore wind a better match to electricity demand profiles than onshore wind. This can be particularly valuable in serving coastal load centres, where fewer infrastructure investments are needed to enable the connection to offshore wind.

Technical potential for offshore wind is substantial (e.g., NREL (2017) and Wind Europe (2017) respectively found a large potential in the United States east coast and in Northern Europe). But in order to exploit this potential, offshore wind costs will have to substantially decrease. Planning and construction costs of offshore wind farms are

---

[3] Of which the United Kingdom with installed capacity of 6.8 GW and Germany with 5.4 GW were the two largest countries (IEA, 2018g).

higher than in the case of onshore wind farms due to higher technical complexity. Furthermore, given their location, offshore wind farms also have higher grid connection costs and higher operation and maintenance costs than onshore wind farms (IRENA, 2018a). As a result of all this, in 2018, the levelised cost of offshore wind stood at USD 92/ MWh, while the levelised cost of onshore wind spanned between USD 29–56/MWh (Lazard, 2018). The development and implementation of internationally harmonised standards will be particularly important to drive offshore wind energy costs down, and therefore to foster its global scale-up (IRENA, 2018b).

7.2 SOLAR ENERGY

The sun has produced energy for billions of years and could well be defined as the ultimate source for all energy sources and fuels we utilise. Biomass energy derives from solar energy through the photosynthesis process, hydraulic energy derives from it as the sun is the motor of the water cycle, and wind energy derives from it as solar radiation drives the winds. Fossil fuels also derive from it, through chemical–physical alterations of prehistoric living organisms containing solar energy.

The sun produces its heat by transforming hydrogen (which currently composes 75 per cent of its mass) into helium (which composes 23 per cent of its mass) in its inner core, where temperatures reach 15 million degrees Celsius. This transformation is called nuclear fusion and joins together four nuclei of hydrogen (protons) to create a helium nucleus, freeing a large quantity of energy, which, as photons, is irradiated towards space. A photon is a neutral particle that spreads into the air at a speed of 300,000 km per second, with an energy that depends on its frequency and a mass that is considered as void when at rests.

A solar constant is the radiation that perpendicularly hits a unit surface positioned at the top limit of the atmosphere of the earth and amounts to 1,367 watts per square metre. This heat, multiplied by the surface of the earth's section (the squared earth's average radius multiplied by pi Greco) calculates the quantity of energy the earth receives from the sun every second: 173,000 TW. Of this, 50,000 TW are reflected by the top layers of the atmosphere and 30,000 TW are absorbed by the atmosphere. Only 90,000 TW finally reach the earth's surface. A big part of this is reflected or absorbed, while a small part is transformed: 400 TW make seawater evaporate and transform it into clouds, 370 TW activate the wind, and 80 TW are transformed by the plant's photosynthesis into chemical energy. These radiations – representing an infinitesimal part of the total energy produced by the sun – enable life on earth, maintaining the planet's average temperatures suitable for living organisms, and providing the energy flows that feed the plants through photosynthesis and that ultimately represent the basis of the food chain of all living beings.

The sun's radiation reaches the earth in a non-homogeneous way as a result of its interaction with the atmosphere and the angle of incidence of sunrays. The angle of incidence varies according to two factors: the earth's rotation around its axis and the inclination of the earth's axis as compared to the plane of its orbit. When the sun is perpendicular to the earth's surface, the maximum concentration of sunrays on the ground is obtained. On the other hand, if the sunrays reach the earth's surface with a certain inclination, the same amount of energy is dispersed over a larger surface. Therefore, solar energy can be highly exploited only within a belt included between 45° latitude south and north.

Only a part of the huge energy flow that gets from the sun to the earth can then be transformed into useful energy. The quantity of solar energy that arrives to the earth's surface and that can be usefully collected depends on irradiation on the area. Irradiation is the quantity of solar energy that arrives at a surface within a determined time interval, typically one day (it is measured in kWh by square metre by day). Instead, the value of solar radiation that arrives on the surface unit (at a determined moment) is called radiance (it is measured in kW/m^2). Irradiation is influenced by local climatic conditions (e.g., clouds, mist) and depends on the latitude: as it is well known, it increases when it gets closer to the equator.

On a clear day, the solar radiation reaching the earth's surface is at most about 1,000 W/m². In order to know how much solar energy will be available on average in a given location, measurements of the total solar radiation are made using instruments called pyranometers. From the data measured at various points on the earth's surface, solar maps are constructed (World Bank, 2016).

Today, the observations made by meteorological satellites are a great help in the production of these maps. More sophisticated measurements distinguish between direct sunshine (i.e., from the sun's rays) and indirect sunshine (i.e., from the diffusion of sunlight into the atmosphere, from clouds, etc.). The clearer the sky is and the fewer clouds are present, the greater the percentage of direct sunlight in the total. The distinction is important for all applications that require light concentration, since only direct radiation can be concentrated.

Solar energy can be collected using solar radiation to generate electricity, and also directly using it to generate heat. The first method of solar energy use involves harvesting the sunlight to generate electricity through photovoltaic panels. As described by the US Department of Energy (2013), 'a photovoltaic cell is composed of semiconductor material, which combines some properties of metals and some properties of insulators. That makes it uniquely capable of converting light into electricity. When photons from the Sun are absorbed into the semi-conductor, they knock a few electrons loose from their atoms; these electrons then move through the semi-conductor and generates electricity' (Figure 7.4).

The second involves the use of solar thermal systems, which basically are mirrors that concentrate and reflect the Sun's rays to heat a fluid. The invention of the solar collector is due to Horace de Saussure, a Swiss geologist and physicist, also often considered as the founder of alpinism and modern meteorology. In 1767, de Saussure built – for cooking purposes – a wooden pot lined with

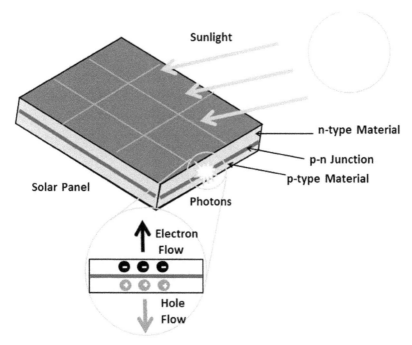

FIGURE 7.4 Photovoltaic solar cell scheme
Source: Shutterstock.

black cork capable of reaching 110 degrees Celsius by means of a three glass layers placed at the top of the pot. In 1981, the American inventor Clarence Kemp patented the first solar thermal panel for the production of domestic hot water. It was a success, but people already knew cheaper and easier ways to heat water. Only after 80 years, following the energy crisis of 1973 and the resulting increase in the oil prices, did Kemp's water heater develop into a modern solar thermal collector.

A first step in the development of solar photovoltaic was made in 1839, when the French scientist Alexandre Becquerel discovered – by placing an electrode inside a solution that worked as a conductor – that a material like metal would send off sparks of electricity when exposed to sunlight. Since then, solar photovoltaic technology started to be explored, mainly driven by fears of coal scarcity. The world's first rooftop solar array based on selenium cells was installed by the inventor Charles Fritts on a New York roof in 1884. Notwithstanding these early steps, the development of solar technologies stagnated in the first half of the twentieth century, as it became clear that coal – and then oil – were largely available. In 1954, the Bell Telephone Laboratories came up with the first silicon solar cell (i.e., a device that converts sunrays straight into electricity using the photovoltaic effect).[4]

Interest in solar technologies revamped after the oil crises of the 1970s, as oil-importing countries sought to develop alternatives to oil. It is in that context that the United States launched the Federal Photovoltaic Utilization Program, and Japan launched the Sunshine Program. In 1977, the United States also launched the Solar Energy Research Institute – which later became today's National Renewable Energy Laboratory – as a federal facility dedicated to harnessing power from the sun. Such programs helped to improve the manufacturing of solar photovoltaic panels, increasing performance and quality, and reducing costs. During the 1980s, photovoltaics became a popular electricity-generation source for consumer electronic devices, as well as for providing electricity to rural areas without access to the

---

[4]   The photovoltaic effect is a physical phenomenon that consists of the direct conversion of solar radiation into electrical energy. The photovoltaic effect is a subcategory of the photoelectric effect, which was theorised by Albert Einstein in 1905 and earned him the Nobel Prize. In photovoltaic cells, when a photon with a certain level of energy is absorbed into a semiconductor material (of which the photovoltaic cell is composed), it creates a pair of electrical charges of opposite sign: an electron (negative) and a gap (positive). These charges of opposite sign can therefore conduct electricity. However, to produce an electric current, you need a difference in potential. And this difference is generated thanks to the presence of small impurities in the material of which the cells are composed. These modify the electrical properties of the semiconductor material (e.g., silicon). Two layers are then created: one, negatively charged, is called layer 'n', while the other, positively charged, 'p'. The contact area between these two types of layers is called the 'p-n junction'. In this separation zone a strong electric field is formed. The positive and negative charges generated by the bombardment of the photons making up the sunlight are separated by the electric field. These charges produce a correct circulation when the device is connected to a load. But not all photons of sunlight are equal. Those useful for the production of electricity through photovoltaic cells are those that have a certain amount of energy. This value depends on the type of photovoltaic cell used.

grid. During the 1990s, solar photovoltaics technology further developed, paving the way for the take-off of the technology since the early 2000s.

Today, solar energy is mainly used for electricity generation. Of the 4,945 mtoe of energy consumed for heat in 2017 at the global level, only 33 mtoe were indeed produced with solar thermal energy, only 0.7 per cent of the total (IEA 2018f). In the same year, of the 25,551 TWh of electricity consumed in the world, 442 TWh were produced with solar technologies, or 1.7 per cent of the total (BP, 2018a).

Although technology developments started long before the turn of the century, solar power really started to provide a contribution to the global electricity generation mix only in the early 2000s. In 1990, global solar power generation indeed amounted to only 0.4 TWh, corresponding to 0.003 per cent of total electricity generation. Solar output continued to remain marginal throughout the 1990s, reaching 1.2 TWh in 2000, or 0.008 per cent of total generation. Only during the 2000s did solar's contribution to global electricity generation finally scale up, reaching the 442 TWh level in 2017 (BP, 2018a). In the same year, China, the United States, the European Union, and Japan drove this trend, being collectively responsible for around 80 per cent of the world's total solar power generation in 2017 (Figure 7.5).

Solar power can be generated in two main ways: solar photovoltaic systems or concentrated solar power (CSP) systems. In 2017, global solar photovoltaic capacity reached 398 GW, with utility-scale projects accounting for just over 60 per cent of total solar photovoltaic installed capacity, with the rest in distributed applications (e.g., residential, commercial, off-grid). In contrast, the deployment of CSP remains in its infancy, with a cumulative installed capacity of only 4.8 GW in 2017 (IEA, 2018f).

Solar photovoltaic cells are semiconductor devices that generate direct current electricity. As illustrated by the JRC (2016, p.17),

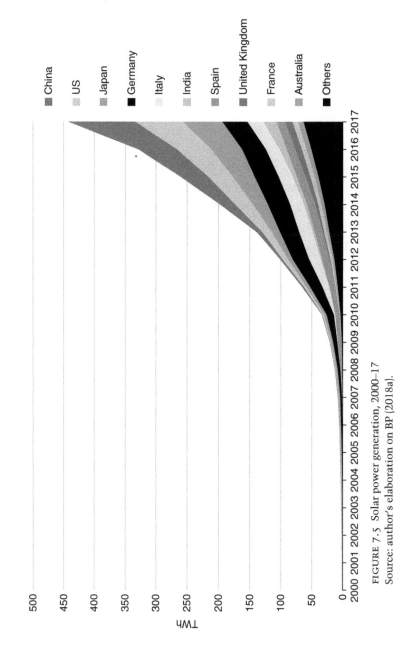

FIGURE 7.5 Solar power generation, 2000–17
Source: author's elaboration on BP (2018a).

Silicon cells are usually sliced from ingots or castings of highly purified silicon. The manufacturing process creates a charge-separating junction, deposits passivation layers and an anti-reflective coating, and adds metal contacts. Cells are then grouped into modules, with transparent glass for the front, a weatherproof material for the back and often a surrounding frame. The modules are then combined to form strings, arrays and systems. Solar photovoltaics can be used for on-grid and off-grid applications of capacities ranging from less than 1 watt to gigawatts. Grid-connected systems require inverters to transform direct current power into alternating current. The balance of system includes inverters, transformers, wiring and monitoring equipment, as well as structural components for installing modules, whether on building rooftops or facades, above parking lots, or on the ground. Installations can be fixed or track the sun on one axis (for non- or low-concentrating systems) or two axes (for high-concentrating systems). Alternative photovoltaic technologies, including thin films, are currently under development'.

The average efficiency of commercial silicon modules has significantly improved in the last decade, reaching 24 per cent in 2018 (Fraunhofer, 2019). Between 2007 and 2017, solar photovoltaic installations increased by a compound annual growth rate of 25 per cent, making it the fastest growing energy market in the world. This trend reflected the strong cost decrease experienced over the period by solar photovoltaics. As previously mentioned, between 2009 and 2018, the mean levelised cost of electricity for utility-scale solar photovoltaic indeed decreased by 88 per cent (Lazard, 2018). Just to provide a real-life example, as illustrated by the Fraunhofer (2019, p.10),

> In Germany prices for a typical 10 to 100 kWp[5] photovoltaic rooftop-system were around 14,000 EUR/kWp in 1990. At the

---

[5] kWp is the peak power of a photovoltaic system. kWp stands for kilowatt 'peak' of a system. The power is calculated under a standardised test for panels across all manufacturers to ensure that the values listed are capable of comparison.

end of 2018, such systems cost about 1,070 EUR/kWp on average. This is a net-price regression of about 90 per cent over a period of 28 years and is equivalent to an annual compound average price reduction rate of 8 per cent. Impressive progress has also been made with respect to manufacturing of photovoltaic cells. The amount of specific materials (e.g., silicon, metal pastes, etc.), the energy consumption and the amount of labour required to assemble modules have all been significantly reduced over time.

CSP systems are a very different technology, concentrating solar rays to heat a fluid, which then directly or indirectly runs a turbine and an electricity generator. As described by the EIA (2019d),

> Concentrating the Sun's rays allows for the fluid to reach working temperatures high enough to ensure fair efficiency in turning the heat into electricity, while limiting heat losses in the receiver. The three predominant CSP technologies are parabolic troughs, linear Fresnel reflectors and towers, also known as central receiver systems. A fourth type of CSP plant is a parabolic dish, usually supporting an engine at its focus. These technologies differ with respect to optical design, shape of receiver, nature of the transfer fluid and capability to store heat before it is turned into electricity. Most installed capacities today replicate the design of the first commercial plants built in California in the 1980s, which are still operating. Long parabolic troughs track the sun on one axis, concentrate the solar rays on linear receiver tubes isolated in an evacuated glass envelope, heat oil to 390 degrees Celsius, then transfer this heat to a conventional steam cycle.

CSP plants also have the capacity to store heat energy for limited periods of time, a feature that allows smoothing of the variability characterising solar photovoltaic electricity production. In practice, thermal storage works as follow: during the day, excess heat is redirected to a storage material such as molten salts. After sunset, this stored heat is released into the steam cycle, so to allow the plant to keep producing electricity even in absence of the sun.

Electricity from CSP remains significantly expensive compared with that generated from solar photovoltaic and wind. In 2018, the levelised cost of electricity for a solar thermal tower with storage stood at USD 98–181/MWh, compared to USD 40–46/MWh for solar photovoltaic crystalline utility scale and to USD 29–56/MWh for wind (Lazard, 2018). However, significant cost reduction potential does exist for CSP. It should also be considered that CSP should not just be compared to the electricity generation costs of other technologies, as it provides ancillary services to electricity systems, starting with storage. This aspect should be properly taken into consideration, as the need for power system flexibility will increase in the future, in order to facilitate the integration of variable renewable technologies such as solar photovoltaic and wind into electricity systems.

Solar heat can be harnessed with different technologies. The most mature technology is represented by solar domestic hot water systems. This technology has a long history, but it was first deployed on a large scale only throughout the 1960s in a few countries, such as Australia, Japan, and Israel. Since then, some markets have strongly increased solar domestic hot water systems, notably as a result of public policy support (e.g., this is the case in Austria and Germany), regulations mandating the use of the technology (e.g., this is the case in Israel), or simply as a result of their competitive advantage over alternative technologies (e.g., this is the case in Cyprus). Over the past fifteen years, Europe and China have become key markets for these technologies.

A solar thermal system normally consists of a panel that receives solar energy, an exchanger in which circulates the fluid used to transfer solar energy to the tanker, and the tanker itself, which is used to store the accumulated energy. A solar thermal panel can have two systems of circulation: natural circulation or forced circulation.

Natural circulation solar thermal panels are systems that provide hot water for sanitary use without having to be integrated with pumps, expansion tanks, or other components. The operating principle of this type of solar system is based on the convection of the heated fluid that tends to decrease its weight and therefore to trigger convective motion from bottom to top. The domestic hot water tank must be positioned above the solar panel, in order to ensure maximum efficiency of the system. The natural cycle is triggered only at a higher temperature than the forced circulation. The technology of natural circulation is cheaper in operating costs as there is no electricity consumption due to the pump and it does not require electronic control systems. This technology requires placing the tank at a height higher than that of the panels, with increased costs for the construction of adequate structures to support the tanks themselves.

In forced circulation systems, the exchange between the collector and the accumulation system is guaranteed by mechanical parts for the circulation of the vector fluid and for control of the management of the flow rates and temperatures of the fluid itself. To regulate the circulation, sensors are used to compare the temperature of the vector fluid in the collector with that in the storage tank, in order to avoid an opposite process whereby heat is taken away from the user and dissipated by the solar panel. In such plants, the possibility of regulating the speed of the vector fluid according to the design parameters allows a greater heat exchange and therefore the efficiency of the panel is slightly higher than that of a natural circulation system. For this reason, forced circulation collectors are preferred for installations designed to provide service throughout the year, bringing benefits in terms of efficiency, especially in the cooler months. The hydraulic circuit connected to the panel is closed and separated from the heating water circuit by means of a coil in the tank as a heat exchanger. There can also be two coils to integrate the production of domestic hot water with an additional heat generator. In some applications, the hot water supplied by the forced circulation panels can be used to make a contribution to the building's heating system.

Solar thermal systems supplying heating or cooling to the building sector can also be found in large-scale applications used for district heating, multifamily buildings or block heating plants. Historically, solar heating networks started to be developed during the 1970s in Northern European countries such as Sweden, Denmark, and the Netherlands. These systems consist of large fields of solar thermal collectors supplying the solar heat produced to a heating network. Solar energy can be an attractive option for district heating systems, where typical working temperatures range between 40 and 100 degrees Celsius. District cooling systems, which are starting to become more common in order to reduce peak load demand on the electricity system, can also utilise large-scale solar thermal plants. Another possible application of solar thermal energy is desalinisation. As illustrated by IRENA (2012, p.3), 'Demand for water desalination is expected to keep growing in regions that are known for water shortages – which often have very good solar resources. Desalination can come from distillation or reverse osmosis technology, with the first being preferred for more saline water. Distillation requires large amounts of thermal energy, which could come from concentrating solar technologies'.

7.3 MARINE ENERGY

Marine energy is in its infancy and today still does not provide a significant contribution to the global electricity generation mix. In 2017, global marine power capacity only amounted to 0.6 GW, generating a modest 1.4 TWh (IEA, 2018g). In the same year, two countries accounted for 90 per cent of the installed capacity: France and South Korea.

Today's main marine generation technology is tidal range, with 99 per cent of total capacity. As illustrated by IEA (2018g, p.19), 'Tidal range technology shares characteristics similar to hydropower, essentially leveraging the height difference of two bodies of water created by a dam or barrier in order to produce electricity. Its main advantage is that is it very predictable. However, its capacity factor of

25 per cent is not as high as offshore wind due to the nature of tidal cycles and current turbine efficiency'. Tidal range is evolving with the concept of tidal lagoons: these are artificial basins built in bays and estuaries (WEC, 2016).

Other ocean energy technologies in various stages of development include tidal stream, wave power, and ocean thermal energy conversion. As illustrated by the SETIS (2014),

> Tidal current energy is created by local regular diurnal (24-hour) or semi-diurnal (12+ hour) flows of ocean water caused by the tidal cycle. Kinetic energy can be harnessed, usually nearshore and particularly where there are constrictions, such as straits, islands and passes. Wave energy is created as kinetic energy from the wind is transmitted to the upper surface of the ocean. Ocean thermal energy conversion uses the temperature difference between surface and deep water in a heat cycle to produce electricity. Although tropical areas are most favourable for the exploitation of this source of energy, the potential resources are enormous'.

Given most marine power technologies are still in the early stages of development, they are not expected to contribute significantly to global energy supply in the foreseeable future. However, it should be mentioned that they might provide a significant contribution at specific sites for local needs, such as in case of island communities.

7.4   RENEWABLES' SYSTEM INTEGRATION CHALLENGE

In their initial phase of deployment, wind and solar energy sources have been developed across the world with a fit-and-forget logic, having priority dispatch and access to the electricity grid. This provision, generally mandated by governments to favour a quick up-take of wind and solar energy in their electricity systems, has been key to allowing the take-off of these technologies. However, as the shares of wind and solar energy becomes increasingly significant, system integration challenges arise – urging a rethink of the way electricity systems are structured and operated.

Electricity systems have traditionally been structured in a way to balance fluctuations in electricity demand and to deal with potential unexpected losses of some generating unit (e.g., for maintenance activities at a power plant). Flexibility has been typically ensured with supply-side assets, such as thermal power plants with advanced cycling capabilities (e.g., open-cycle gas turbines), with a flexible renewable source as hydropower, or with pumping hydro storage if available.

But wind and solar energy are technically different from conventional forms of electricity generation. Their maximum instantaneous output depends on how much wind and sunlight are available at any given moment, which makes their output variable and only partially predictable. Considering that a reliable supply of electricity requires supply and demand to be balanced continuously across all timescales, from sub-seconds to years, these properties can make it difficult for electricity systems to accommodate higher amounts of wind and solar energy. Key to ensuring a smooth integration of higher shares of wind and solar energy into electricity systems is to foster system flexibility. This can be done by making use of various options that facilitate the reliable and cost-effective management of variability and uncertainty in both supply and demand (Figure 7.6).

Conventional electricity generation sources play an important role in ensuring the stability of the system, being able to provide the rapid increases and decreases in electricity output necessary for accommodating increasing amounts of variable and non-dispatchable renewable energy sources into the system. Natural gas power plants are particularly suitable for this role, as they can be quickly switched on and off.[6] As the role of wind and solar increase in a system, conventional power plants might then progressively switch from their traditional electricity generation role to a new back-up role. This switch clearly undermines the established business model of conventional

---

[6]   For instance, the cold start-up time of an open-cycle gas turbine is 5–11 minutes, and that of a combined-cycle gas turbine is 3–4 hours. In comparison, that of a hard coal-fired power plant is 5–10 hours (IRENA, 2018c).

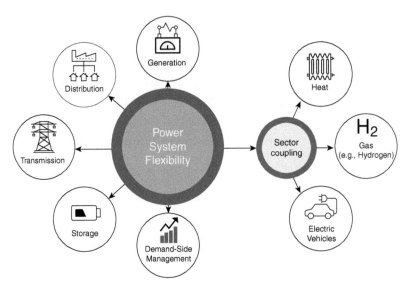

FIGURE 7.6 Power system flexibility enablers in the energy sector
Source: International Renewable Energy Agency (2018c).

electricity producers, as it implies that power plants should remain on
stand-by for most of the time, just waiting to be eventually called into
the system at a moment when wind and solar energy output is not
sufficient to meet electricity demand. Under normal market circumstances, conventional power plants would close down, having no
economic rationale to be always ready to operate – with all the related
costs implied – but then actually utilised only on limited occasions.
To overcome this issue, and ensure that conventional plans remain
operative to provide security of electricity supply, governments have
designed specific regulatory tools, called capacity mechanisms. These
are payments made by the state to electricity utilities to simply keep
their conventional power plants ready to enter into operation, in case
a back-up is required. Capacity mechanisms – which some consider to
be a sort of state aid to private companies – therefore find their legal
rationale in a public good such as energy security.

An additional option to deal with wind and solar energy intermittency is to aggregate their outputs over a wider geographical area,
notably through a robust distribution and transmission grid. In fact,

wind and solar intermittency at site level (e.g., at the single wind or solar farm) is increasingly smoothed once moved up to the regional, national, or even continental level. As illustrated by Hafner and Tagliapietra (2017, p.7), 'This results from different weather patterns that do not correlate into single electricity generation peaks, yielding geographical smoothing effects that ultimately transform intermittency at local level in variability at broader level. With a solid electricity grid, differing production peaks across countries thus enable exports to regions where the load is not covered'. As pointed out by the IEA (2018f, p.45), 'Grid flexibility also refers to the existence of advanced controls to enhance communication among system elements that enables, for example, automated control of generators, automatic activation of demand response or advanced power flow control'.

Other options are energy storage and demand-side management, but they face major challenges. As outlined by EPO (2016), 'Energy storage is challenged by a persistent technological gap. To date, the only operative option is represented by pumped storage hydropower, which indeed represented 99 per cent of on-grid electricity storage'. Other technologies such as battery systems, compressed air energy storage, flywheels, and hydrogen storage are not yet competitive due to technology cost vis-à-vis revenues, but as their costs decline, they are expected to become key contributors to flexibility in the future. Demand-side management seeks to change the way end users consume energy using technological solutions, or regulatory or financial incentives. Entailing consumer behavioural changes, this might be challenging for the residential sector, but certainly easier – due to clear economic incentives – for the industry and services sectors.

Another way to enhance power system flexibility is to interconnect the power sector itself with the broader energy sector, including the heating, natural gas, and mobility sectors. This process of interconnection, called sector coupling, also includes – for instance – the charging of battery-electric cars and production of heat and hydrogen from electricity. Battery-electric cars can indeed act as battery storage devices if regulations and technologies are aligned, and they can provide short-term storage and grid services. Likewise, the electrification of heat and fuels can also provide a storage option for the power system in the future.

As the share of wind and solar energy grows in the electricity system, all these flexibility options will have to be utilised in order to ensure the stability of the system, and therefore to guarantee energy security.

7.5   KEY TAKEAWAYS

Wind Energy

- Wind is a well-established and cost-competitive energy technology.
- Wind turbine capacity has strongly increased over time as technology developed.
- Some 95 per cent of wind generation currently occurs onshore, but offshore has a great potential.
- Wind currently contributes to 4 per cent of global electricity generation.
- China, the United States, and the European Union cover 80 per cent of global wind generation.

Solar Energy

- Solar energy can be collected to generate electricity mainly through photovoltaic cells.
- Solar energy can also be collected to produce heat through solar thermal systems.
- Solar is mainly used for electricity generation and accounts for 1.7 per cent of total generation.
- China, the United States, the European Union, and Japan cover 80 per cent of solar generation.

Marine Energy

- Marine energy is in its infancy and currently does not play a significant role.
- Global marine capacity is very limited and mainly installed in France and South Korea.
- Tidal range currently covers 99 per cent of marine energy generation.

- Other technologies include tidal stream, wave power, and ocean thermal energy conversion.

Renewables' System Integration Challenge

- Initially, wind and solar have been deployed with priority dispatch and access to the grid.
- As the shares of wind and solar grow, system integration challenges arise due to their variability.
- To ensure smooth integration of wind and solar, is key to foster system flexibility.
- Conventional electricity generation sources play an important role in ensuring flexibility.
- Distribution and transmission grids allow to smooth wind and solar intermittency at site level.
- Energy storage is also important, albeit today it remains concentrated in pumping hydro plants.
- Demand side management can modify end-user energy demand profile and smooth peaks.
- Linking electricity with other sectors (e.g., transport, heating) is also a flexibility enabler.

8 Energy Consumption and Energy Efficiency

8.1 INTRODUCTION TO ENERGY CONSUMPTION AND ENERGY EFFICIENCY

Between 1971 and 2016, the world's total final energy consumption more than doubled. However, energy consumption by most economy sectors did not change and has been fairly stable for several years. Industry has traditionally been the largest energy consuming sector (37 per cent of the world's total final energy consumption in 2016), followed by transport (29 per cent) and residential (22 per cent). Other relevant consuming sectors are commerce and public services (8 per cent) and agriculture and forestry (2 per cent).[1] In industry, energy consumption is largely driven by a long-term trend of rising production in energy-intensive industry subsectors, such as chemicals, iron and steel, cement, pulp and paper, and aluminium. Since 2010, India saw the highest rate of industrial energy consumption growth (3.9 per cent annual growth), while China had the largest absolute increase, accounting for 60 per cent of the total net increase. In Europe and the Americas industrial energy use has in the meanwhile slightly declined. In transport, energy consumption is largely driven by cars, vans, and trucks, reflecting the major share of the road segment in the sector. In the residential sector, energy is consumed for heating, cooling, lighting, and cooking purposes, with shares that largely depend on geographical conditions.

Often named as the world's potential 'first fuel', energy efficiency entails 'using technology that requires less energy to perform the same function. A typical example of energy efficiency is

---

[1]   IEA, World Energy Balances database, accessed in June 2019.

using a light-emitting diode (LED) light bulb that requires less energy than an incandescent light bulb to produce the same amount of light' (EIA, 2019c). Energy efficiency should therefore not be confused with energy conservation, which refers to 'any behaviour resulting in the utilisation of less energy' (EIA, 2019c). For instance, turning the lights off while leaving a room is a way of conserving energy.

The level of a country's energy efficiency can be measured through energy intensity, an indicator that refers to the ratio between a country's energy consumption and its GDP. This indicator can also be applied to individual sectors, such as industry, transport, buildings, etc. At the global level, energy intensity is generally expressed in tonnes of oil equivalent (toe) per thousand dollars of GDP.

Every economy needs energy to produce wealth. However, energy intensity varies greatly from one country to another. It depends, among other things, on the structure of the economy in question (e.g., weight of industries and services), on the energy efficiency of transport systems and buildings, on the policies implemented to control energy consumption, as well as on overall climatic factors and on the population's standard of living.

Energy intensity is an indicator to be carefully handled. Given the structure of the economy is an important factor in determining a country's energy intensity, it should be noted that improvements in the indicator might indeed not be driven by real energy efficiency improvements, but rather by shifts of economic activities from energy intensive industries towards less energy intensive services.

As illustrated by the IEA (2017b, p.20), 'the world's energy intensity is declining – indicating that we are able to produce more GDP for each unit of energy consumed. This is the case for both developed and developing countries, as in both groups energy intensity has declined almost without interruption since 2000' (Figure 8.1).

According to the IEA (2017b, p.17),

Between 2000 and 2016, in OECD countries primary energy demand fell by 1 per cent, despite a 32 per cent increase in GDP.

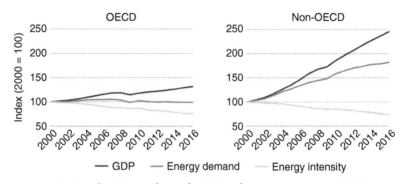

FIGURE 8.1 Energy demand, GDP, and energy intensity in OECD and Non-OECD
Source: International Energy Agency, Energy Efficiency 2017. All rights reserved.

In the same period, in non-OECD countries energy demand rose 80 per cent while GDP increased 150 per cent. Globally, energy efficiency improved 13 per cent between 2000 and 2016. Without this improvement, global final energy use in 2016 would have been 12 per cent higher – equivalent to adding the annual final energy use of Europe to the global energy market.

These improvements deliver an energy productivity bonus, as the world is able to produce more GDP for each unit of energy demand. To provide an idea of its order of magnitude, the IEA (2017b) measured

the difference between the world's actual GDP in 2016 and the notional level of GDP that would have been generated in the same year had energy intensity stayed at the previous year's level. The result is clear: the world's energy productivity bonus due to energy efficiency amounted in 2016 to USD 2.2 trillion, i.e., twice the size of the Australian economy. This bonus in China was larger than that of any other country, at around USD 1.1 trillion; in the United States, it amounted to around USD 500 billion. Combined, the two countries accounted for over three-quarters of the total world bonus.

Other relevant factors include the benefits related to energy efficiency improvements (Figure 8.2), ranging from climate change

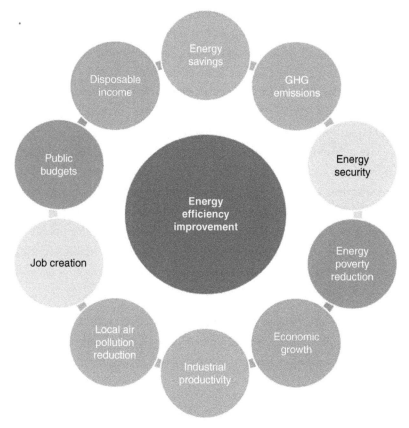

FIGURE 8.2 Multiple benefits of energy efficiency
Source: author's elaboration.

mitigation to job creation, from energy poverty reduction to the fostering of energy access in developing countries.

For instance, a major benefit of energy efficiency is climate change mitigation, as it plays an important role in steadying and reducing GHG emissions. As calculated by the IEA (2017b), 'global energy savings from efficiency improvements since 2000 led to a reduction in GHG emissions of over 4 billion tonnes of CO_2 equivalent in 2016. Without these efficiency improvements, emissions in 2016 would have been 12.5 per cent higher. The avoidance of fuel combustion that results from efficiency improvements also reduces local air pollutants, benefiting air quality and public health'.

Energy efficiency can also bolster energy security, for instance reducing an oil-and-gas importing country's reliance on external suppliers. The IEA (2017b, p.28) calculated that 'efficiency improvements between 2000 and 2016 are estimated to have avoided nearly USD 50 billion in expenditure on energy imports'.

It is important to outline that energy efficiency also generates a number of social benefits. First of all, by reducing per-unit energy consumption, energy efficiency can reduce a household's energy bill – therefore making energy services more affordable to all. Secondly, energy efficiency has a key role to play in facilitating the uptake of energy access in developing countries, as it basically enables serving more people with the same amount of available energy.

As noted by the IEA (2013, pp.28–9),

As with other energy resources, energy efficiency activity takes place as part of a market – where forces of demand and supply operate, buyers and sellers interact, and transactions occur [Figure 8.3]. In its

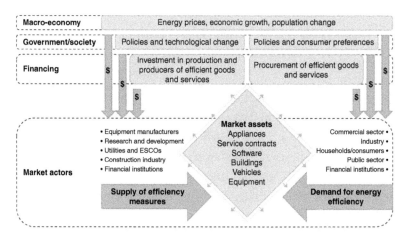

FIGURE 8.3 The market for energy efficiency
Source: International Energy Agency, Energy Efficiency Market Report 2013. All rights reserved.

most basic form, investments are made in energy efficiency that lead to avoided energy consumption (e.g., for demand-side interventions such as improved vehicle efficiency) or avoided energy losses (e.g., for supply-side interventions such as improvements to the efficiency of electricity distribution). Delivering the same level of energy services (e.g., lighting, heating, transport) while using less energy has a value related to the cost of the energy saved. The market for energy efficiency is as diffuse as energy consumption patterns themselves. It is composed of many market actors who demand more efficient provision of energy services, and those that supply the necessary goods and know-how. Describing the energy efficiency market in terms of the drivers of supply and demand helps to reveal the key factors, including policy interventions, that shape the market and show how their interactions deliver investments and outcomes. The actors and dynamics driving the energy efficiency market are numerous and diverse. Production and consumption decisions, as in other markets, occur within a particular economic and socio-political context. In the case of the energy efficiency market, the broader economic environment is particularly sensitive to energy prices. In addition to energy prices, government policy plays an especially critical role. The ways in which policies affect the decision-making processes of a variety of private and public sector investors are complex and require careful understanding. The energy efficiency market is also characterised by a range of market agents acting in a variety of economic sub-sectors (both as direct producers and consumers).

Energy prices are a key driver underpinning demand for energy efficiency. This is the reason why energy prices should always reflect real costs, and therefore not be subject to universal subsidies schemes. Just to make an example, oil-and-gas producing countries in the MENA region have traditionally largely subsidised fossil fuel consumption as part of their social contracts. Iran's fossil fuel subsidies are the largest in the world, with an estimated value of USD 45 billion in 2017 (i.e., equivalent to 10 per cent of the country's GDP). In the same year, fossil fuel subsidies amounted, for instance, to USD 37 billion in Saudi Arabia, to USD 9 billion in the United Arab Emirates, and to around USD 7 billion in both Iraq and Kuwait (IEA, 2018b). These high fossil fuel subsidies distort the economics of energy and the price signals of energy resources, and lead to the inefficient allocation of resources, encouraging rent-seeking behaviour and excessive energy consumption. Not by coincidence, MENA hydrocarbon producers are among the least energy-efficient countries in the world (Tagliapietra, 2017b).

Energy policies also play a key role in fostering demand for energy efficiency. Energy policies can indeed influence energy prices, and also create demand for energy efficiency through awareness programmes and regulation. As illustrated by REN21 (2018, p.15),

> Policy interventions can address market failures and technical
> barriers, along with behavioural and organisational barriers that
> may reinforce existing market failures. Energy policies in the field
> can be divided into three broad categories: regulation, provision of
> information, and economic instruments. Governments across the
> world have increasingly adopted energy efficiency policies. By end-
> 2017, at least 145 countries had enacted some kind of energy
> efficiency policy, and at least 157 countries had enacted one or more
> energy efficiency target.

The energy efficiency supply/demand relationship is characterised by numerous behavioural and market failures that are recognised as deterring demand and, by extension, investment. Even in cases where the financial benefits of an efficiency measure are clear, consumers often do not select it. One reason why consumers may not undertake cost-effective efficiency measures relates to behavioural preferences, such as avoiding the perceived inconvenience of, for example, building renovations. Another reason may relate to imperfect information; for example, consumers may undervalue energy efficiency because they do not understand the opportunity it presents. Market failures tend to attenuate energy price signals and can act to increase the perceived cost and risk of energy efficient technology, hindering the full potential of cost-effective energy efficiency improvements.

8.2 ENERGY CONSUMPTION AND ENERGY EFFICIENCY IN INDUSTRY

Industry has a double role in energy efficiency, as it both produces energy-consuming goods and as it consumes large amounts of energy for their production. Industry has traditionally been the main energy consuming sector in the world, and it accounted for 37 per cent of global final energy consumption in 2017.[2]

As noted by the IEA (2013, p.37),

> Energy consumption by heavy industry is often related to large, energy-hungry equipment that can be responsible for a high share of operational costs and have lifetimes of over 40 years.
> Refurbishment of this equipment is generally only undertaken if the payback period is in the order of two to five years. The energy efficiency market in industry is therefore unevenly distributed, largely driven by economic growth, and comprises many globally active players. Most investments have shifted towards emerging economies with expanding industrial sectors. Industrial firms often have competitiveness pressures that drive autonomous energy efficiency measures, especially in times of stable demand for industrial output. In addition to efficiency measures, strategies to reduce energy consumption in the manufacturing sector include the recovery of waste energy, as well as recycling, substitution and re-use of materials and products.

Between 2000 and 2016, energy intensity in industry (i.e., measured as final energy consumption per unit of gross value added – GVA) decreased at the global level by 30 per cent (IEA, 2017b). This makes industry a global success story in terms of energy efficiency.

---

[2]   IEA, World Energy Balances database, accessed in June 2019.

According to the IEA (2017b, p.67) calculations,

> Energy intensity improvements were largest in the chemicals and
> vehicles sub-sectors, where there has been a clear divergence
> between energy use and GVA. This reflects ongoing technological
> improvements, such as automation and the use of industrial robots,
> and strong demand for outputs, particularly plastics and vehicles.
> Globally, vehicles manufacturing is the largest user of industrial
> robots, which improve the sector's energy productivity through
> greater automation of production. In 2015, the global supply of
> industrial robots was 50 per cent higher to the vehicles
> manufacturing industry than to the second largest sector (i.e.,
> electronics manufacturing). Deployment of industrial robots is also
> evident in the metals and chemicals manufacturing sub-sectors,
> which are the third- and fourth largest sectors for deployment,
> globally.

Energy prices and activity levels in energy-intensive industrial
sectors are the key determinants of a country's industrial energy
intensity. As illustrated by the IEA (2017b, p.70),

> Countries with high energy prices tend to have much lower energy
> intensities than countries with lower prices. While this highlights
> the tendency of higher energy prices to foster industry efficiency, it
> also shows that countries with cheap energy are favoured locations
> for energy-intensive sub-sectors. On average, the contribution of
> energy-intensive subsectors to total industry GVA is 40 per cent
> higher in countries with lower energy prices than in countries with
> higher prices.

A sensible way to foster industrial energy efficiency is to adopt
an energy management system. This basically entails the creation of
a structure to monitor a company's energy consumption in view of
finding potential ways to improve efficiency. In this field, the
International Organization for Standardization (ISO) 50001 standard
provides an internationally benchmark for implementation. First

published in 2011, ISO 50001 was revised in 2018 to reflect a desire to promote adoption of the standard not only among large firms, but also among small and medium-sized enterprises. Data contained in more than forty case studies from various European countries show that implementing ISO 50001 allow firms to achieve an average annual energy saving of 26 per cent (IEA, 2017b).

There are large opportunities for industry to keep enhancing its energy efficiency through improved equipment and process design as well as through a wider adoption of energy management systems and practices. Governmental policies play an important role in pushing industry to adopt energy data management systems as well as minimum performance standards for industrial equipment.

8.3 ENERGY CONSUMPTION AND ENERGY EFFICIENCY IN BUILDINGS

In buildings, households consume energy for a number of different reasons, spanning from heating and cooling to cooking, from lighting to the powering of appliances. Buildings have long lifetimes: according to the IEA (2013, p.36), 'more than half of the current global building stock will still be standing in 2050. While the overall building stock turnover rate is only 1 to 2 per cent per year, heating and cooling systems are generally upgraded or replaced every 10 to 30 years'. Policies aimed at introducing new energy efficiency standards in buildings can therefore take a very long time before starting to generate actual energy savings. This is the reason why these policies are complemented by policies aimed at encouraging the refurbishment of existing buildings. This is particularly key in developed countries, where the building stock does not grow at the rate of emerging countries. With regard to household appliances, the IEA (2013, p.37) estimates that

> [Household appliances] are generally purchased every 5 to 20 years, while consumables (e.g., mobile telephones), have much shorter life spans. The level of investment related to each energy service is

therefore dictated by the lifetime of the appliance stock. Energy costs for individual appliances are often small relative to the total cost of the appliance. Energy-efficient appliances will generate the highest energy savings and financial flows in market segments with high energy consumption, more rapid stock turnover and where technological change can significantly reduce energy consumption without increasing lifecycle costs.

As a result of these complexities, and of the related behavioural issues, promoting energy efficiency in buildings has proven to be much more difficult than in the industrial sector. At the global level, buildings' final energy consumption is indeed growing steadily as a result of increasing floor area growth, which outpaces energy intensity reduction. As indicated by the IEA (2017b, p.78),

> Progress on energy efficiency policies for buildings has increased since 2010, though the share of progress on building envelopes by country varies compared with progress on heating, ventilation and air conditioning (HVAC) equipment. In some countries, such as Denmark and Germany, building envelope policy has been the key driver for policy progress, while in other countries, such as Japan and Korea, HVAC equipment has been a key driver. A combination of both envelope and equipment policies is critical for the transition to sustainable buildings. Highly efficient building envelopes indeed enable the use of higher-efficiency equipment and energy sources, such as low temperature waste heat, heat pumps and renewable energy. Energy efficiency in buildings can be delivered by both technology and policies – and ideally by a mix of the two.

On the technology side, building envelopes, smart meters, building energy storage, and heat pumps represent the key elements to foster energy efficiency.

Building envelopes are key to ensure that buildings maintain the desired indoor temperature better and over a longer period, independently of the external temperature. Smart meters can empower end users by allowing them to have better understanding and control over their energy system, ultimately promoting energy conservation. In an increasingly complex energy environment, energy storage is key to allowing a building to adapt to operating loads and absorb or release energy when needed. Batteries are likely to become an important part of future building-related storage, also fostering the up-take of domestic solar photovoltaic installations. Heat pumps are increasingly being recognised as an important solution to foster energy efficiency in buildings.

To put it simply, a heat pump is an air conditioner that can also run in reverse. It relies on the fact that a liquid absorbs heat as it is vaporised into a gas and that a gas releases heat as it condenses into a liquid. In winter, the heat pump heats the house taking the heat stored in the air, water, or soil from the outside and transferring it to the inside of the room. In winter, therefore, the heat pump uses the thermal energy of the main elements present in nature – even at low temperatures – to raise the temperature (hence the name of 'pump') cooling and sending it inside the rooms to get their heating. Conversely, in summer, thanks to the possibility of reversing the cycle, the heat pump follows the principle of operation of the domestic refrigerator. If we put a hand behind our refrigerator, we will feel heat, because the refrigerator takes it away from the food, keeping it fresh, and disperses it in the kitchen environment through the coil that is located on the outside, on the back. In the summer, therefore, our house becomes the 'container' from which, in function of conditioning, the pump's production of hot water removes the excess heat and expels it outside, cooling the rooms. The heat pump, just like the boilers we have in our apartments, is also able to produce domestic hot water, which is the water we use in our bathrooms and kitchens. This hot water is heated in special storage tanks and distributed through the normal hydraulic pipes inside the buildings. According to the IEA (2017b, p.66), 'today's heat pumps can reduce a household's electricity use for heating by approximately 50 per cent compared to electric resistance heating such as furnaces and baseboard heaters.

They can also enable energy savings of 60 to 80 per cent compared with typical instantaneous and storage water heaters'.

On the policy side, a wide range of measures can be adopted by governments to foster energy efficiency in buildings. First of all, minimum energy performance requirements for materials used in building constructions and renovations can be mandated through building codes. Likewise, minimum energy efficiency standards can be mandated for domestic appliances and equipment. Another measure to foster energy efficiency in buildings relates to energy benchmarking and disclosure. As noted by the EIA (2019c),

> this represents a market-based policy tool used to increase building energy performance awareness and transparency among key stakeholders and create demand for energy efficiency improvements. Such improvements may be offered through voluntary programs, or take the form of mandated policies for private and/or public sector buildings. This policy tool represents an effort by policymakers to overcome barriers that prevent the commercial real estate marketplace and public sector institutions from identifying and valuing the energy efficiency of existing buildings.

8.4   ENERGY CONSUMPTION AND ENERGY EFFICIENCY IN TRANSPORT

The transport sector accounts for 30 per cent of global energy consumption and for half of global oil demand. As a result, the sector accounts for a quarter of energy-related CO_2 emissions, and also represents a major contributor to air pollution in cities. Energy efficiency improvements in the sector (i.e., reduce energy use per transport unit – passenger-km or tonne-km) could thus provide substantial reductions in energy consumption as well as in CO_2 emissions and air pollution.

To date, energy efficiency has had a limited impact in the transport sector. Transport growth, reflecting increased demand for both mobility and freight transport, lower occupancy rates in passenger vehicles and structural shifts between modes of transport, has indeed continued to drive up final energy use for both passenger and freight transport all over the world.

Passenger transport energy efficiency is measured by passenger transport intensity, which indicates the amount of energy used to move one passenger over a distance of one kilometre. As illustrated by the IEA (2019h),

> Passenger transport intensity levels vary across countries
> depending on the share of modes (e.g., road, air, water, rail), vehicle
> types in the mix (e.g., passenger cars, buses, etc.) and on the average
> occupancy (e.g., passengers per vehicle) – which in many countries
> has decreased over time as people increasingly drive their vehicles
> alone. Passenger transport intensity is particularly high in countries
> like the United States, due to the large use of passenger cars (of
> which a high share are SUVs) and domestic flights as compared to
> more efficient transportation modes like buses and trains.
> Conversely, this indicator is comparatively low in countries like
> France, where rail transport is relatively common.

Rail indeed continues to be the most energy-efficient mode of passenger transport, while aviation continues to be the least efficient mode. Over the last decades, the fuel efficiency of new vehicles has improved for all modes. However, the introduction of more powerful and heavier cars, as well as a decrease in the occupancy rates of cars, have absorbed much of the impact in most countries. Since 2000, in developed countries, a decrease in the average number of passengers for each vehicle and transport mode greatly contributed to increase energy demand in the sector. According to the IEA (2017b, p.24), 'energy efficiency did improve by 7 per cent between 2000 and 2016 – largely due to mandatory fuel efficiency policies. However, this was not sufficient to entirely offset other effects, resulting in a net 4 per cent increase in energy use'. Meanwhile, in emerging countries the growth in passenger transport led to a 180 per cent increase in energy demand between 2000 and 2016, which was further boosted by increased vehicle ownership and reduced average vehicle occupancy. Always according to the IEA (2017b, p.25), 'energy efficiency improvements, linked to policy and technology, did reduce demand, but nevertheless net passenger transport energy use ultimately more than tripled between 2000 and 2016'.

As far as freight transport is concerned, it is important to outline the difference between heavy-duty trucks, medium-duty trucks, and light trucks. As noted by the IEA (2018i, p.38),

> While heavy-duty trucks consume much more fuel on average per kilometre driven than smaller trucks, this does not necessarily mean that they represent a less efficient mode of freight transport. In terms of useful service (i.e., per tonne-kilometre), heavy-duty trucks are most efficient at transporting goods and require an average of about 3.8 litres of diesel equivalent (lde) to transport 1 tonne of good over a distance of 100 kilometres. Medium freight trucks require about 4.3 lde to perform the same service, while light commercial vehicles require about 19.5 lde. However, road transport remains far more inefficient than other modes, such as rail and maritime. Both rail and ships indeed use on average 85 per cent less energy (i.e., between 0.4 lde and 0.5 lde respectively) as heavy-duty trucks per 100 tonne-kilometre. Energy efficiency improvements have so far been small in freight transport, partly because policy efforts to improve the fuel efficiency of trucks have been limited across the world. As a result, between 2000 and 2016 the final energy use in the sector augmented by 9 per cent in developed countries and by more than 250 per cent in emerging countries.

There are two main ways to foster energy efficiency in transport: shift person and good transport towards low carbon and energy efficient transport modes (i.e., modal shift), and improve energy efficiency and fuel economy standards of vehicles.[3]

[3]   This part of the section develops and updates an analysis previously elaborated by the author in Tagliapietra and Zachmann (2018).

Modal shift entails the promotion of more efficient solutions such as public transport, walking, and cycling, as well as more integrated modes of mobility. New mobility such as 'mobility-as-a-service'[4] can be enabled by ongoing developments in digital technologies. For instance, smartphone apps can allow information about transportation services from public and private providers to be better combined through a single gateway that creates and manages the trip, for which users can pay via a single account. New approaches could help overcome a major comparative disadvantage of public transport – the longer door-to-door travel times – which mainly arises from the first and the last mile in the transport chain. Energy consumption in freight transport could be reduced by promoting a switch from road to rail and maritime[5], and including the environmental cost of transport in the final purchase price of goods.

But all this is challenging, as reducing demand for passenger transport means changing people's daily habits and taking an integrated policy approach. The governance issue is particularly relevant, considering that road transport is governed by a complex series of policy frameworks developed separately at different levels – cities, national, and federal/supranational (Table 8.1).

And national and local policies on taxation, infrastructure choices, and other matters seem to determine road transport demand. Just to make the example of Europe, Belgians used 741 kilogrammes of oil equivalent of diesel and gasoline in 2016, while Germans used 623 kg, and French drivers only used 581 kg.[6]

---

[4]   Mobility-as-a-service describes a shift away from personally owned modes of transportation and towards mobility solutions that are consumed as a service. The key concept behind it is to offer travellers mobility solutions based on their travel needs.

[5]   It must be noted that freight transport systems have changed radically over the past 200 years. The colonial economies of the eighteenth century were built on maritime transport. Businesses clustered close to sea and river ports to minimise the cost of freight transportation. The introduction of rail technology in the mid-nineteenth century freed business and industry from the need to locate near sea, river, and canal ports. The development of truck and highway technologies in the early twentieth century freed business and industry again, this time from the need to locate near rail lines and terminals. As a result, trucking became the dominant mode of freight transportation.

[6]   IEA, World Energy Balances database, accessed in June 2019.

Table 8.1 *The governance of road transport: Who regulates what?*
The case of Europe

	City level	Country level	EU level
Ban on diesel and petrol vehicles			
Emissions standards			
Alternative fuels infrastructure			
Car-sharing			
Car-pooling			
Ride-sharing			
Walking and biking			
Public transport			
Public procurement			
Parking fee			
Congestion areas			
Speed limits			
Energy taxation			
Road charging			
Spatial planning			
Rail activity			
Maritime activity			

Source: author's elaboration.

Cities are responsible for a wide range of transport policies, such as public transport, enabling car-sharing, congestion charges, parking management, and cycling and walking zones. Countries have different transport taxes and charges, and different policies in relation to the development of transport infrastructure and the creation of alternatives to road transport for freight and in urban areas. On top of this, federal/supranational authorities might also develop – as in the case of the EU – a wide range of policies aimed at making transport systems more connected, competitive, and sustainable. Such fragmented governance risks impeding the promotion of modal shift, as policy measures implemented at the various levels without coordination can neutralise or even hinder each other.

Over the last decades, improvements in vehicle efficiency have been achieved thanks to expanding fuel economy standards – even if emissions reductions have been much less than intended. At the global level, fuel economy standards delivered a 1.7 per cent annual average decline in consumption per kilometre of new cars and light-duty trucks between 2005 and 2017. Between 2005 and 2011, average fuel consumption in advanced economies improved at a rate of 2.7 per cent per year compared with 0.3 per cent per year in emerging economies. Conversely, in the period between 2011 and 2017, emerging economies improved at a faster rate (2.0 per cent) than advanced economies (1.3 per cent). This notably reflects recent strong efficiency gains in China, which improved by nearly 3 per cent per year (IEA, 2019a). Fuel economy standards for light-duty vehicles are now applied in around 40 countries, albeit they have been offset by global consumer trends for larger cars and trucks and need to be improved. The policy coverage for heavy-duty vehicles is a decade behind light-duty vehicles, but is catching up because of an increased focus on the sector in regions like the EU and India. It should be noted that a determining factor in recent global fuel economy developments is the shift in market structures of advanced economies. There has been a decline in the market share of North America (which has larger and, therefore, less-efficient vehicles), and a subsequent growth of the relevance of markets characterised by the smaller and more efficient vehicles sold in Europe, Japan, and Korea. This has been accompanied by a contextual increase, for emerging economies, of the relevance of China – where fuel economy is subject to regulations requiring significant fuel economy improvements – and India, a market that has traditionally been characterised by large shares of small and fuel-efficient cars. Policies play a vital role in fuel economy standards. The impact of the introduction of mandatory fuel economy standards or efficiency-based incentives for vehicle purchase is indeed visible in the market. The average fuel economy improvement rate of countries after implementing fuel consumption standards or efficiency-based purchase incentives after 2005 was nearly 60 per cent higher than countries without standards and incentives – albeit improvement rates continue to be insufficient to meet global climate change mitigation targets. Korea, China, and the EU have achieved the fastest rates of improvement since their fuel economy regulations came into force with annual improvement rates of 1.7–2.3 per cent. The average improvement rate prior to the regulations was 1.1 per cent per year (IEA, 2019a). This underlines the potential of fuel efficiency gains when regulations are implemented.

The electrification of cars also plays a crucial role in ensuring that fuel economy can be effectively improved. Electric motors are indeed more efficient compared to conventional power trains, contributing in parallel to compliance with energy efficiency standards and diversifying the fuel mix of the transport sector (even if this largely depends on the electricity generation mix powering an electric car). Electric cars are already contributing positively to improving the country-weighted average fuel consumption by up to 3.5 per cent (IEA, 2019a). Japan experienced the largest gains due having to the largest market share globally for hybrids, followed by the United States with a mix of electrified vehicle types. Electrification in China was also very relevant to improving average fuel economy, thanks to a fast-growing market share for battery electric cars. The electrification of vehicles has over the last few years become a key trend in the automotive sector, driven by clean energy and climate change concerns and policy interventions – such as support for zero-emission vehicles and carbon taxes – intended to reduce GHG emissions. As electric car technology has developed, technological improvements have reduced production costs, in particular by reducing battery costs, further nurturing the development of the electric car market. Lithium-ion is currently the technology of choice for electric car batteries, and is expected to retain this dominant position during the next decade. Prices for Li-ion batteries have significantly decreased since their introduction in the 1990s, whether for electronics, residential and utility storage, or electric car–related purposes. Alongside the falling cost of Li-ion technology, the scaling up of battery manufacturing capacities in recent years has been a key driver of cost reductions for batteries. Electric cars are expected to proliferate in the future, as governments will increase their support for zero-emission vehicles, ban dirty vehicles, and support the deployment of electric cars and their charging infrastructure. At the same time, electric car technology and manufacturing costs are likely to continue to fall as production expands, further boosting the development of the market for electric cars across the world.

Another potential alternative to oil in transport is represented by hydrogen. Hydrogen is – as electricity – an energy carrier; that is, it allows the transport of energy in a useable form from one place to another. Hydrogen must thus be produced from another substance, such as water, fossil fuels, or biomass. As indicated by Hydrogen Europe (2019), 'hydrogen has the highest energy content of any common fuel by weight (i.e., about three times more than gasoline), but it has the lowest energy content by volume (i.e., about four times less than gasoline).' Today, it takes more energy to produce hydrogen (i.e., by separating it from other elements in molecules) than hydrogen provides when it is converted to useful energy. According to the IEA (2019b),

> Around 70 million tonnes of hydrogen are currently used, mostly for oil refining and chemical production. This hydrogen is currently produced from fossil fuels, with significant associated CO_2 emissions. However, hydrogen is useful as an energy source/fuel because it has a high energy content per unit of weight, which is why it is used as a rocket fuel and in fuel cells to produce electricity on some spacecraft. Hydrogen is not widely used as a fuel now, but it has the potential for greater use in the future. Some in the energy industry look at electrolyses as a cross-cutting technology that might enable the production of clean-burning and storable hydrogen fuel from electricity and water. While electrolysers are a well-known and long-used technology in a variety of industry sectors, the fastest-growing market is for new purposes relating to energy and climate: storing electricity, fuelling vehicles, injecting hydrogen into the gas grid, making synthetic fuels and using cleaner hydrogen inputs in industrial processes.

A major application of hydrogen would be transport, with fuel-cell electric cars. These cars use a fuel cell, instead of a battery, to power an on-board electric motor. A fuel cell is an electrochemical device able to obtain electricity directly from certain substances, typically hydrogen and oxygen, without any process of thermal combustion. Fuel-cell cars are generally classified as zero-emission cars that only emit water and heat. In 2018, the global fuel-cell cars stock amounted to only 11,200 units – concentrated in California, Japan, Korea, and Germany. While deployment of fuel-cell cars remains very low compared with plug-in hybrids and battery electric cars, several countries have announced ambitious deployment targets towards 2030, based on the assumption that by then fuel cell cars technology will be mature.

8.5   KEY TAKEAWAYS

Introduction to Energy Demand and Energy Efficiency

- Energy demand is driven by industry, transport, and residential sectors.
- Efficiency entails using technology that requires less energy to perform the same function.
- Efficiency is seen as the world's potential 'first fuel', a source of energy in its own right.
- The level of a country's energy efficiency can be measured through energy intensity.
- Energy intensity is a measure of the amount of energy used to produce a unit of GDP.
- Energy intensity is declining in both developed and emerging countries.
- Efficiency has multiple benefits, spanning from climate change mitigation to economic growth.

Energy Demand and Energy Efficiency in Industry

- Energy demand in industry is led by chemicals, iron and steel, cement, pulp and paper, and aluminium.
- Industry is an efficiency success story, as global intensity in the sector is sharply declining.
- Automation and industrial robots significantly contribute to efficiency gains in the sector.

- Industries tend to be more efficient in countries with higher energy prices.
- Adopting an energy management system is a key way to improve efficiency in an industry.

Energy Demand and Energy Efficiency in Buildings

- Energy demand in buildings is led by heating, cooling, lighting, and cooking.
- Promoting efficiency in buildings is difficult, due to a number of behavioural issues.
- Both building envelope and home equipment are critical to foster efficiency in the sector.
- Digital technologies can open new opportunities for efficiency in buildings.
- The role of policies is particularly important, in both public and private buildings.

Energy Demand and Energy Efficiency in Transport

- Energy demand in transport is largely driven by road transport – and is it mainly based on oil.
- Energy efficiency progress in transport has been rather limited so far.
- Efficiency gains have been outpaced by strong global transport demand growth.
- Two ways to foster efficiency in the sector are modal shift and improved vehicle efficiency.
- Modal shift entails the promotion of more efficient modes, as public transport or rail.
- Governance is key in modal shift, as various levels regulate various road transport elements.
- Vehicles' fuel economy standards have brought efficiency gains, albeit still not sufficient.
- Electric cars are more efficient than conventional power trains and could boost efficiency.
- Hydrogen (i.e., fuel-cell electric cars) could also boost energy efficiency in the sector.

9   In-Depth Focus 1: Energy and Climate Change

Climate change is a long-term change in the earth's average climate. The earth's climate did change throughout history: as illustrated by NASA (2019), 'in the last 650,000 years, there have been seven cycles of glacial advance and retreat, with the abrupt end of the last ice age about 7,000 years ago marking the beginning of the modern climate era'. However, since the Industrial Revolution, the average climate has changed at an unprecedented rate. According to the IPCC (2018, p.6), 'human activities are estimated to have caused approximately 1 degree Celsius of global warming above pre-industrial levels' (Figure 9.1).

As illustrated by the IPCC (2018, p.6), 'warming greater than the global annual average is being experienced in many land regions and seasons, including two to three times higher in the Arctic'. Furthermore, as described by the IPCC (2014, p.53), 'temperature rise to date has already resulted in profound alterations to human and natural systems, including increases in droughts, floods, and some other types of extreme weather, sea level rise and biodiversity loss'.

Global warming is anthropogenic – in other words, it is the result of human activities that, like the combustion of fossil fuels, propel carbon dioxide (CO_2), methane (CH_4) and nitrous oxide (N_2O) emissions into the atmosphere. These greenhouse gas (GHG) emissions increase the earth's natural GHG effect,[1] compromising the planet's specific

---

[1]   As described by NASA (2019), 'Sunlight passes through the atmosphere and warms the earth's surface. This heat is radiated back toward space. Most of the outgoing heat is absorbed by GHG molecules and re-emitted in all directions, warming the surface of the earth and the lower atmosphere, allowing life in the planet. That is, the earth does require a certain level of this GHG effect. Without enough GHG effect, the earth would indeed be like planet Mars, with a largely frozen surface that shows no evidence of life.

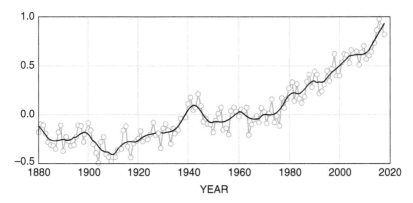

FIGURE 9.1 Global temperature anomaly, 1880–2019 (Degree Celsius)
Source: NASA (2019).

energetic equilibrium between the radiation it receives from the sun and the radiation it emits out to space. This creates the enhanced GHG effect that ultimately causes global warming (Figure 9.2).

GHG emissions have substantially increased as a result of human activities since the Industrial Revolution, and according to the IPCC (2007, p.5) 'today far exceed pre-industrial values determined from ice cores spanning many thousands of years' (Figure 9.3).

The abundant empirical evidence on the unprecedented rate and global scale of the impact of human activities on the earth system has led many scientists to call for the introduction of a new epoch in the geological time scale: the Anthropocene (Zalasiewicz et al., 2017). This – still not official – interval of geologic time would then be characterised as the time in which human activities began to significantly impact the earth's surface, atmosphere, oceans, and systems of nutrient cycling.

As show by the IPCC (2014), among anthropogenic GHG emissions, CO_2 is by far the most important, accounting for 76 per cent of the total, followed by CH_4 (16 per cent) and N_2O (6.2 per cent) (Figure 9.4).

On the contrary, with too much GHG effect the earth would be like planet Venus, which having an extremely high level of carbon dioxide in the atmosphere has a surface temperature hot enough to melt lead'.

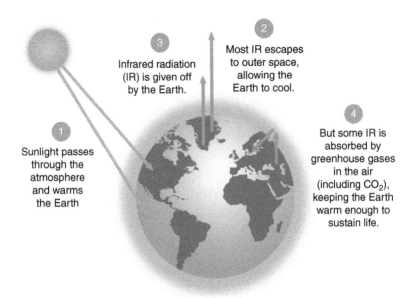

FIGURE 9.2 Diagram describing the mechanism of the greenhouse effect
Source: Shutterstock.

Based on estimations made by NASA (2019), 'the global atmospheric concentration of CO_2 has increased from a pre-industrial value of about 280 parts per million (ppm) to 411 ppm in 2019'. This level of atmospheric concentration exceeds historical levels by far. The IPCC (2007) indeed reports 'atmospheric concentration of CO_2 in the natural range over the last 650,000 years of 180 to 300 ppm as determined from ice cores'. Further, according to the IPCC (2007, p.37), this signifies that 'the annual CO_2 concentration growth rate was larger during the last 10 years, than it has been since the beginning of continuous direct atmospheric measurements'. The use of fossil fuels represents the primary source of this increased atmospheric concentration of CO_2.

As NASA (2019) estimated, 'global atmospheric concentration of CH_4 has increased from a pre-industrial value of about 715 parts

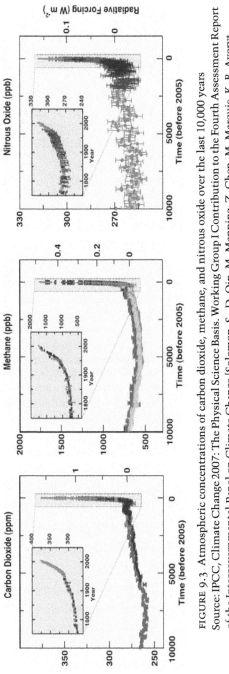

FIGURE 9.3 Atmospheric concentrations of carbon dioxide, methane, and nitrous oxide over the last 10,000 years
Source: IPCC, Climate Change 2007: The Physical Science Basis. Working Group I Contribution to the Fourth Assessment Report
of the Intergovernmental Panel on Climate Change [Solomon, S., D. Qin, M. Manning, Z. Chen, M. Marquis, K. B. Averyt,
M. Tignor, and H. L. Miller (eds.)]. Cambridge, UK and New York, NY: Cambridge University Press.

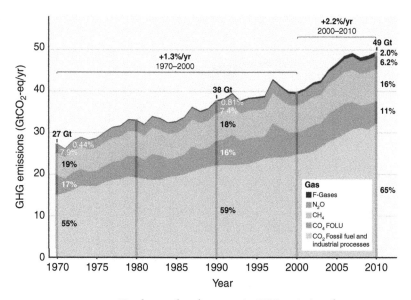

FIGURE 9.4 Total annual anthropogenic GHG emissions by gases, 1970–2010
Source: IPCC, Climate Change 2014: Mitigation of Climate Change. Contribution of Working Group III to the Fifth Assessment Report of the Intergovernmental Panel on Climate Change [Edenhofer, O., R. Pichs-Madruga, Y. Sokona, E. Farahani, S. Kadner, K. Seyboth, A. Adler, I. Baum, S. Brunner, P. Eickemeier, B. Kriemann, J. Savolainen, S. Schloemer, C. von Stechow, T. Zwickel and J.C. Minx (eds.)]. Cambridge, UK and New York, NY: Cambridge University Press. Note: F-Gases: fluorinated gases; FOLU: Forestry and Other Land Use.

per billion (ppb) to 1,840 ppb in 2019'. Again, this level of atmospheric concentration exceeds historical levels by far. The IPCC (2007, p.5) indeed reports atmospheric concentration of CH_4 'in the natural range over the last 650,000 years of 320 to 790 ppb as determined from ice cores'. The increase in methane concentration is predominantly due to agriculture activities and fossil fuel use.

According to NASA (2019), 'the global atmospheric concentration of N_2O increased from a pre-industrial value of about 270 ppb to 329 ppb in 2019.' The growth rate has been approximately constant since 1980. More than a third of all N_2O emissions are primarily due to agriculture.

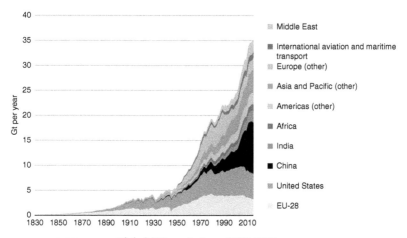

FIGURE 9.5 Global CO_2 emissions, 1830–2015
Source: author's elaboration on Carbon Dioxide Information Analysis
Center, accessed in June 2019.

But which countries historically emitted the most? The first
industrial-scale CO_2 emitter was the United Kingdom, being at the
centre of the coal-based Industrial Revolution. Emissions in other
European countries and North America shortly followed. Other
regions – Latin America, Asia, and Africa – started contributing to
global emissions much later, largely contained to the twentieth and
twenty-first centuries. As an overall trend, between 1830 and 2015,
the United States and Europe have been the world's key CO_2 emitters.
China's CO_2 emissions impressively increased over the last three
decades, making it the second largest historical emitter after the
United States (Figure 9.5).

It is interesting to note how global emissions shifted over time.
Europe dominated global emissions for most of the nineteenth cen-
tury. The United States' emissions substantially emerged in
the second half of the nineteenth century, and peaked around 1950.
Since then, the country's emissions declined by approximately
26 per cent in 2015, albeit remaining the world's largest. By 2015,
China accounted for 12 per cent of total cumulative emissions, and
India for 3 per cent.

An historical view on global emissions is useful not only to understand the genesis of climate change, but also to better comprehend the international debate on how to tackle it. However, it is also relevant to clearly outline current trends. Today, China, the United States, and the EU are the world's top three emitters. Together, these three blocs contribute to more than half the world's total GHG emissions, while the 100 smallest-emitting countries collectively add up to only 3.5 per cent of emissions[2].

It must be outlined that a key issue with measuring total national emissions relates to the fact that it does not take into consideration countries' population sizes. To make a fair comparison of countries' contributions to global emissions, it is therefore useful to introduce a per capita perspective on emissions. Just to provide some examples, CO_2 emissions per capita stand at 17 metric tonnes (mt) in the United States; at 10 mt in Russia, Japan, and Germany; at 7 mt in China and the EU; at 2 mt in Brazil and India; and at far less than 1 mt in most sub-Saharan African countries (BP, 2019).

Another major drawback of the commonly utilised emissions measurement system is that it takes into account their production rather than consumption. This accounting method reports emissions as those emitted within a country's given geographical boundaries. As a consequence, the emissions that might have been imported or exported in the form of traded goods are not taken into consideration. A 'consumption-based' accounting method would thus reflect more accurately the global emission landscape as, for instance, some of the CO_2 produced (and therefore reported) in emerging economies is due to the production of goods consumed in developed countries. Such a reporting system would then significantly change the global emissions picture, notably increasing global emission shares of developed countries while reducing the ones of emerging countries.

[2]   Author's elaboration on Carbon Dioxide Information Analysis Center, accessed in June 2019.

The following sections discuss the two – complementary – ways to respond to climate change: mitigation (i.e., reducing climate change) and adaptation (i.e., adapting to life in a changing climate).

9.2 CLIMATE CHANGE MITIGATION

Mitigation is defined by NASA (2019) as the activity aimed at

> reducing the flow of heat-trapping GHGs into the atmosphere, either by reducing sources of these gases (e.g., the burning of fossil fuels for electricity, heat or transport) or enhancing the 'sinks' that accumulate and store these gases (e.g., oceans, forests and soil). The goal of mitigation is to avoid significant human interference with the climate system, and stabilize GHG levels in a timeframe sufficient to allow ecosystems to adapt naturally to climate change, ensure that food production is not threatened and to enable economic development to proceed in a sustainable manner.

The Paris Agreement set the target 'to keep the increase in global average temperature to well below 2 degrees Celsius above pre-industrial levels and to pursue efforts to limit the temperature increase to 1.5 degree Celsius, recognizing that this would significantly reduce the risks and impacts of climate change' (UNFCCC, 2015, p.3). As outlined by Gao et al. (2017, p.1), 'the setting of the long-term goal for addressing climate change has been a long process, and the 2 degrees Celsius global temperature target represents a political consensus on the basis of scientific assessment'.

Scientists calculated the amount of CO_2 the world can emit while limiting global warming to the agreed thresholds, and refer to it as the world's 'carbon budget'. According to the IPCC (2018, p.14),

> Limiting global warming requires limiting the total cumulative global anthropogenic emissions of CO_2 since the preindustrial period, that is, staying within a total carbon budget. By the end of 2017, anthropogenic CO_2 emissions since the pre-industrial period are estimated to have reduced the total carbon budget for 1.5 degree

Celsius by approximately 2200 ± 320 billion tonnes of CO_2 ($GtCO_2$). The associated remaining budget is being depleted by current emissions of 42 ± 3 $GtCO_2$ per year. The choice of the measure of global temperature affects the estimated remaining carbon budget. [...] Using growing season mean temperature gives estimates of 770 and 570 $GtCO_2$, for 50 per cent and 66 per cent probabilities, respectively.

This signifies that to have a medium chance (i.e., 50 per cent) of limiting global warming to 1.5 degrees Celsius, the world can still emit only 770 $GtCO_2$, while to have a likely chance (i.e., 66 per cent), the remaining carbon budget drops to 570 $GtCO_2$. As suggested by the World Resources Institute (2018) this implies that

Even if countries fulfil their current [Paris Agreement] unconditional emissions-reduction pledges, we're on track to blow through the entirety of the remaining carbon budget for a likely chance of limiting warming to 1.5 degree Celsius by 2030. Even in the overly optimistic scenario in which current levels of CO_2 emissions are held constant, we would still exhaust the budget in 2030 (for a likely chance of limiting warming to 1.5 degrees Celsius). This clearly illustrates the need to peak global emissions before 2030 to have a better chance of avoiding the worst climate impacts.

This overall situation clearly illustrates the urgent need to reduce the world's GHG emissions through mitigation actions.

Examples of climate change mitigation actions are switching the global energy system from fossil fuels to clean energy sources, promoting energy efficiency and conservation, promoting afforestation and reforestation, promoting carbon capture utilisation and storage, promoting geoengineering solutions, and shifting food consumption patterns. Since renewable energy sources and energy efficiency and conservation have already been discussed in dedicated chapters, it might now be useful to quickly review the other options.

Forests retain and absorb CO_2, playing a key role in mitigating climate change. Afforestation (i.e., planting of plants where there have never been any) and reforestation (i.e., reforestation of deforested areas) can therefore contribute to the sequestration of CO_2 from the atmosphere, and to its storage – through photosynthesis – in the form of wood and vegetation. This is particularly the case in tropical regions, where vegetation grows more rapidly – thus quickly absorbing CO_2 from the atmosphere. In these regions, planting trees can remove large amounts of CO_2 from the air in a relatively short time: an annual amount of 15 tonnes of CO_2 per hectare could indeed be stored in these forests. Typically, trees are made up of about 20 per cent of their weight of carbon, and the entire forest biomass acts as a 'carbon sink'. The organic matter present in the soil of forests – such as the humus produced by the decomposition of dead plant material – also acts as a carbon reservoir. As a result, forests capture huge amounts of carbon: the planet's forests and their undergrowth absorb more than a trillion tonnes of carbon in total – twice as much as in the atmosphere. Forest destruction, on the other hand, adds nearly 6 billion tonnes of CO_2 to the atmosphere every year (Crowther et al., 2015).[3] Preventing this stored carbon from being released is crucial to mitigate climate change and to preserve the environment.

Carbon capture, utilisation, and storage (CCUS), is defined by the IEA (2019d) as

> an important emissions reduction technology that can be applied in the industrial sector and in power generation. These technologies involve the capture of CO_2 from fuel combustion or industrial processes, the transport of CO_2 via ship or pipeline, and either its use as a resource to create valuable products or services or its permanent storage deep underground in geological formations.

CCUS entails three integrated steps: the capture of the CO_2, through a plant capable of separating it from the rest of the wastewater

---

[3]   It is estimated that over 15 billion trees are cut down each year, and the global number of trees has fallen by approximately 46 per cent since the start of human civilisation.

emitted from large sources; the transport of the CO_2, by either pipes or ship; and the storage of the CO_2 in a suitable underground site.

The capture of CO_2 produced by industry can be carried out before combustion (i.e., pre-combustion capture chain) or after combustion (i.e., post-combustion capture chain). This process takes place through chemical absorption with reactive and regenerable solvents, or through the removal of the nitrogen component of the atmosphere during combustion itself (i.e., oxyfuel capture chain) through a special system unit called 'air separation unit' tasked of confining combustion to oxygen only, in order to produce exhaust gases with a high concentration of easily extractable CO_2. In general, the capture of CO_2 from the flue-gas is carried out by means of physical or chemical methods: the most studied and adopted one uses amines in which absorption takes place using amine-based solvents as the most developed afterburning technology.

CO_2 storage sites can be: (i) depleted or depleting oil or natural gas fields, where CO_2 injection can also facilitate the release of residual hydrocarbons after the primary production period, by increasing secondary recovery (this process is named enhanced oil/gas recovery), where CO_2 also acquires an economic value; (ii) deep diffuse layers of coal, in which the injection of CO_2 facilitates the release of CH_4 present there, promoting an easier and faster recovery (this process is named enhanced coal bed methane) due to the different coefficient of adsorption of CO_2 and CH_4 in the coal itself; and (iii) deep saline aquifers of large dimensions, for quantity of CO_2 stored in the order of magnitude of 100–1000 Mt for each deep geological structure.

CCUS technologies are still at an early stage of commercialisation. In 2018, there were only two large-scale CCUS power projects and sixteen large-scale CCUS projects in industry and fuel transformation across the world.[4]

Geoengineering refers to deliberate and large-scale human intervention in the earth's climate system, with the aim of mitigating

---

[4]   IEA, Tracking Clean Energy Progress, accessed in June 2019: www.iea.org/tcep/

climate change. This entails, for example, the deployment of technologies aimed at cooling the planet by reflecting sunlight away from earth or at siphoning CO_2 out of the atmosphere. The idea of cooling the planet by reflecting sunlight away entails the release of small particles of sulphur dioxide into the stratosphere to reflect incoming rays. Scientists have already witnessed this principle in action in 1991, when Mount Pinatubo erupted in the Philippines injecting an estimated 20 million tonnes of sulphur dioxide into the stratosphere. The eruption created a haze of sulphate particles that cooled the planet by around 0.5 degree Celsius. For about 18 months, the earth's average temperature returned to what it was before the industrial revolution. The idea that humans might turn down the earth's average temperature by similar, artificial, means (e.g., using high-flying planes) dates back several decades, and researchers are continuously working on it. However, predicting the knock-on effects – both positive and negative – remains a major challenge (i.e., solar geoengineering could alter precipitation patterns and even lead to more droughts in some regions) and for this reason the option currently remains only theoretical (Tollefson, 2018b). Siphoning CO_2 out of the atmosphere requires the use of direct air capture technology. This technologies captures CO_2 from the atmosphere, and provides it in purified form that can be either utilised or stored underground – as in the case of CCUS. Direct air capture technologies are today still at an experimental stage. In 2018, there were across the world only few companies pursuing direct air capture technologies, with only few pilot plants (Tollefson, 2018a).

As far as food consumption patterns are concerned, it must be outlined that the environmental impact of the global food system is substantial and increasing. Increasing living standards in emerging countries, as well as rapid urbanisation trends, are pushing higher the consumption of meat and dairy – foods with outsized climate impacts. Limiting the global demand for meat (notably beef, lamb, and goat) is particularly important to mitigate climate change. Ruminant meats have indeed the highest resource requirements of any kind of food. As illustrated by the World Resources Institute (2019), 'producing beef, for instance, requires 20 times the land and emits 20 times the emissions as producing beans, per gram of protein'. To put it more bluntly, if cows were a country, they would indeed rank third in GHG emissions after China and the United States (Gates, 2018).

9.3 CLIMATE CHANGE ADAPTATION

Alongside mitigation actions, measures must also be implemented to adapt to the various impacts of climate change, which occur or may occur in many areas of the planet – for example, modification of the precipitation regime, reduction of water resources, or increase in the frequency of extreme weather events such as heat waves, floods, and droughts. Economic sectors that depend on climatic conditions, such as agriculture, forestry, fishing, seaside and mountain tourism, health, transport, the energy system, financial services, and insurance, may be severely affected by these impacts. Preventive action through the implementation of measures to adapt to certain impacts of climate change are crucial, as the costs of such preventive actions is less onerous from a socio-economic point of view than those resulting from the damage due to the same impacts (Stern, 2007). Adaptation measures vary widely according to sectors and areas of implementation. Example of adaptation measures are the construction of flood defences and artificial dykes to cope with sea-level rise; the adaptation of existing building standards to cope with future climatic conditions, in particular extreme weather and climate events that may occur in the future; the more efficient use of scarce water resources; the development of drought-resistant crops; the selection of forest species and practices less sensitive to heavy rainfall and fires; and the development of effective spatial plans taking into account possible changes in climatic conditions. Adaptation must be planned with appropriate strategies at local, regional, and national levels, with the aim of making societies more resilient to climate change, and implemented through plans that present appropriate allocations of financial resources and systems for monitoring the effectiveness of the measures implemented. As illustrated by the IPCC (2014, p.8),

In Europe adaptation policy has been developed across all levels of government, with some adaptation planning integrated into coastal and water management, into environmental protection and land planning, and into disaster risk management. Likewise, in North America governments are engaging in incremental adaptation assessment and planning, particularly at the municipal level. Some proactive adaptation is occurring to protect longer-term investments in energy and public infrastructure. In Asia, adaptation is being facilitated in some areas through mainstreaming climate adaptation action into subnational development planning, early warning systems, integrated water resources management, agroforestry, and coastal reforestation of mangroves. In Africa, most national governments have also initiated governance systems for adaptation.

It is important to stress the point that, as noted by the IPCC (2012, p.10),

adaptation is place- and context-specific, with no single approach for reducing risks appropriate across all settings. Effective risk reduction and adaptation strategies consider the dynamics of vulnerability and exposure and their linkages with socioeconomic processes, sustainable development, and climate change. Adaptation planning and implementation can be enhanced through complementary actions across levels, from individuals to governments. National governments can play an important role in coordinating adaptation efforts with local and subnational governments, for example by protecting vulnerable groups, by supporting economic diversification, and by providing information, policy and legal frameworks, and financial support. Local government and the private sector are increasingly recognized as critical to progress in adaptation, given their roles in scaling up adaptation of communities, households, and civil society and in managing risk information and financing.

It should also be noted that, as remarked by the IPCC (2014), 'significant co-benefits, synergies, and trade-offs exist between mitigation and adaptation and among different adaptation responses. Efforts to mitigate and adapt to climate change also imply complex cross-sectorial interactions between energy, water, land use, and biodiversity'.

9.4 CARBON PRICING

Carbon pricing, the instrument favoured by many economists to tackle climate change, entails the application of a cost to CO_2 emissions in order to encourage emitters to reduce the amount of their emissions into the atmosphere. Instead of directly mandating who should reduce emissions where and how, a sensible carbon price gives an economic signal, and leaves to the emitters the decision on whether to reduce their emissions, or continue polluting and pay for it. This should allow the achievement of environmental goals in a flexible and least-cost manner for society. Furthermore, a sensible price on carbon should provide a clear sense of direction to energy and other industries about decarbonisation, and in theory also foster innovation in low-carbon technologies.

Two are the main types of carbon pricing: carbon taxes and cap-and-trade systems.

A carbon tax is a fiscal policy instrument according to which every tonne of CO_2 (or CO_2-equivalente GHG emissions) released in the atmosphere would be subject to a payment, the rate of which is set by the government. Since it is directed against a negative externality, a carbon tax can be classified as a Pigouvian tax.[5] A carbon tax thus aims at providing to firms and households (depending on whom it is applied, as a government could either adopt an upstream approach, a downstream approach, or both) a clear incentive to reduce their CO_2 emissions. As pointed by Aldy and Stavins (2011, p.4), 'a carbon tax

---

[5]   A tax on any market activity that generates negative externalities, which is named after Arthur Cecil Pigou, an economist of the University of Cambridge, who first introduced the concept of externalities and the idea of correcting them with a tax.

would be administratively simple and straightforward to implement in most industrialised countries, since the tax could incorporate existing methods for fuel-supply monitoring and reporting to the regulatory authority'. However, this administrative simplicity goes in tandem with political complexity, as the introduction of a new – very visible – tax can hardly be met with enthusiasm by society. An example of this is provided by the EU. As reported by Delbeke and Vis (2015, p.1),

> In the 1990s, economists were actively looking at how to improve environmental policymaking, and made a strong case for putting a price on the impacts of pollution that are not otherwise paid for by the polluter. Their preferred way to do this was through taxation, and the EU tried for almost a decade to get a carbon-energy tax adopted. This failed for political reasons, as the notion of creating new taxes was an unpopular message at a time when many people already felt over-taxed.

The EU indeed finally opted for an alternative approach: the introduction of a cap-and-trade system.

A cap-and-trade system sets a maximum level of emission, a cap, and distributes emissions permits among firms that produce emissions. As eloquently illustrated by Aldy and Stavins (2011, p.5), 'faced with the choice of surrendering an allowance or reducing emissions, firms place a value on an allowance that reflects the cost of the emission reductions that can be avoided by surrendering an allowance'. Whilst the maximum emission quantity is set in advance, the trading price of permits fluctuates, becoming more expensive when demand is high relative to supply and cheaper when demand is lower. The setting a cciling on overall quantity of emissions thus defines in this system the price on emissions. A cap-and-trade system is more complex, from an administrative perspective, than a carbon tax. Policymakers must indeed decide the size of the emissions cap, the types of emissions covered by the cap, and the system regulation methods, and then decide whether to freely distribute allowance or sell them through auctions (Aldy and Stavins, 2011). However, being less visible than a carbon tax, it might be more feasible politically. The largest cap-and-trade system in the world currently is the EU's Emissions Trading System (ETS).

As pointed by the High-Level Commission on Carbon Pricing (2017, p.3),

> Explicit carbon-pricing instruments can raise revenue efficiently because they help overcome a key market failure: the climate externality. The revenue can be used to foster growth in an equitable way, by returning the revenue as household rebates, supporting poorer sections of the population, managing transitional changes, investing in low-carbon infrastructure, and fostering technological change. ... Carbon pricing by itself may not be sufficient to induce change at the pace and on the scale required for the Paris Agreement targets to be met, and may need to be complemented by other well-designed policies tackling various market and government failures, as well as other imperfections. A combination of policies is likely to be more dynamically efficient and attractive than a single policy.

But what can be a sensible carbon price level? According to the High-Level Commission on Carbon Pricing (2017), a carbon price level consistent with achieving the Paris Agreement is US\$40–80/tCO$_2$ by 2020 and US\$50–100/tCO$_2$ by 2030. In 2018, forty-five countries and twenty-five subnational jurisdictions had carbon pricing initiatives in place, covering around 20 per cent of global GHG emissions and with three quarters of covered emissions being priced at less than US \$10/tCO$_2$, which is substantially lower than price levels consistent with achieving the Paris Agreement. According to the World Bank (2018c), in 2018, only the carbon taxes in Finland, Liechtenstein, Sweden, and Switzerland had carbon price rates consistent with the 2020 price range recommended by the High-Level Commission on Carbon Prices. However, it should be noted that emissions covered by carbon pricing have increased almost fourfold over the past decade.

It must be noted that an increasing number of public and private organisations are using internal carbon pricing to inform corporate strategic investment decision-making. Some governments also use internal carbon pricing as a tool for in their procurement process, project appraisals, and policy design in relation to climate change impacts. Financial institutions have also begun using internal carbon pricing as a tool to evaluate their investments by including the cost of carbon in economic analyses of new projects.

It must be noted that carbon pricing might have significant distributional consequences; in other words, might affect different parts of the population differently (Zachmann et al., 2018). For instance, in a poor country, road fuel taxes fall on the richer part of the population that can afford a car – and hence tend to reduce inequality. On the other hand, in a relatively rich country, where people outside the big cities tend to be less well-off but need a car to be mobile, road fuel taxes can increase inequality. Taxing carbon can have very different distributional consequences, depending on the sector the emissions are from: taxing carbon in aviation is likely to reduce inequality as it will fall more strongly on high-income households. By contrast, taxing carbon from heating tends to increase inequality. Road fuel taxes are somewhere in between, often seen as mainly falling on the middle-class – as really poor households typically own no cars and high-income households only spend a very small fraction of their income on road fuel. Policymakers can chose different instruments to decarbonise a certain sector, and those can have different distributional consequences: decarbonising road transport through forcing car companies to ensure that the average emissions of all cars they are selling is below a certain threshold – as implemented in the United States and the EU – can increase inequality even more than road fuel pricing. The reason is, that car companies will make expensive hydrogen, electric, and hybrid cars – that were typically bought by higher-income households – cheaper in order to sell more of them, and increase the price of less efficient vehicles that were typically bought by low-income households in order to meet the average fleet emission targets. Finally, the specific implementation of policies can have a significant impact on the distributional effects. For example, in the EU ETS between 2013 and 2017, the cost of the carbon price was largely passed through to final consumers, while large emitters were getting free allowances worth EUR 50 billion and industrial consumers received compensation worth EUR 8 billion. These choices were made deliberately to protect industry, but they had significant distributional consequences. Hence, policymakers should carefully select the right mix of climate policies in the right sectors and places, and design them in the right way to minimise adverse distributional effects. Furthermore, policymakers should also be more creative in deploying climate policies that are actively helping low-income households. Investment subsidies typically target high-income households that have the ability to invest – but public investments into energy efficiency measures in social housing or energetically modernising schools and kindergartens in disfavoured areas would not only reduce emissions, but also inequality. Finally, carbon taxes generate revenues that can be used to compensate low-income households for the adverse effects. Recycling some of the revenues from the road fuel carbon tax through transfers to the most affected households can limit their distributional effects. Properly assessing the distributional effects of carbon pricing and other climate policies, and assuming the adequate measures to address them, is the only way to ensure the achievement of climate change mitigation goals in a socially sustainable manner.

9.5   INTERNATIONAL CLIMATE REGIME

Climate change is a global commons problem. As stated by Edenhofer et al. (2013, p.1), 'the atmosphere is a global common-pool resource in its function as a sink for GHGs, and it is openly accessible and appropriated by everyone free of charge in most regions of the world'. The geographical origin of GHG emissions into the atmosphere has no effect on impacts: any jurisdiction taking action against climate change thus incurs the costs of its actions, while climate benefits are distributed globally. Therefore, as defined by Stavins (2011, p.1), 'for virtually any jurisdiction, the climate benefits it reaps from its actions will be less than the costs it incurs, despite the fact that the global benefits may be greater – possibly much greater – than the global costs. This presents a classic free-rider problem, which is why international cooperation on climate change is essential'.

The international community convened for the first time to discuss how to reconcile worldwide economic development with protection of the environment in Rio de Janeiro in June 1992, at the United Nations Conference on Environment and Development (generally known as Earth Summit). As illustrated by the Britannica (2019b),

> the Summit was the largest gathering of world leaders as of 1992, with 117 heads of state and representatives of 178 nations in all attending. By means of treaties and other documents signed at the conference, most of the world's nations nominally committed themselves to the pursuit of economic development in ways that would protect the earth's environment. The main documents agreed upon at the Earth Summit were the Convention on Biological Diversity (i.e., a binding treaty requiring nations to take inventories of their plants and wild animals and protect their endangered species) and the United Nations Framework Convention on Climate Change (UNFCCC).

The aim of the UNFCCC is to stabilise GHG concentrations in the atmosphere at a level that prevents dangerous anthropogenic disturbance of the climate system. All UNFCCC parties have an obligation to protect the climate system for the benefit of present and future generations, on an equitable basis and in relation to their common but differentiated responsibilities and respective capabilities. Developed countries are expected to take the lead in combating climate change and its adverse effects, while full consideration shall be given to the specific needs and special circumstances of developing countries, in particular those which are already exposed to the problem and which would be disproportionately or abnormally burdened under the Convention. A mechanism of regular meetings (i.e., Conferences of Parties – COP) has been established under the Convention to take stock of the implementation of the Convention and to take the necessary decisions to facilitate such implementation.

The UNFCCC treaty did not include any emissions reduction targets. Such targets were eventually established in an amendment to the UNFCCC: the Kyoto Protocol of 1997. The Protocol was based on a principle of common but differentiated historical responsibilities, and put an obligation to reduce GHG emissions only on developed countries. In particular, these countries had to ensure that, between 2008 and 2012, their anthropogenic emissions of six gases (carbon dioxide, methane, nitrogen oxide, hydrofluorocarbons, perfluorocarbons, and sulphur hexafluoride) would have been reduced by at least 5 per cent compared to 1990 levels. To this end, the Protocol attributed to each developed country a certain percentage of emissions. The Protocol therefore did not include developing countries in the list of countries obliged to reduce emissions, and not even the ones which – having important industrial apparatus such as China – were already important contributors to global GHG emissions. This disparity of obligations has led to the non-ratification of the Kyoto Protocol by the United States, at the time the world's main GHG emitter.

The inadequacy of the Kyoto Protocol led to an increasingly generalised lack of confidence in the ability of countries to agree on mechanisms on a global scale that could go beyond short-term policies and the exclusive pursuit of national interests. Nor did the poor results of the numerous meetings, including those held in the framework of the COP to the UNFCCC, to renew the commitments arising from the Protocol after the expiry of 2012 or to establish different and fairer mechanisms for sharing emission reductions contribute to improving the situation. There were also those who considered it unrealistic to agree on an effective global mechanism, even if there was a problem with a global dimension, and suggested a shift towards bilateral or regional strategies, in which countries with common interests would participate.

The fact that in December 2015, after complex negotiations, the Paris Agreement was adopted by the 195 parties of the UNFCCC substantially changed the international climate change regime. The Paris Agreement – which came into force on 4 November 2016 after the ratification of fifty-five countries accounting for 55 per cent of global GHG emissions – is the first-ever universal, legally binding, agreement on climate change. It aims at 'holding the increase in the global average temperature to well below 2 degrees Celsius above pre-industrial levels and pursuing efforts to limit the temperature increase to 1.5 degrees Celsius above pre-industrial levels, recognising that this would significantly reduce the risks and impacts of climate change' (UNFCCC, 2015, p.3).

The Paris Agreement is a complex international climate policy architecture, presenting both bottom-up and top-down elements. Bottom-up elements are the Nationally Determined Contributions (NDCs), being non-binding targets and actions voluntarily designed by countries. Top-down elements are the centralised oversight, guidance, and coordination architecture of the Agreement. The Paris Agreement is therefore a legal hybrid, blending non-binding emissions targets with binding elements of accountability (e.g., the revision of NDCs every five years in view of increasing their level of ambition). The Paris Agreement therefore bets on the force of rising norms and ambitions rather than legally binding and effective rules to achieve its aims. It remains a risky bet, particularly when considering that about 78 per cent of the NDCs – notably of developing countries – contained within the Agreement are conditional to external financial and technical support. The Paris Agreement thus provides an important framework to tackle climate change, albeit we will not know about ultimate success of the Agreement for many years, as international cooperation is important, but actions ultimately have to be undertaken at national levels.

9.6   KEY TAKEAWAYS

Introduction to Climate Change

- Climate change entails a long-term change in the earth's weather patterns or average climate.
- Global warming is anthropogenic, and it is mainly due to fossil fuel combustion.
- Global temperature has risen approximately 1 degree Celsius above pre-industrial levels.
- Among GHG emissions, CO_2 is by far the most important accounting for 76% of the total.
- Today, China, the United States, and the EU are the world's top three emitters.
- The United States emits 17 metric tonnes of CO_2 per capita, while China emits 7 metric tonnes.

Climate Change Mitigation

- Mitigation involves reducing the flow of GHG emissions into the atmosphere.
- This can be done by reducing sources of these or by enhancing the 'sinks' that store these gases.
- Paris Agreement aims at keeping the increase in global temperatures to well below 2 degrees.
- Switching the global energy system from fossil fuels to renewables is a key mitigation action.
- Energy efficiency and energy conservation are also key mitigation actions.
- Afforestation and reforestation contribute to the sequestration of CO_2 from the atmosphere.
- Carbon capture, utilisation, and storage can reduce emissions in industry and power generation.
- Geoengineering refers to large-scale artificial interventions in the earth's climate system.
- Food consumption patterns are key to climate change; cows are the third largest GHG emitters.

Climate Change Adaptation

- Measures to adapt to climate change impacts are crucial in certain sectors depending on climate.
- An example is the construction of flood defences and artificial dykes to cope with sea-level rise.
- Adaptation measures vary widely according to sectors and areas of implementation.
- Costs of such preventive actions is less onerous than those resulting from the damage.
- Adaptation must be planned with appropriate strategies at local, regional, and national levels.
- Adaptation is place- and context-specific, with no one-size-fits-all approach for reducing risks.

Carbon Pricing

- Application of a cost to CO_2 emissions in order to encourage emitters to reduce their emissions.
- Sensible carbon price gives economic signal to emitters and stimulates low-carbon innovation.
- Carbon tax system entails the imposition of a tax on each unit of emissions.
- Cap-and-trade system sets a maximum level of emissions and distributes emissions permits.
- To achieve Paris targets, US$40–80/$tCO_2$ by 2020 and US$50–100/$tCO_2$ by 2030 are needed.
- In 2018, pricing initiatives covered 20 per cent of global emissions, and with less than US$10/$tCO_2$.
- Public and private organisations are using internal carbon pricing to guide decision-making.

International Climate Regime

- Climate change is a 'global commons' problem.
- Being a classic free-rider problem, international cooperation is essential in the field.
- International community first addressed the problem in the 1992 Rio's Earth Summit.

- UNFCCC was established in Rio in view of stabilising GHG concentrations in atmosphere.
- First GHG emissions reduction targets were introduced by the Kyoto Protocol in 1997.
- Kyoto was based on the principle of common but differentiated historical responsibilities.
- Kyoto introduced an obligation to reduce GHG emissions only for developed countries.
- In 2015, the Paris Agreement was adopted by the 195 parties to the UNFCCC.
- It is the first-ever universal agreement on climate change.
- It aims at holding the increase in global temperature to well below 2 degrees Celsius.
- It aims at pursuing efforts to limit the temperature increase to 1.5 degrees Celsius.
- It is based on voluntary and non-binding nationally determined contributions.
- It is a legal hybrid, blending non-binding emissions targets with binding procedures.
- It bets on the force of rising ambitions rather than legally binding rules to achieve its aims.
- While international cooperation is essential, key climate action will be at national levels.

10 In-Depth Focus 2: Energy Access in Africa

Africa is on the move.[1] Since 2000, the continent has seen rapid economic growth (e.g., with real GDP growth rates outperforming other major regional economic blocs), improving social conditions (e.g., with falling infant mortality rates and rising life expectancies) and progressive political liberalisation (e.g., if in the 1990s only about 5 per cent of African nations were considered to be democracies, today only a handful of the fifty-five African states do not have a multiparty constitutional system). In this context, making energy reliable and widely affordable for the population has been and continues to be a key challenge in the continent (Hafner et al., 2018).

In energy terms, Africa can be divided into three different zones – defined by radically different levels of energy access (Table 10.1). North Africa is almost entirely electrified and most households also have access to clean cooking technologies. The situation is similar in South Africa, which is predominantly electrified. In the rest of sub-Saharan Africa (SSA)[2], however, most people have no access to electricity – 573 million in 2017 – and still rely on solid biomass for cooking – 900 million in 2017 (IEA et al., 2019).

In the case of electricity, it should also be emphasised that – beyond access – an important problem is the quality of access. For instance, wide disparities in electricity consumption levels exist

---

[1]   This chapter develops, enlarges, and updates previous analyses carried out by the author in Tagliapietra (2017c), Tagliapietra and Bazilian (2019), as well as in Hafner, Tagliapietra, and de Strasser (2018).

[2]   Throughout the chapter, 'SSA' will be used to refer to the sub-Saharan region excluding South Africa. Any reference to the 'subcontinent' will indicate the whole region.

Table 10.1 *Africa: Three different energy zones (share of population, 2016)*

	Access to electricity	Access to clean cooking
North Africa	100%	99%
Sub-Saharan Africa (excl. South Africa)	42%	12%
South Africa	86%	83%

Source: author's elaboration on International Energy Agency, Energy Access database, accessed in June 2019.

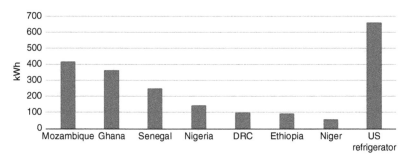

FIGURE 10.1 Electricity consumption per capita in selected African countries, 2016
Source: author's elaboration International Energy Agency, World Energy Balances database, accessed in June 2019 and US Department of Energy (2019).

between populations with access to electricity in SSA, and in other world regions. Just to provide an example, in Nigeria the average person consumes 140 kWh per year of electricity. This compares to 4,300 kWh/year of the average Chinese, to 6,000 kWh/year of the average European and to 13,000 kWh/year of the average American.[3] To put it even clearer, in many SSA countries an average person consumes 10 times less electricity than a refrigerator cooling coke bottles in a random kitchen in the United States (Figure 10.1).

---

3   World Bank, World Development Indicators database, accessed in June 2019.

Energy access in SSA thus represents the key energy issue in the continent. Energy access is a fundamental prerequisite for human development. Without energy, our lives would be dramatically different: we couldn't light our homes, access clean water, provide quality health care, operate machinery, or use technology to instantly communicate with the world. This fact is intuitive, but it has also been formally illustrated by a wide range of empirical studies. Looking at different country-cases around the world, various studies have indeed illustrated the correlation between energy consumption – and notably electricity consumption – and economic growth.[4] Likewise, several studies have also illustrated the causal effects of access to electricity on labour market, household welfare, and business activities.[5] Lack of access to modern energy solutions hinders socio-economic development, and it even represents a primary cause of mortality due to indoor household air pollution resulting from the utilisation of solid biomass for cooking. Overcoming the barrier of access to electricity and clean cooking thus represents a fundamental prerequisite to unleash the subcontinent's socio-economic potential.

From an energy demand perspective, it should firstly be noted that while SSA accounts for 14 per cent of the world population, it only account for 4.5 per cent of global primary energy demand (IEA, 2017b). The residential sector leads SSA's energy sector, implying that more productive sectors like industry and transport consume small amounts of energy (i.e., not only if compared to OECD countries, but also to other developing regions). This reflects a deep infrastructural gap: the penetration of railways, paved roads, and ports is very low in the subcontinent, as is the diffusion of energy distribution systems. The implications of this infrastructural underdevelopment include low human mobility and low accessibility of goods (including among others, fuels and energy equipment), which in turn explains the low

---

[4]   Bonan et al. (2017).

[5]   See, for instance, Bensch et al. (2011); Bernanrd (2012); Chakvravorty et al. (2014); Dasso and Fernandez (2015); Dinkelman (2011); Khandker et al. (2012); Rud (2012); van de Walle et al. (2013).

levels of productive energy use. In SSA, the share of electricity in total energy consumption remains very low, and electricity is mainly consumed to power two key industrial activities: mining and refining, while the rest is more or less equally distributed between services and the residential sector. To a certain extent, small businesses like carpentry or tailoring can get by with little or no electricity, but of course scaling them up becomes impossible without it, and it is impossible to start industrial activities without access to it. As electrification tends to develop around centres of demand that can function as anchor loads for the benefit of surrounding communities, the small consumption of productive sectors is clearly a missed opportunity for broader development, and electrification in particular.

On the supply side, solid biomass (i.e., fuelwood, charcoal, and dung) dominates SSA's energy sector. This is in contrast with North Africa and South Africa, where the biggest part of the energy supply comes from fossil fuels – notably oil and gas in North Africa and coal in South Africa. This is due to the fact that free or very cheap fuel is simply more appealing to low-income users: fuelwood can be directly harvested or bought for a cheap price in local markets, while agricultural waste is produced at home or farm. Even in the event that the price of charcoal and firewood increases, other alternatives typically remain more expensive – or just not available. This reliance on solid biomass has strongly negative human, environmental, and in turn economic, consequences. Indoor air pollution caused by the inefficient use of solid biomass for cooking kills around 600 thousand people every year, and as population increases this number follows. Women and young children are the most affected by air pollution because they spend the longest time next to the stove while food is being cooked. Also, women and girls are often those in charge of household management and this includes the collection of water and energy. All in all, they can spend several hours a day fetching water and fuelwood and preparing food, tasks that keep them out of school or employment, and ultimately contribute to hinder women's empowerment and socio-economic development. This problem concerns not only rural populations: worryingly, biomass holds a significant share in cities as well, where other fuels are more accessible. Charcoal is in many cases a more convenient choice than fuelwood for urban households because it is more accessible far from forests: it has a higher energy content, and it is easier to transport and commercialise. In fact, around 80 per cent of urban households in SSA use charcoal. But charcoal is often a product of fuelwood, and its production process can be highly inefficient. In this context, the penetration of fossil fuel–based cooking (e.g., with LPG or kerosene) is limited, and largely concentrated in a few countries.

SSA's energy access challenge should also be considered in view of the subcontinent demographic trends. Demographers have indeed long observed a continued, sometimes accelerated, population growth in SSA, with no sign of a reversal in fertility rates. According to United Nations projections, following these trends, by 2100, the African population could reach 4.7 billion, or about 40 per cent of the forecasted global population of 11 billion.[6] Today, Africa is 'still' at 1.2 billion, but the population grows so fast (and urban planning and infrastructure so slow in comparison) that challenges like overcrowding, traffic congestion, pollution, and localised resource depletion are already worrying. That is, booming populations and urbanisation, industrialisation, and expansion of the middle class, will require more energy, putting further pressure on the already vast challenge of energy access in the subcontinent.

10.2 FOSTERING ACCESS TO ELECTRICITY

Responding to SSA's electrification challenge requires comprehensive action, targeting both on-grid and off-grid solutions. First, SSA's on-grid electricity generation, transmission, and distribution infrastructure should be substantially enhanced and expanded. The current infrastructure is either insufficient or unreliable, with unavailability running at about 540 hours per year on average (IEA, 2014b). Several

---

[6]   United Nations, World Population Prospects database, accessed in June 2019.

factors are behind this, such as drought affecting hydropower capacity, poor maintenance causing power plants to fall into disrepair, lack of reliable fuel supply, and insufficient transmission and distribution capacity. As a result, blackouts and brownouts are the norm in all SSA countries. This clearly represents a major barrier to SSA economic and social development. In order to meet future electricity demand growth, SSA's on-grid electricity infrastructure has to be reinforced, modernised, and expanded. This has to happen at the national and regional levels. Developing SSA's four regional power pools (i.e., Southern Africa, Western Africa, Central Africa, and Eastern Africa) will be key to the full exploitation of SSA's vast untapped potential for both large-scale hydropower and gas.

In parallel with on-grid solutions, alternative solutions such as off-grid systems, mini-grid systems, and back-up generators represent an increasingly important element of electricity generation in SSA. Diesel-fuelled back-up generators are a traditional part of SSA's electricity landscape, but use of new off-grid and mini-grid systems based on solar photovoltaic, small hydropower, and small wind is rapidly expanding across the continent. These solutions are very important because they represent the most viable means of access to electricity for the large rural population that is distant from the grid.

SSA countries should lead their own energy transformations. They have the resources, but this potential can only be unleashed by reforming the governance of their energy sectors. In particular, electricity utilities (which are generally state owned) and energy subsidies should be structurally reformed across the subcontinent.

SSA's electricity utilities have failed to develop flexible energy systems to provide firms with a reliable power supply and people with access to electricity. This is mainly the result of governments often viewing electricity utilities as opportunities for political patronage and vehicles for corruption. Changing this situation would be a fundamental prerequisite to unleashing the SSA energy transformation. As shown by Trimble et al. (2016), across SSA, only the utilities of two countries fully cover their operational and capital expenditures. All other SSA utilities run in quasi-fiscal deficit (i.e., defined as the difference between the actual revenue collected and the revenue required to fully recover the operating costs of production and capital depreciation), and thus need to be subsidised by the state. Reform is the only way to reduce these deficits and make utilities financially viable. To reach operational efficiency, utilities should reduce transmission, distribution, and bill collection losses while tackling overstaffing. Utilities then need to increase tariffs, starting with their large- and medium-sized customers, for whom affordability is not as significant a challenge as for small-consumption households. The introduction of innovative solutions, such as prepaid meters, could also improve overall revenue collection. Finally, in order to reform electricity utilities and ensure implementation, SSA countries should create robust and independent regulatory bodies with the authority to hold electricity utilities to account.

SSA countries spend about USD 25 billion each year in energy subsidies (IMF, 2015). This substantial amount of budgetary resource is mainly used to subsidise inefficient and wasteful electricity utilities and, in certain cases, to subsidise old forms of energy, such as kerosene. Redirecting these resources into productive energy investments would be a vital step in reshaping SSA's energy systems. There are two main reasons why energy subsidies should be reformed. First, energy subsidies are inequitable. Being universal rather than targeted schemes, energy subsidies in SSA mostly benefit higher-income groups, which consume the most. Electricity subsidies are particularly regressive because connection to the electricity grid is highly skewed towards higher-income groups. Second, energy subsidies are profoundly detrimental for the development of energy systems. Subsidies create disincentives for maintenance or investment in the energy sector, perpetuating energy shortages and low levels of access. Therefore, energy subsidies should be reformed across SSA, to allow for better use of budgetary resources for pro-poor and development spending and to facilitate the expansion of electricity output. As shown by experiences elsewhere (IMF, 2013), reforming energy sub-sides is challenging, but possible.

Putting the governance of the SSA energy sector in order thus represents the starting point for expanding the region's electricity systems. Without such reforms, international energy companies and investors would have no incentive to enter SSA energy markets. For this reason, SSA governments should be the first movers. Then, support of the international community will be necessary to ensure progress, particularly in terms of off-grid rural electrification.

Investing in on-grid, utility-scale, projects is indeed relatively easier for energy companies and investors than investing in off-grid projects, as high densities of electricity demand guarantee more stable revenue streams. Should sound reforms of electricity utilities and energy subsidies be put in place, there should be no major problem in the future to ensure the bankability of the expansion of on-grid electricity infrastructure in SSA. It will be far more problematic to ensure the development of the small-grid and off-grid solutions that are needed to bring electricity to the three-fifths of the SSA population who live in rural areas, including areas that are unlikely to be reached by the national grid, because of either geographical constraints and/or the lack of business cases for grid expansion.

Grids, mini-grids, and stand-alone systems indeed have very different underpinning economic models even though, technically, at least, grids and mini-grids look similar. A grid brings power from a number of centres of production to many users through a capillary system of transmission and distribution lines, hence it basically differs from a mini-grid in terms of the amount of power that it carries to users. However, building grids require huge financial effort (and risk) so that this business is ultimately in the hands of governments and public companies, while mini-grids can be built by private companies, local entrepreneurs, or even cooperatives of users, as long as there is a clear return on investment and an enabling business environment to support them. Stand-alone systems, finally, are typically distributed by private companies to single users. The business model that is proving to be most successful so far in Africa is that of solar photovoltaic modules that users rent and gradually come to own, through pay-as-you-go payment schemes.

With the declining costs and better performance of small-scale hydro installations, solar photovoltaic, and wind turbines, and with declining costs and technological improvements in electricity storage and control systems, small-grid and off-grid renewable energy systems could become game-changers for rural electrification in SSA – in a decentralised and modular manner. However, these innovative energy solutions face two major barriers. First, they are characterised by low operating expenses and by high up-front capital investment expenditure. This is a major barrier to investment, because in an environment like SSA, country, regulatory, and commercial risks substantially increase the expectations investors have of returns, and thus any project's cost of capital. This discourages capital-intensive energy options and encourages less capital-intensive, conventional energy technologies. Second, innovative energy solutions are characterised by high transaction costs. For instance, the transaction cost per kWh of electricity produced by a hydropower plant will be lower than the sum of the costs of the hundreds of transactions required for comparable capacity from solar photovoltaics or wind power. In this context, reforming the governance of SSA's energy markets will not be sufficient to attract international investors into small-grid and off-grid energy solutions in rural areas. International support will be necessary to crowd-in private investors, most notably via public–private partnerships.

10.3   FOSTERING ACCESS TO CLEAN COOKING

Policies aimed at modernising access to clean cooking across SSA have so far proved largely insufficient, and the challenge of universal access to clean cooking still receives less attention than that of electrification. One of the reasons for this is that there has been no real market breakthrough of innovative stand-alone technologies (e.g., solar or biogas cookers) yet, and the alternatives to traditional cooking today are more or less the same as we had decades ago, most importantly petroleum-based fuels and electricity. In other words, the main challenges of clean cooking remain improving the logistics, and increasing the affordability and cultural acceptance of alternative solutions to rudimentary stoves.

Providing an alternative to solid biomass for everyone means stimulating the use of all available alternatives. Fossil fuels, and in particular LPG, have an important role to play. Today, LPG is already the most utilised alternative to solid biomass in SSA; still, only 7 per cent of SSA's population have access to it, and LPG use is mostly concentrated in a few countries: Angola, Ghana, Nigeria, and Sudan (IEA, 2017b). LPG can be used for multiple purposes, including transport, but in SSA its real potential probably lies in its use as a modern cooking fuel – as well as, once available, as heat for small income-generating activities like food processing, brick making, metal casting, and so on. Together with ethanol, methanol, biogas, and electricity, LPG is among the few cooking fuels that can meet the indoor pollution standards set by the World Health Organization, and several studies point at its suitability for cooking in the developing world. In particular, when compared to kerosene, which is the second most utilised fossil fuel–based cooking fuel, LPG is much less hazardous to handle. However, the case for LPG can – and should – be made even without claiming that it is the best available option. LPG thus is a valuable option, though of course its wide uptake requires a significant policy effort. In fact, consumers (both urban and rural) base their choices not only on the availability of alternatives, but also on opportunity costs and cooking preferences. That is, subsidies play a major role in determining which fuel is preferred. The experience of Senegal is emblematic: after a successful strategy, LPG ended up reaching as much as 70 per cent of urban users, but as soon as the government decided to lift subsidies there was a massive drop in consumption. If the ambition is to bring LPG cooking also to rural users, the most critical elements of success will be the existence of far-reaching LPG value chains on the one hand and the effectiveness of targeted pro-poor cross-subsidisation on the other. Particularly for rural customers, accessibility remains highly problematic. The distribution of LPG from production sites or import stations to the single users requires the careful handling, storage, and transport of pressurised gas (in comparison, the transport of liquid kerosene is less complicated). Clearly, this type of supply chain cannot be improvised for safety reasons, and a multitude of factors like the poor state of roads in rural SSA or the handling of pressurised cylinders by untrained people, can become significant elements of risk. Despite these issues, there is ample evidence that – once available and affordable – LPG responds to the needs of customers, which is not trivial. For instance, the experience of South Africa shows that (subsidised) LPG cooking can take root even where electrical cooking is available and cheap. At the same time in India – where the use of solid biomass is also widespread – LPG seems to be responsible for the first signs of reduction in solid biomass consumption after decades of promotion of improved biomass stoves, which ended up delivering poor results (IEA 2017b). LPG is not a new solution, and its promotion in different parts of the world has already resulted in both success stories and failures. Some SSA countries, like Ghana, Cameroon, and Senegal, are already embarking on ambitious LPG programmes, but experience is also accumulating on larger scales in countries like China, Brazil, India, and Indonesia as well as in North Africa, where LPG is commonly used. In sum, promoting LPG requires a high level of economic, infrastructural, and logistic commitment, but it is also a fairly effective solution not to be missed for resolving the pressing problem of unsafe cooking. Notably, women are the best-positioned promoters of clean cooking solutions because they are the first beneficiaries of improved indoor pollution and reduced time for cooking, which is why linking LPG programmes to gender-focused and women-led development initiatives could be crucial.

The effect of electrification can also have a major impact on the way people cook: today, for instance, electricity is already widely used in urban areas in South Africa, and assuming sufficient affordability, it can become a key fuel in the future cooking fuel mix of other countries too.

Modern forms of bioenergy, including the product of biomass-residues treatment (e.g., biogas, pellets) and liquid biofuels (i.e., bioethanol and biodiesel) are potentially very promising options, although their theoretical potential is often restricted by a number of factors such as high costs, complexity of fuel production, storage, and transport, or even competition with food. Pushing these solutions will require an explicit effort to establish whole new value chains for products coming from agriculture, forestry, and waste management.

Advanced biomass stoves can offer an important transition technology that reduces emissions levels common to traditional biomass stoves. Other benefits of more efficient cooking appliances include fuel cost or collection savings, injury reduction, and better temperature and indoor environment control.

It should be noted that the use of fuelwood is difficult to eradicate even where alternatives are available: it is possible, and indeed common, to own more than one type of stove and fuel ('fuel-stacking') and using one or another depending on fuel availability, price, or even to satisfy food taste preferences. However, this challenge should be addressed, as the benefits of achieving universal access to clean cooking would be immense and would include improvement of health conditions, local job creation, and gender empowerment. Furthermore, it would also reduce deforestation (i.e., Africa lost 12 per cent of its forest area between 1990 and 2015), in turn contributing to global climate mitigation.

10.4   THE ROLE OF INTERNATIONAL INSTITUTIONS
IN THE FIELD

International institutions, such as multilateral development banks and national development agencies, could channel international private investments into Africa's energy sector by establishing dedicated blended finance tools and/or risk-sharing mechanisms.

The combination of political risks (e.g., corruption), commercial risks (e.g., capacity of consumers to pay their bills), the lack of stable power market regulatory frameworks, and the lack of adequate power infrastructure are factors that currently discourage private investment. On the other hand, international official development assistance and other official flows to the African power sector have quadrupled over the last decade, increasing from USD 2 billion in 2005 to USD 8 billion in 2015 (Tagliapietra and Bazilian, 2019).

The World Bank Group, EU institutions and member states, and the African Development Bank disbursed most of the funds in the sector, while other players – including the United States, the Climate Investment Funds, the Arab Fund for Economic and Social Development, and the OPEC Fund for International Development played a far smaller role.

Investors have focused on different energy sectors, with the World Bank Group investing mainly in non-renewable electricity generation, the EU in renewable electricity generation, and the African Development Bank in electricity transmission and distribution infrastructure.

China has also played a substantial role in Africa's energy sector, but that country does not disclose precise information about its development finance flows to Africa, and only unofficial estimates exist. According to IEA (2017b), Chinese companies (90 per cent of which are state owned) were responsible for 30 per cent of new power capacity in SSA between 2010 and 2015, with a total investment of around USD 13 billion. Chinese contractors have built or are contracted to build 17 gigawatts of power generation capacity in SSA from 2010 to 2020, equivalent to 10 per cent of existing installed capacity. These projects are widespread across SSA, in at least thirty-seven of the region's fifty-four countries. Chinese contractors primarily focus on large projects involving traditional forms of energy like hydropower (49 per cent of projects 2010–20), coal (20 per cent), and gas (19 per cent); their involvement in modern renewables remains marginal (7 per cent).

Africa is also part of China's 'One Belt, One Road' initiative. That initiative includes not only the 'Silk Road economic belt' stretching from Asia to Europe, but also the 'maritime Silk Road' linking China and Europe via the Indian Ocean littoral and East Africa. China has invested about USD 128 billion in energy projects in Belt-and-Road countries since 2001. Of this investment, USD 4.1 billion has targeted Africa – predominantly to develop coal-fired power plants. In this initiative, China thus seems not to consider the environmental and social issues that currently prevent the majority of international financing institutions from supporting coal projects in Africa. China's focus on coal and big hydropower projects makes international financing institutions' support for solar and wind energy projects in Africa even more important.

The increasing international support for Africa's energy sector is good news for the continent, but it is not sufficient to bridge the gap between current investments and those required to provide universal energy access by 2030. The most promising way to bridge this gap is to scale up international private investment; and for that to occur, domestic reforms are needed to create a viable and attractive investment environment.

International financial assistance for Africa's energy sector should also evolve to assert more leverage over private investors, and over African governments by incentivising energy market reforms. In this regard, the main issue is coordination. Around sixty international initiatives – originating in Europe, America, the Middle East, and Asia – are currently contributing to the development of energy markets and the improvement of access to power in Africa. As outlined by the Africa Progress Panel (2015), Africa's energy needs are poorly served by such a fragmented system. This is so because funding is generally delivered through overly bureaucratic structures that combine high transaction costs with low impact, resulting in most finance being earmarked for small-scale projects rather than sizeable programmes.

Global financing initiatives for Africa's electrification are broad in scope and eclectic in focus. Taken in isolation, this might be considered good news, as it signals widespread global support for Africa's electrification. However, when considering that 92 per cent of the last decade's international financial support to Africa's electrification came from only three sources (World Bank Group, African Development Bank, and EU), there likely remains a coordination issue between these large well-established funders and the multitude of new initiatives.

The EU's presence appears particularly fragmented, while the World Bank Group, the African Development Bank, and the United States have streamlined their activities, focusing resources on a few initiatives, and thus do not appear to be contributing to the fragmentation problem. For instance, the African Development Bank, in addition to its traditional financing tools, has established two initiatives: 'The New Deal on Energy for Africa' (a public–private partnership between the Bank, African governments, and the global private sector aimed at establishing innovative financing for energy projects), and 'Africa50' (an infrastructure fund owned by the Bank, African governments, and global institutional investors, created to mobilise long-term savings to promote infrastructure development). The United States mainly acts through 'Power Africa', a public–private partnership launched in 2013 involving twelve US government agencies, African governments, other multilateral partners, and more than one hundred private-sector partners including energy companies, investment banks, equity funds, and institutional investors.

Energy access is a major requirement for socioeconomic development in SSA. Achieving it requires joint action by SSA countries and the international community. SSA countries should reform the governance of their energy sectors – in particular, of power utilities and energy subsidies. Without this, they will not attract international private investment at the scale needed to achieve universal energy access by 2030.

International financial and development institutions need to offer more than financial support for SSA's energy development. Increased technical assistance is also critical. International institutions with solid experience in infrastructure financing could enhance Africa's 'soft' infrastructure of national governments and institutions by supporting the development of sound energy policies, regulations, incentive systems, sector reforms, corporate governance, and transparency and accountability best practices. Programmes like the 'New Deal on Energy for Africa' and 'Power Africa' are already contributing to this effort.

Calls for better coordination and cohesion in the development arena are ubiquitous, and there are relatively few success stories. Still, the way to make the most of the global financing initiatives for Africa's electrification could be to establish a coordination or information-sharing mechanism to better track the sector's rapid changes and keep key actors and stakeholders informed.

International financial support is particularly vital for the three-fifths of the SSA population living in rural areas. Developing small-grid and off-grid power solutions in rural areas is often highly challenging due to geographical or economic constraints. With declining costs and increasing performance for small hydro, solar photovoltaic, and wind power generation as well as electricity storage and control systems, small-grid and off-grid renewable energy systems could become game changers for SSA rural electrification, in a decentralised and modular manner. However, these innovative energy solutions face two major barriers. First, while their operating expenses are low, they require substantial up-front capital investment. In SSA, country, regulatory, and commercial risks substantially increase the return expectations of investors and thus any project's capital costs. This discourages capital-intensive energy options and encourages less-capital-intensive, conventional energy technologies. Second, they are characterised by high transaction costs. For instance, the transaction cost per kWh of electricity produced from a hydropower plant is lower than the sum of the costs of the hundreds of transactions required for comparable capacity from solar photovoltaic or wind power. International financing institutions could play a truly vital role in making a stronger case for investment in rural electrification solutions.

In addition to its relevance for SSA's socioeconomic development, electrification has important implications for climate change. The United Nations has predicted that Africa will experience greater population growth than any other region by 2050. Energy demand is likely to grow accordingly. Thus, ensuring a sustainable energy mix for Africa is crucial to avoiding a negative impact on climate, and efficiently supporting Africa's sustainable electrification should be seen by international actors as an important component of their overall climate change mitigation effort.

In this regard, the potential for a new global North–South financial cooperation should also be considered. Financial resources from Europe and North America could be invested in green assets in the global South, and notably in Africa. This would allow investors to earn higher returns, while helping to improve living conditions for the world's poorest and to mitigate climate change. It is up to African countries themselves to initiate this virtuous cycle – by making the reforms necessary to create a favourable investment environment.

10.5 KEY TAKEAWAYS

Energy Access: the Key Energy Issue in the Continent

- North Africa and South Africa are well electrified and with high shares of clean cooking.
- In sub-Saharan Africa (SSA), electrification rate is only 42 per cent and the clean cooking rate is 12 per cent.
- In many SSA countries, an average person consumes 10 times less electricity than a US fridge.
- SSA accounts for 14 per cent of global population but only for 4.5 per cent of global energy demand.
- SSA energy supply is dominated by solid biomass, which is socio-economically damaging.

Fostering Access to Electricity

- Responding to SSA's electrification challenge requires both on-grid and off-grid solutions.

- On-grid electricity infrastructure has to be reinforced and expanded across SSA.
- Off-grid solutions are the most viable means to reach rural populations.
- SSA electricity utilities are financially unsustainable and must be reformed to foster growth.
- SSA countries must switch resources from energy subsidies to productive investments.
- Good energy sector governance is key to attract international investments.

Fostering Access to Clean Cooking

- SSA clean cooking policies have so far not delivered satisfactory results.
- Key challenges in the field are logistics, affordability, and social acceptance of modern solutions.
- LPG, electricity, and modern bioenergy are all valid solutions depending on the circumstance.
- Advanced biomass stoves represent an important transition technology.

The Role of International Institutions in the Field

- International institutions play a key role, both in terms of financing and capacity building.
- Blended finance is key to leverage private investments in SSA, due to political/commercial risks.
- Capacity building is key to promote better governance and regulations.
- International support is particularly relevant to foster energy access in rural areas.
- Energy access in SSA represents a unique opportunity for global North–South cooperation.

Bibliography

Africa Progress Panel (2015), *Power People Planet: Seizing Africa's Energy and Climate Opportunities*, Africa Progress Report, Geneva, https://reliefweb .int/sites/reliefweb.int/files/resources/APP_REPORT_2015_FINAL_low1.pdf

Agora Energiewende (2015), *The European Power System in 2030: Flexibility Challenges and Integration Benefits*, www.agora-energiewende.de/en/publica tions/the-european-power-system-in-2030-flexibility-challenges-and-integration-benefits-2/

Aldy, J., and Stavins, R. (2011), *The Promise and Problems of Pricing Carbon: Theory and Experience*, National Bureau of Economic Research, Working Paper 17569, www.nber.org/papers/w17569.pdf

Asafu-Adjaye, J. (2000), 'The relationship between energy consumption, energy prices and economic growth: Time series evidence from Asian developing countries', *Energy Economics*, 22(6), 615–25.

Beblawi, H., and Luciani, G. (eds.) (1987), *The Rentier State: Nation, State and the Integration of the Arab World*, Croom Helm, London.

Ben Ali, M. S. (ed.) (2016), *Economic Development in the Middle East and North Africa: Challenges and Prospects*, Palgrave Macmillan, London.

Bensch, G., Kluve, J., and Peters, J. (2011), 'Impacts of rural electrification in Rwanda', *Journal of Development Effectiveness*, 3(4), 567–88.

Bernard, T. (2012), 'Impact analysis of rural electrification projects in sub-Saharan Africa ', *The World Bank Research Observer*, 27(1), 33–51.

Bilgili, F., Koçak, E., Bulut, Ü., and Sualp, M. N. (2016), 'How did the US economy react to shale gas production revolution? An advanced time series approach', *Energy*, 116, 963–77.

Bonan J., Pareglio, S., and Tavoni, M. (2017), 'Access to modern energy: a review of barriers, drivers and impacts', *Environment and Development Economics*, 22 (5), 491–516.

Bosch (2019), *Synthetic Fuels: The Next Revolution?*, www.bosch.com/stories/ synthetic-fuels/

BP (2018a), *Statistical Review of World Energy 2018*, London, www.bp.com/content/ dam/bp/business-sites/en/global/corporate/pdfs/energy-economics/statistical-review/bp-stats-review-2018-full-report.pdf

BP (2018b), *Energy Outlook 2018*, London, www.bp.com/content/dam/bp/business-sites/en/global/corporate/pdfs/energy-economics/energy-outlook/bp-energy-outlook-2018.pdf

BP (2019), *Oil Reserve Definitions*, www.bp.com/content/dam/bp/business-sites/en/global/corporate/pdfs/energy-economics/statistical-review/bp-stats-review-2019-oil-reserve-definitions.pdf

Britannica (2019a), *9 of the Biggest Oil Spills in History*, www.britannica.com/list/9-of-the-biggest-oil-spills-in-history

Britannica (2019b), *United Nations Conference on Environment and Development*, www.britannica.com/event/United-Nations-Conference-on-Environment-and-Development

British Library (2017), *James Blyth and the World's First Wind-Powered Generator*, London, https://blogs.bl.uk/science/2017/08/james-blyth-and-the-worlds-first-wind-powered-generator.html

Carbon Tracker (2018), *Statement on BP Energy Outlook 2018*, London, www.carbontracker.org/statement-bp-energy-outlook-2018/

Chakravorty, U., Pelli, M., and Marchand, B. (2014), 'Does the quality of electricity matter? Evidence from rural India', *Journal of Economic Behavior and Organization*, 107, 228–47.

CIA (Central Intelligence Agency) (2019), *The World Factbook*, www.cia.gov/library/publications/the-world-factbook/

Concawe (2019), *Review*, www.concawe.eu/wp-content/uploads/Concawe-Review-27-2-web-resolution-2.pdf

Crowther, T. W., Glick, H. B., Covey, K. R. et al. (2015), 'Mapping tree density at a global scale', *Nature*, 525(7568), 201–5.

Dadush, U., and Demertzis, M. (2018), *Youth Unemployment: Common Problem, Different Solutions?*, Bruegel Blogpost, November 29, Brussels, http://bruegel.org/2018/11/youth-unemployment-common-problem-different-solutions/

Dasso, R., and Fernandez, F. (2015), 'The effects of electrification on employment in rural Peru', *IZA Journal of Labor and Development*, 4(1).

Delbeke, J., and Vis, P. (2015), *EU Climate Policy Explained*, https://ec.europa.eu/clima/sites/clima/files/eu_climate_policy_explained_en.pdf

Dinkelman, T. (2011), 'The effects of rural electrification on employment: New evidence from South Africa', *The American Economic Review*, 101(7), 3078–108.

Dodson, J., Xiaoqiang L., Nan, S., et al. (2014), 'Use of coal in the Bronze Age in China', *The Holocene*, 24(5), 525–30.

Edenhofer, O., Flachsland, C., Jakob, M., and Lessmann, K. (2013), *The Atmosphere as a Global Commons: Challenges for International Cooperation and*

Governance, The Harvard Project on Climate Agreements, August 2013, Discussion Paper 13–58, www.belfercenter.org/sites/default/files/legacy/files/hpcadp58_edenhofer-flachsland-jakob-lessmann.pdf

EIA (Energy Information Administration) (2011), *The Geology of Natural Gas Resources*, www.eia.gov/todayinenergy/detail.php?id=110

EIA (Energy Information Administration) (2014), *World Oil Transit Chokepoints Critical to Global Energy Security*, www.eia.gov/todayinenergy/detail.php?id=18991

EIA (Energy Information Administration) (2017a), *Global Transportation Energy Consumption: Examination of Scenarios to 2040 using ITEDD*, www.eia.gov/analysis/studies/transportation/scenarios/pdf/globaltransportation.pdf

EIA (Energy Information Administration) (2017b), *World Oil Transit Chokepoints*, www.eia.gov/beta/international/regions-topics.php?RegionTopicID=WOTC

EIA (Energy Information Administration) (2018a), Europe's Liquefied Natural Gas Imports Have Increased Lately, but Remain below 2011 Peak, Washington, DC, www.eia.gov/todayinenergy/detail.php?id=37354

EIA (Energy Information Administration) (2018b), How Much Carbon Dioxide Is Produced When Different Fuels Are Burned?, Washington, DC, www.eia.gov/tools/faqs/faq.php?id=73&t=11

EIA (Energy Information Administration) (2018c), Annual Energy Outlook 2018 with Projections to 2050, Washington, DC, www.eia.gov/outlooks/aeo/

EIA (Energy Information Administration) (2019a), Levelized Cost and Levelized Avoided Cost of New Generation Resources in the Annual Energy Outlook 2019, Washington, DC, www.eia.gov/outlooks/aeo/pdf/electricity_generation.pdf

EIA (Energy Information Administration) (2019b), Oil: Crude and Petroleum Products, Washington, DC, www.eia.gov/energyexplained/index.php?page=oil_home

EIA (Energy Information Administration) (2019c), Energy Efficiency and Conservation, Washington, DC, www.eia.gov/energyexplained/index.php?page=about_energy_efficiency

EIA (Energy Information Administration) (2019c), Solar Thermal Power Plants: Basics, Washington, DC, www.eia.gov/energyexplained/print.php?page=solar_thermal_power_plants

Energy Charter (2007), *Putting a Price on Energy*, Brussels, https://energycharter.org/fileadmin/DocumentsMedia/Thematic/Oil_and_Gas_Pricing_2007_en.pdf

Eni (2013), Annual Report 2013, Rome, https://report.eni.com/annual-report-2013/en/annual-report/operating-and-financial-review.html

Eni (2018a), *World Oil Review 2018*, Rome, www.eni.com/en_IT/investors/global -energy-scenarios/world-oil -gas-review-eng.page

Eni (2018b), *World Gas and Renewables Review 2018*, Rome, www.eni.com/en_ IT/investors/global-energy-scenarios/world-gas -e-renewables-review-2018 .page

EPO (European Patent Office) (2016), *Energy Storage: Added Stability for Electrical Grids*, www.epo.org/news-issues/technology/sustainable-technologies/storage .html

European Commission (2019), *Energy Prices and Costs in Europe*, Brussels, https://ec.europa.eu/transparency/regdoc/rep/10102/2019/EN/SWD-2019-1-F1- EN-MAIN-PART-1.PDF

European Parliament (2016), *The Quest for Natural Gas Pipelines*, Brussels, www .europarl.europa.eu/RegData/etudes/STUD/2016/586626/EPRS_STU(2016)58 6626_EN.pdf

Eurostat (2019), *Glossary: Tonnes of Oil Equivalent (TOE)*, https://ec.europa.eu/ eurostat/statistics-explained/index.php/Glossary:Tonnes_of_oil_equivalent_ (toe)

Falchetta, G., Gernaatcd, D., Hunte, J., Sterlfgh, S. (2019), 'Hydropower dependency and climate change in sub-Saharan Africa: a nexus framework and evidence-based review', *Journal of Cleaner Production*, 231, 1399–417.

Fraunhofer (2019), *Photovoltaics Report*, Freiburg, www.ise.fraunhofer.de/con tent/dam/ise/de/documents/publications/studies/Photovoltaics-Report.pdf

Gao, Y., Gao, X., and Zhang, X. (2017), 'The 2 °C Global Temperature Target and the Evolution of the Long-Term Goal of Addressing Climate Change: from the United Nations Framework Convention on Climate Change to the Paris Agreement', *Engineering*, 3(2), 272–8.

Gates, B. (2018), *Climate Change and the 75% Problem*, GatesNotes, www.gatesnotes.com/Energy/My-plan-for-fighting-climate-change

Griffiths, S. (2017), 'A review and assessment of energy policy in the Middle East and North Africa region', *Energy Policy*, 102, 249–69.

G20 (2015), *Leaders' Communique' Agreed in Antalya*, http://g20.org.tr/g20- leaders-commenced-the-antalya-summit/

Hafner, M., and Tagliapietra, S. (2013), *The Globalization of Natural Gas Markets: New Challenges and Opportunities*, Claeys & Casteels, Deventer.

Hafner, M., and Tagliapietra, S. (eds.) (2017), *The European Gas Markets. Challenges and Opportunities*, Palgrave Macmillan, London.

Hafner, M., Tagliapietra, S., and de Strasser, L. (2018), *Energy in Africa: Challenges and Opportunities*, Springer, Berlin.

Hertog, S. (2013), *The Private Sector and Reform in the Gulf Cooperation Council*, London School of Economics, London, http://eprints.lse.ac.uk/54398/1/Hertog_2013.pdf

High-Level Commission on Carbon Pricing (2017), *Report of the High-Level Commission on Carbon Pricing*, International Bank for Reconstruction and Development, International Development Association, The World Bank, Washington, DC, https://static1.squarespace.com/static/54ff9c5ce4b0a53decccfb4c/t/59b7f2409f8dce5316811916/1505227332748/CarbonPricing_FullReport.pdf

Hydrogen Europe (2019), *Hydrogen Basics*, https://hydrogeneurope.eu/hydrogen-basics-0

Hvidt, M. (2013), *Economic Diversification in GCC Countries: Past Record and Future Trends*, London School of Economics, London, http://eprints.lse.ac.uk/55252/1/Hvidt%20final%20paper%2020.11.17_v0.2.pdf

IAEA (International Atomic Energy Agency) (2015), *Technology Roadmap: Nuclear Energy*, Vienna, www.oecd-nea.org/pub/techroadmap/techroadmap-2015.pdf

IAEA (International Atomic Energy Agency) (2018), *Charting the International Roadmap to a Demonstration Fusion Power Plant*, Vienna, www.iaea.org/newscenter/news/charting-the-international-roadmap-to-a-demonstration-fusion-power-plant

IAEA (International Atomic Energy Agency) (2019), *Power Reactor Information System*, Vienna, https://pris.iaea.org/PRIS/home.aspx

IEA (International Energy Agency) (2010), *Technology Roadmap Concentrating Solar Power*, IEA/OECD, Paris.

IEA (International Energy Agency) (2011), *Technology Roadmap Geothermal*, IEA/OECD, Paris.

IEA (International Energy Agency) (2012), *Technology Roadmap Hydropower*, IEA/OECD, Paris.

IEA (International Energy Agency) (2013), *Energy Efficiency Market Report*, IEA/OECD, Paris.

IEA (International Energy Agency) (2014a), *Capturing the Multiple Benefits of Energy Efficiency*, IEA/OECD, Paris.

IEA (International Energy Agency) (2014b), *Africa Energy Outlook*, IEA/OECD, Paris.

IEA (International Energy Agency) (2015), *Technology Roadmap Nuclear*, IEA/OECD, Paris.

IEA (International Energy Agency) (2017a), *Technology Roadmap Delivering Sustainable Bioenergy*, IEA/OECD, Paris.

IEA (International Energy Agency) (2017b), *Energy Efficiency*, IEA/OECD, Paris.

IEA (International Energy Agency) (2018a), *CO$_2$ Emissions from Fuel Combustion 2018*, IEA/OECD, Paris.

IEA (International Energy Agency) (2018b), *World Energy Outlook 2018*, IEA/OECD, Paris.

IEA (International Energy Agency) (2018c), *The Future of Petrochemicals*, IEA/OECD, Paris.

IEA (International Energy Agency) (2018d), *Gas 2018*, IEA/OECD, Paris.

IEA (International Energy Agency) (2018e), *Coal 2018*, IEA/OECD, Paris.

IEA (International Energy Agency) (2018f), *Renewables 2018*, IEA/OECD, Paris.

IEA (International Energy Agency) (2018g), *Offshore Energy*, IEA/OECD, Paris.

IEA (International Energy Agency) (2018h), *Outlook for Producer Economies*, IEA/OECD, Paris.

IEA (International Energy Agency) (2018i), *Future of Trucks*, IEA/OECD, Paris.

IEA (International Energy Agency) (2019a), *Fuel Economy in Major Car Markets*, IEA/OECD, Paris.

IEA (International Energy Agency) (2019b), *Hydrogen. Tracking Clean Energy Progress*, IEA/OECD, Paris.

IEA (International Energy Agency) (2019c), *Carbon capture, utilisation and storage. A critical tool in the climate energy toolbox*, IEA/OECD, Paris.

IEA (International Energy Agency) (2019d), *What Is Energy Security?*, www.iea.org/topics/energysecurity/whatisenergysecurity/

IEA (International Energy Agency) (2019e), *Key World Energy Statistics*, www.iea.org/statistics/kwes/supply/

IEA (International Energy Agency) (2019f), *Methodology: Defining Energy Access*, www.iea.org/energyaccess/methodology/

IEA (International Energy Agency) (2019g), *Bioenergy and Biofuels*, www.iea.org/topics/renewables/bioenergy/

IEA (International Energy Agency) (2019h), *Energy Efficiency Statistics*, www.iea.org/statistics/efficiency/

IEA (International Energy Agency) and FAO (Food and Agriculture Organization) (2017), *How2Guide for Bioenergy*, IEA/OCED, Paris.

IEA (International Energy Agency), IRENA, UNSD, WB, WHO (2019), *2019 Tracking SDG 7: The Energy Progress Report 2019*, Washington DC, http://trackingsdg7.esmap.org/data/files/download-documents/2019%20Tracking%20SDG7%20Report.pdf

IFC (International Finance Corporation) (2017), *Overcoming Constraints to SME Development in MENA Countries and Enhancing Access to Finance*, Washington, DC, http://documents.worldbank.org/curated/en/581841491392213535/Overcoming-constraints-to-SME-development-in-MENA-countries-and

-enhancing-access-to-finance-IFC-advisory-services-in-the-Middle-East-and-North-Africa

IGU (International Gas Union) (2018), *Wholesale Gas Price Survey 2018*, www.igu.org/sites/default/files/node-news_item-field_file/IGU_Wholesale%20Gas%20Price%20Survey%202018%20Final.pdf

ILO (International Labour Organization) (2018), *World Employment Social Outlook 2018*, Geneva, www.ilo.org/wcmsp5/groups/public/–dgreports/–dco mm/–publ/documents/publication/wcms_670542.pdf

IMF (International Monetary Fund) (2013), *Energy Subsidy Reform in Sub-Saharan Africa: Experiences and Lessons*, Washington, DC, www.imf.org/external/pubs/ft/dp/2013/afr1302.pdf

IMF (International Monetary Fund) (2015), *How Large Are Global Energy Subsidies?*, Washington, DC, www.imf.org/en/Publications/WP/Issues/2016/12/31/How-Large-Are-Global-Energy-Subsidies-42940

IMF (International Monetary Fund) (2016), *Economic Diversification in Oil-Exporting Arab Countries*, Washington, DC, www.imf.org/external/np/pp/eng/2016/042916.pdf

IMF (International Monetary Fund) (2017), *Public Wage Bills in the Middle East and Central Asia*, Washington DC, www.imf.org/en/Publications/Departmental-Papers-Policy-Papers/Issues/2018/01/09/Public-Wage-Bills-in-the-Middle-East-and-Central-Asia-45535

IMF (International Monetary Fund) (2019), *Financial Inclusion of Small and Medium-Sized Enterprises in the Middle East and Central Asia*, Washington DC, www.imf.org/en/Publications/Departmental-Papers-Policy-Papers/Issues/2019/02/11/Financial-Inclusion-of-Small-and-Medium-Sized-Enterprises-in-the-Middle-East-and-Central-Asia-46335

IPCC (International Panel on Climate Change) (2007), *Climate Change 2007 – The Physical Science Basis*, Cambridge University Press, Cambridge, www.ipcc.ch/site/assets/uploads/2018/05/ar4_wg1_full_report-1.pdf

IPCC (International Panel on Climate Change) (2011a), *Renewable Energy Sources and Climate Change Mitigation*, Geneva, www.ipcc.ch/report/renewable-energy-sources-and-climate-change-mitigation/

IPCC (International Panel on Climate Change) (2011b), *Fact Sheet: Climate Change Science – the Status of Climate Change Science Today*, Geneva, https://unfccc.int/files/press/backgrounders/application/pdf/press_factsh_science.pdf

IPCC (International Panel on Climate Change) (2012), *A Special Report of Working Groups I and II of the Intergovernmental Panel on Climate Change (IPCC)*, Geneva, www.ipcc.ch/site/assets/uploads/2018/03/SREX-Chap8_FINAL-1.pdf

IPCC (International Panel on Climate Change) (2014), *Climate Change 2014: Synthesis Report*, Geneva, www.ipcc.ch/site/assets/uploads/2018/05/SYR_AR5_FINAL_full_wcover.pdf

IPCC (International Panel on Climate Change) (2018), *Global Warming of 1.5°C: Summary for Policymakers*, Geneva, www.ipcc.ch/site/assets/uploads/sites/2/2018/07/SR15_SPM_version_stand_alone_LR.pdf

IRENA (International Renewable Energy Agency) (2012), *Water Desalination Using Renewable Energy*, Abu Dhabi, www.irena.org/-/media/Files/IRENA/Agency/Publication/2015/IRENA-ETSAP-Tech-Brief-I12-Water-Desalination.ashx?la=en&hash=9AFC238EA8FAEB8CDBB5305D77E4624A26B1D239

IRENA (International Renewable Energy Agency) (2016a), *Scaling up Variable Renewable Power: the Role of Grid Codes*, Abu Dhabi, www.irena.org/publications/2016/May/Scaling-up-Variable-Renewable-Power-The-Role-of-Grid-Codes

IRENA (International Renewable Energy Agency) (2016b), *Boosting Biofuels: Sustainable Paths to Greater Energy Security*, Abu Dhabi, www.irena.org/publications/2016/Apr/Boosting-Biofuels-Sustainable-Paths-to-Greater-Energy-Security

IRENA (International Renewable Energy Agency) (2018a), *Renewable Power Generation Costs in 2017*, Abu Dhabi, www.irena.org/publications/2018/Jan/Renewable-power-generation-costs-in-2017

IRENA (International Renewable Energy Agency) (2018b), *Nurturing Offshore Wind Markets*, Abu Dhabi, www.irena.org/publications/2018/May/Nurturing-offshore-wind-markets

IRENA (International Renewable Energy Agency) (2018c), *Power System Flexibility for the Energy Transition*, Abu Dhabi, www.irena.org/publications/2018/Nov/Power-system-flexibility-for-the-energy-transition

IRENA (International Renewable Energy Agency) (2019a), *A New World: the Geopolitics of the Energy Transformation*, Abu Dhabi, http://geopoliticsofrenewables.org/assets/geopolitics/Reports/wp-content/uploads/2019/01/Global_commission_renewable_energy_2019.pdf

IRENA (International Renewable Energy Agency) (2019b), *Bioenergy*, www.irena.org/bioenergy

IRENA (International Renewable Energy Agency), IEA and REN21. (2018), *Renewable Energy Policies in a Time of Transition*, www.irena.org/-/media/Files/IRENA/Agency/Publication/2018/Apr/IRENA_IEA_REN21_Policies_2018.pdf

ITER (2019), *What is ITER?*, www.iter.org/proj/inafewlines

JRC (Joint Research Center) (2016), *Analysis of Material Recovery from Silicon Photovoltaic Panels*, https://ec.europa.eu/jrc/en/publication/analysis-material-recovery-silicon-photovoltaic-panels

Khandker, S. R., Barnes, F., and Samad, H. (2012), 'Are the energy poor also income poor? Evidence from India', *Energy policy*, 47, 1–12.

Kingdom of Saudi Arabia (2019), *Budget Statement Fiscal Year 2019*, Riyadh, www.mof.gov.sa/en/financialreport/budget2019/Documents/Budget%20Statement%202019.pdf

Kissinger, H. (2009), *The Future of the IEA*. Speech for the 35th Anniversary of the International Energy Agency, www.henryakissinger.com/speeches/the-future-role-of-the-iea/

Lazard (2018), *Lazard's Levelized Cost of Energy Analysis – Version 12.0*, New York, www.lazard.com/media/450784/lazards-levelized-cost-of-energy-version-120-vfinal.pdf

Luciani, G. (ed.) (2012), *Resources Blessed: Diversification and the Gulf Development Model*, Gerlach Press, Berlin.

Lynn Kar, T. (1997), *Paradox of Plenty*, University of California Press, Oakland.

Mahdavy, H. (1970), 'Patterns and problems of economic development in rentier states: the case of Iran', in Cook, M. A. (ed.), *Studies in Economic History of the Middle East*, Oxford University Press, Oxford.

NASA (National Aeronautics and Space Administration) (2019), *Global Climate Change, Facts*, https://climate.nasa.gov/evidence/

NREL (National Renewable Energy Laboratory) (2017), *An Assessment of the Economic Potential of Offshore Wind in the United States from 2015 to 2030*, www.nrel.gov/docs/fy17osti/67675.pdf

Nuclear Energy Agency (2016), *Small Modular Reactors: Nuclear Energy Market Potential for Near-term Deployment*, OECD-NEA, Paris, www.oecd-nea.org/ndd/pubs/2016/7213-smrs.pdf

PIF (Public Investment Fund) (2017), *The Public Investment Fund Program (2018–2020)*, Riyadh, www.arabia-saudita.it/files/news/2018/07/pif_program_en.pdf

Qatar Planning and Statistics Authority (2018), *Qatar Economic Outlook 2018–2020*, Issue Number 11, Doha, www.mdps.gov.qa/en/knowledge/Doc/QEO/Qatar-Economic-Outlook-2018-2020-En.pdf

REN21, *Renewables 2018. Global Status Report*, www.ren21.net/gsr-2018/

Reuters (2017), *Saudi Sovereign Fund Creates $1.07 bln 'Fund of Funds' to Back SMEs*, London, www.reuters.com/article/saudi-fund-funds/saudi-sovereign-fund-creates-1-07-bln-fund-of-funds-to-back-smes-idUSL8N1MK3XH

Righter, R. W. (1996), *Wind Energy in America: A History*, University of Oklahoma Press, Norman.

Rud, J. P. (2012), 'Electricity provision and industrial development: Evidence from India', *Journal of Development Economics*, 97(2), 352–67.

SETIS (2014), *Ocean Energy*, https://setis.ec.europa.eu/system/files/Technology_ Information_Sheet_Ocean_Energy.pdf

Singh, C. (2012), 'Variable Speed Wind Turbine', *International Journal of Engineering Science and Advanced Technology*, 2(3), 652–6.

Stavins, R. (2011), *The National Context of State Policies for a Global Commons Problem*, Harvard Project on Climate Agreements, www.belfercenter.org/sites/ default/files/legacy/files/Stavins_AB_32_Viewpoint_3.pdf

State Council of People's Republic of China (2018), *Three-year action plan for cleaner air released*, http://english.gov.cn/policies/latest_releases/2018/07/03 /content_281476207708632.htm

Stern, N. (2007), *The Economics of Climate Change: the Stern Review*, Cambridge University Press, Cambridge.

Stern, J., and Rogers, H. (2017), The evolution of European gas pricing mechanisms, in Hafner, M., and Tagliapietra, S. (eds.), *The European Gas Markets: Challenges and Opportunities*, Palgrave Macmillan, London.

Sulzer (2019), *Gas-Fired Power Generation*, www.sulzer.com/en/applications/ power-generation/fossil/gas-fired-power-generation

Swank, J. M. (1892), *History of the Manufacture of Iron in All Ages, and Particularly in the United States from Colonial Times to 1891*, The American Iron and Steel Association, Philadelphia.

Tagliapietra, S. (2017a), *The Political Economy of Middle East and North Africa Oil Exporters in Times of Global Decarbonisation*, Bruegel Working Paper, Issue 05/2017, Brussels, http://bruegel.org/wp-content/uploads/2017/04/WP-2017_05 .pdf

Tagliapietra, S. (2017b), *Beyond Coal: Facilitating the Transition in Europe*, Bruegel Policy Brief, Issue 05/2017, Brussels, http://bruegel.org/wp-content/ uploads/2017/11/PB-2017_05_SimoneTagliapietra-1.pdf

Tagliapietra, S. (2017c), *Electrifying Africa: How to Make Europe's Contribution Count*, Bruegel Policy Contribution, Issue 17/2017, Brussels, http://bruegel.org /wp-content/uploads/2017/06/PC-17–2017_1.pdf

Tagliapietra, S., and Bazilian, M. (2019), 'The role of international institutions in fostering sub-Saharan Africa electrification', *The Electricity Journal*, 32, 13–20.

Tagliapietra, S., and Zachmann, G. (2016), *Rethinking the Security of the European Union's Gas Supply*, Bruegel Policy Contribution, Issue 2016/01, Brussels, http://bruegel.org/2016/01/rethinking-the-security-of-the-european-unions-gas-supply/

Tagliapietra, S., and Zachmann, G. (2018), *Addressing Europe's Failure to Clean Up the Transport Sector*, Bruegel Policy Brief, Issue 2018/02, Brussels, http://bruegel.org/wp-content/uploads/2018/04/PB-2018_02.pdf

Trimble, C., Kojima, M., Perez Arroyo, I., and Mohammadzadeh, F. (2016) *Financial Viability of Electricity Sectors in Sub-Saharan Africa: Quasi-Fiscal Deficits and Hidden Costs*, Policy Research Working Paper 7788, World Bank, Washington DC, http://documents.worldbank.org/curated/en/182071470748085038/pdf/WPS7788.pdf

Tollefson, J. (2018a), 'Sucking carbon dioxide from air is cheaper than scientists thought, *Nature*, June 7, www.nature.com/articles/d41586-018-05357-w

Tollefson, J. (2018b), 'First sun-dimming experiment will test a way to cool Earth', *Nature*, November 27, www.nature.com/articles/d41586-018-07533-4

UNFCCC (United Nations Framework Convention on Climate Change) (2015), *Paris Agreement*, New York and Geneva, https://unfccc.int/sites/default/files/english_paris_agreement.pdf

UNFCCC (United Nations Framework Convention on Climate Change) (2017), *National Inventory Submissions 2017 – European Union*, New York and Geneva, http://unfccc.int/national_reports/annex_i_ghg_inventories/national_inventories_submissions/items/10116.php

UNFCCC (United Nations Framework Convention on Climate Change) (2019), *Nationally Determined Contributions Interim Registry*, New York and Geneva, www4.unfccc.int/sites/ndcstaging/Pages/Home.aspx

United Nations (2015), *Resolution adopted by the General Assembly on 25 September 2015. Transforming our world: the 2030 Agenda for Sustainable Development*, New York and Geneva, www.un.org/ga/search/view_doc.asp?symbol=A/RES/70/1&Lang=E

US Bureau of Reclamation (2019), *The History of Hydropower Development in the United States*, www.usbr.gov/power/edu/history.html

US Department of Energy (2013), *Solar Photovoltaic Cell Basics*, www.energy.gov/eere/solar/articles/solar-photovoltaic-cell-basics

US Department of Energy (2014), *How a Wind Turbine Works*, www.energy.gov/articles/how-wind-turbine-works

US Department of Energy (2019), *Estimating Appliance and Home Electronic Energy Use*, Washington, DC, www.energy.gov/energysaver/save-electricity-and-fuel/appliances-and-electronics/estimating-appliance-and-home

US Geological Survey (2019), *What Are the Types of Coal?*, www.usgs.gov/faqs/what-are-types-coal?qt-news_science_products=0#qt-news_science_products

Van de Walle, D. P., Ravallion, M., Mendiratta, V., and Koolwal, G. B. (2013), *Long-Term Impacts of Household Electrification in Rural India*, World Bank, Washington DC, http://documents.worldbank.org/curated/en/9784414682594 64720/Long-term-impacts-of-household-electrification-in-rural-India

WEC (World Energy Council) (2016), *World Energy Resources: Marine 2016*, Tilburg, www.worldenergy.org/wp-content/uploads/2017/03/WEResources_ Marine_2016.pdf

WEF (2019), *Poor Access to Finance Is Holding Back Businesses in MENA: This Is How We Can Help Them*, Geneva, www.weforum.org/agenda/2019/03/scaling-up-sme-access-finance-mena-region/

Wind Europe (2017), *Unleashing Europe's Offshore Wind Potential: a New Resource Assessment*, Brussels, windeurope.org/wp-content/uploads/files/about-wind/ reports/Unleashing-Europes-offshore-wind-potential.pdf

Wingas (2019), *In Search of Gas with High-Tech Tools*, www.wingas.com/en/ raw-material-natural-gas/natural-gas-production.html

World Bank (2016), *MENA Economic Monitor: Economic and Social Inclusion to Prevent Violent Extremism*, Washington, DC, http://documents.worldbank.org /curated/en/409591474983005625/pdf/108525-REVISED-PUBLIC.pdf

World Bank (2016b), *Global Solar Atlas*, Washington, DC, https://globalsolaratlas .info/

World Bank (2018a), *Managing Coal Mine Closure: Achieving a Just Transition for All*, Washington, DC, www.worldbank.org/en/topic/extractiveindustries/ publication/managing-coal-mine-closure

World Bank (2018b), *World Wind Atlas*, Washington, DC, https://globalwindatlas .info/

World Bank (2018c), *State and Trends of Carbon Pricing*, Washington, DC, https:// openknowledge.worldbank.org/bitstream/handle/10986/29687/978146481292 7.pdf?sequence=5&isAllowed=y

World Bank (2019), *Ease of Doing Business Report 2019*, Washington, DC, www .worldbank.org/content/dam/doingBusiness/media/Annual-Reports/English/ DB2019-report_web-version.pdf

World Bank, IMF and OECD (2015), *Capital Market Instruments to Mobilize Institutional Investors to Infrastructure and SME Financing in Emerging Market Economies. Report for the G20*, Washington, DC and Paris, http:// documents.worldbank.org/curated/en/192061468179954327/Capital-market -instruments-to-mobilize-institutional-investors-to-infrastructure -and-SME -financing-in-emerging-market-economies-report-for-the-G20

World Resources Institute (2018), *According to New IPCC Report, the World Is on Track to Exceed Its 'Carbon Budget' in 12 Years*, www.wri.org/blog/2018/10/ according-new-ipcc-report-world-track-exceed-its-carbon-budget-12-years

World Resources Institute (2019), *6 Pressing Questions about Beef and Climate Change, Answered*, www.wri.org/blog/2019/04/6-pressing-questions-about-beef-and-climate-change-answered

WHO (World Health Organization) (2018), *Household Air Pollution and Health*, Geneva, www.who.int/news-room/fact-sheets/detail/household-air-pollution-and-health

WHO (World Health Organization) (2019), *Air Pollution: Invisible Killer*, www.who.int/airpollution/en/

WMO (World Meteorological Organization) (2019), *WMO Confirms Past 4 Years Were Warmest on Record*, Geneva, https://public.wmo.int/en/media/press-release/wmo-confirms-past-4-years-were-warmest-record

Yergin, D. (1990), *The Prize: the Epic Quest for Oil, Money & Power*, Simon & Schuster, New York.

Yergin, D. (2011), *The Quest: Energy, Security and the Remaking of the Modern World*, Penguin Press, New York.

Zachmann, G., Fredriksson, G., and Claeys, G. (2018), *The Distributional Effects of Climate Policies*, Bruegel, Brussels, http://bruegel.org/2018/11/distributional-effects-of-climate-policies/

Zalasiewicz, J., Waters, C. N., Wolfe, A., et al. (2017), 'Making the case for a formal Anthropocene Epoch: an analysis of ongoing critiques', *Newsletters on Stratigraphy*, 50(2), 205–26.

Index

For EU product safety concerns, contact us at Calle de José Abascal, 56–1°,
28003 Madrid, Spain or eugpsr@cambridge.org.